STUDIES IN PUBLIC COMMUNICATION

MASS MEDIA AND COMMUNICATION
Edited by Charles S. Steinberg

THE LANGUAGES OF COMMUNICATION
A Logical and Psychological Examination
by George N. Gordon

TO KILL A MESSENGER
Television News and the Real World
by William Small

INTERNATIONAL COMMUNICATION
Media—Channels—Functions
Edited by Heinz-Dietrich Fischer and John Calhoun Merrill

THE COMMUNICATIVE ARTS
An Introduction to Mass Media
by Charles S. Steinberg

PERSUASION
The Theory and Practice of Manipulative Communication
by George N. Gordon

MASS MEDIA AND THE SUPREME COURT
The Legacy of the Warren Years
Edited by Kenneth S. Devol

THE PEOPLE'S FILMS
A Political History of U.S. Government Motion Pictures
by Richard Dyer MacCann

STUDIES IN PUBLIC COMMUNICATION

THE PEOPLE'S FILMS

A Political History of U.S. Government Motion Pictures

by

RICHARD DYER MacCANN

COMMUNICATION ARTS BOOKS

HASTINGS HOUSE, PUBLISHERS

NEW YORK

To John Gaus
and
Walter Sandelius

Library of Congress Cataloging in Publication Data

MacCann, Richard Dyer.   The people's films.

(Studies in public communication)   (Communication arts books)
   Based on the author's thesis, Harvard, 1951.
   Includes bibliographical references.
   1. Moving-pictures, Documentary—United States
—History. 2. Moving-pictures in propaganda.
3. Moving-pictures—Political aspects. I. Title.
II. Title: Government motion pictures.
PN1995.9.D6M3   791.43'53   72-13665
ISBN 0-8038-5795-0   ISBN 0-8038-5796-9 (pbk)

Published simultaneously in Canada by
Saunders of Toronto, Ltd., Don Mills, Ontario

Printed in the United States of America

CONTENTS

v

Contents

PREFACE

In the years since 1951, when the bulk of this book was completed and shelved among the Ph.D. dissertations at Harvard, there have been a good many requests for it from specialized students of film and of history. It was a somewhat unconventional dissertation subject at the time. The rapidly mounting interest in motion pictures today—reflected in the expansion of university courses and enrollments and a rising tide of new books—suggests that a history of U.S. government activity in film-making will now find a wider readership.

The first chapter has been rewritten from three in the original and the second brought more up to date. The last three chapters are entirely new. The basic history of the federal government use of films from 1908 to 1945 remains essentially unchanged.

Apart from including British and Canadian experience as precedent and parallel, I have not attempted to deal with the shaky business of "influences." Russian films of the 1920's, for example, had great influence on early documentary directors, especially Joris Ivens and John Grierson. The Russian history is well known, thanks to the Museum of Modern Art archives and the writings of such scholars as Paul Rotha and Jay Leyda. But it is fair to say, I think, that the impact of Eisenstein and Pudovkin in the United States was considerably less than in Europe. Pare Lorentz himself was not the sort to be taught by anybody nor to be a teacher and propagandist about film, as Grierson was. He met Grierson in London on one brief holiday, got help and advice from King Vidor in Hollywood, and must have followed the issues of Louis de Rochemont's theatrical news series, *The March of Time*, after 1935. But he was as lone a wolf as many another American artist or writer; he was always loath to admit that he was influenced by anybody—especially by European high culture—and he was probably right.

Furthermore, it is at least debatable whether the version of history seen in Russian silent films, even in *Potemkin* (with its famous Odessa steps sequence, conceived solely in the fertile intuitive intellect of Sergei Eisenstein) can be called documentary in any but the loosest sense. Dziga Vertov and his theories of the impersonal Kino-Eye are of special interest today, partly because of new techniques of *cinéma vérité*. But among the euphoric reconstructions of the revolutionary past brought to the screen in that extraordinary era, Victor Turin's *Turksib* is probably the nearest to documentary. For all its poetic pictorialism, it does tell the story of building a railroad.

Nor have I tried to draw other obvious European comparisons. The nonfiction propaganda of Leni Riefenstahl, created at the behest of Adolf Hitler, was certainly a landmark example of government persuasion through art. *Triumph of the Will*, as Siegfried Kracauer has so brilliantly explained, was the record of a real fantasy, the Nuremberg Nazi party congress of 1934, planned in large part to satisfy the demands of the camera— a theatrical thriller going by the name of documentary.[1] The challenge to democracy and to the documentary represented by *Triumph of the Will* and its hard-propaganda successors, *Baptism of Fire* and *Victory in the West*, has been stated best by John Grierson: "It puts a heavy burden on democratic statement when the very essence of it is that it should not be melodramatic and should not be spectacular." [2]

Government tasks are diverse and sometimes delicate. When the persuasive purpose is agreed upon and dramatic weapons acceptable, there may occur what can be called a "documentary movement." The great periods of documentary creativity and productivity in the English-speaking world are chronicled in this book.

In my original preface, I listed a few other subjects besides federal government films that deserved to be reported: (1) the story of the American Film Center (1938–47) which was an ineffective attempt, in imitation of the British Film Centre, to bridge the gap between educators and documentary producers outside of government; (2) the promising development of the Southern Educational Film Production Service, then supported by southern state departments of health, agriculture, and educa-

[1] Siegfried Kracauer, "Propaganda and the Nazi War Film," *From Caligari to Hitler*, pp. 298–303.
[2] "Searchlight on Democracy," *Grierson on Documentary*, p. 195 (first U.S. edition, 1947).

tion and by the Tennessee Valley Authority, but shortly afterward stifled
by political and economic pressures; (3) the scattered range of film activities in certain state governments, in the New York City television and motion picture unit, in the United Nations, and in UNESCO.

Today, one might add a dozen more suggestions for further investigation. The North Carolina Film Board had its brief moment in 1962–
65, influenced by the Canadian experience.[3] Many states and cities have
gone beyond the travelog or public relations film to encourage public
understanding or action. It would be useful to know about the films and
the programs, and in recent years, to know to what extent state arts
councils have supported nonfiction film-making.

One adaptable and characteristic American approach is the growth of
film units in the state universities, represented nationally by the University
Film Association. Offering production services to its own institution, to
nonprofit sponsors and to other state agencies—somewhat in the manner
of a university press—the university film production unit has become an
important contributor to the college-level educational film. The University
Film Foundation, working through the UFA, was in fact a contractee of a
government agency, the National Aeronautics and Space Administration,
for ten films about frontiers of space science, produced by university film
units.[4]

Abroad, there have been more extensive governmental operations. The
government of India has long had an elaborate film production program,
supported further in recent years by graduates of the government film
school. Pakistan has also been active, and Indonesian film-makers, many
of them trained at the University of Southern California, have made a
massive contribution to government information, through all the radical
changes of policy there. Puerto Rico had a time of notable creative effort
in documentary in the 1950's when a group of theater-trained people in
the audio-visual branch of the department of education sent away to New
York for some film books and proceeded to persuade rural communities to
build bridges and schools.[5]

The British Colonial Film Unit, with its inheritance of the Grierson
influence, has had a notable effect on certain emerging African states.
Many of them, as they became independent, set up film units in conjunction with television stations, partly for domestic education, partly to
impress foreign visitors and investors. The Australian Film Board, which

[3] See Elmer Oettinger, "The North Carolina Film Board," *Journal* of the Society
of Cinematologists, Vol. V.

[4] Richard D. MacCann, "The NASA Project," *Journal* of the University Film Association, Vol. 18, No. 4, 1966.

[5] Richard D. MacCann, "Canadians, Puerto Ricans Developing Own Traditions,"
The Christian Science Monitor, September 22, 1959. Important U.S. help in Puerto
Rico came through Jack Delano and Ed Rosskam, who were trained in documentary
methods.

was a direct outgrowth of contacts with the Canadian National Film Board, restricted itself until recent years to scientific subjects of use to farmers, fishermen, explorers and businessmen.

The U.S. State Department and the USIA, working together, have had a modest influence in some places. Through the energetic efforts of Professor Don Williams, head of audio-visual education at Syracuse University and later at the University of Missouri at Kansas City, technical teams were sent to Iran and to South Korea. Their teaching and example encouraged the development of outstanding official documentary film groups in both countries.[6]

France, Germany, Italy and Japan get their nonfiction films primarily from private sources, but the East European and Russian official agencies, which turn out vast quantities of carefully planned short films, are known to us only through embassy catalogs or such selected items as turn up in festival showings. China and its satellites are also busy with didactic films of various lengths, little known in the West.

Outside of government, the documentary has become a familiar form of public communication. Network television, a private enterprise operated for profit, served the nation well during the 1950's as a source of information about a changing society.[7] Edward R. Murrow began it with his half-hour weekly program, *See It Now* (Fred Friendly co-producing for CBS). Television's whole approach to news and public affairs was largely formed by this wise and worried man. He saw the chance to adapt to TV the authentic American muckraking tradition in journalism, adding to it his own well-developed sense of humor and of pragmatic fair play. His main stylistic contribution was confrontation through selective film editing, paring to the bone the essential arguments on both sides of an issue.

Irving Gitlin's "specials" at both CBS and NBC were notable contributions to the study of controversy in depth. *Victory at Sea* (NBC), *Twentieth Century* (CBS), and the biographies of Churchill and Roosevelt (ABC) were compilation series that gave viewers a new acquaintance with history. The *Close-Up* series on ABC and "The Making of the President" (1960, 1964) often included political analysis.

Sometimes these private newsmen examined specific functions of government. Murrow did a historical study of "The Vice-Presidency," and CBS later tried to bring judicial processes alive in "Storm Over the Supreme Court." Gitlin's coverage of a town in New York state, "The Battle

[6] Richard D. MacCann, "Korean Cameras Create New Poetry," *The Christian Science Monitor*, January 30, 1964. Also, same author, "Films and Film Training in the Republic of Korea," *Journal* of the UFA, Vol. 16, No. 1, 1964. Viet Nam, of course, gradually became a special case, dominated by Defense Department policies, but in the beginning the combination of U.S. aid and the USIA's example and training followed the pattern of Korea.

[7] See A. William Bluem, *Documentary in American Television*, for an excellent analysis of this period.

of Newburgh," examined the administration of federal welfare programs. Robert Drew and Richard Leacock brought *cinéma vérité* to bear on the Presidency, showing how the Kennedy brothers looked and acted "behind the scenes" during the constitutional conflict with Governor George Wallace of Alabama over desegregation of schools ("Crisis: Behind a Presidential Commitment"). In "Primary"—Kennedy vs. Humphrey in Wisconsin (1960)—the same film-makers managed to convey effectively the tiring pressures of campaigning.

I hope every reader will understand that I could not write about informational and documentary films in government without assuming the continued presence of privately owned newspapers and broadcasting stations. Private agencies of communication will always have a unique responsibility for reporting on government and public affairs—tracking down false impressions, puncturing stuffed shirts, doubting every glittering generality. For daily news and the news of campaigns and elections, the viewer will still turn to the solons of broadcasting for comment and interpretation, for that independence of politics which one expects from the commentator and the columnist in America. Certainly no official agency in society—not even the educational system—is so well equipped to contribute to our general education in contemporary public affairs as are the TV stations, magazines and newspapers.

As a single instance—certainly an outstanding one—among many local and national achievements in public service broadcasting, I should like to call attention to the work of a TV station in Houston, Texas. *Variety* headlined the story (January 1, 1969, page 1): "KPRC-TV Achieves in 7 Days What 20 Years of Ghetto Beefs Couldn't."

Houston had annexed and taxed many outlying county areas but failed to give them water lines or sewer service. Meanwhile many downtown areas had never had sewer maintenance or adequate garbage pickup.

> For seven straight days, KPRC-TV's city hall reporter Lee Tucker filed film stories covering the problems of ghetto neighborhoods and their inability to get Houston's city council action on complaints filed over the last 20 years.
>
> After the fifth special report, Houston Mayor Louis Welch told KPRC-TV that only a city council policy prevented action from being taken. He indicated he was not opposed to a change by the council.
>
> After the sixth Tucker report, a vet councilman declared for a re-study of the blocking policy. The following day, the Houston city council unanimously called for a new policy extending city services to Houston's thousands of "second class citizens," as the newscasts had dubbed the ghetto residents.

It was "a persistent series of special news reports," as *Variety* pointed out, that brought the city council to action. This example of pressure on government not only illustrates the watchdog role of all free enterprise communication but shows what has to be done simply to get attention.

When I checked the story with Jack Harris, KPRC station manager who initiated the series, he called them "mini-documentaries" and emphasized the importance of catching the cumulative attention of viewers who miss it the first day or the second. He recalled an earlier case when a new hospital was standing empty and unused because of a quarrel over funds between the city and the county. That TV news story went on for 36 days before minds were changed and action taken.

"There are other cases just as deserving," Harris told the *Variety* reporter, "and if the local broadcaster fully carries out his community responsibilities by focusing them in the eyes of the general public, the basic fairness of the American people will ensure they are solved when enough people learn what's been going on. That's what local community television is all about."

In my original preface, I find the following:

This thesis deals mainly with the public relations process in the Federal government—specifically, with the medium of the documentary film.

Public relations comes after the decision-making process. And yet there is a kind of decision-making about public relations itself. I am concerned, then, with the questions: What factual motion pictures have been produced by the United States Government? When? How? But I am also concerned with the question: Why? What pressures and personalities produced the decisions which produced these films? And beyond this, it is important to make some attempt at criticism of the "why."

My specific assumption is that some kind of re-enactment of administrative and political experience is possible by visual means, and that the documentary film is one means which is especially promising.

My general assumptions are three-fold: that there is a crisis in communication in our time, that free communication between experts and the people is vital to the health of a democratic society, and that government is one of many agencies in our society which have immediate moral responsibility for action.

If there is a political philosophy behind these assumptions, as I see it now it is one of attachment to the equalitarian ideals of the Declaration of Independence, while accepting as well such practical checks and balances as the American Constitution imposes on men who certainly act as if they were unequal. It implies a faith in the responsiveness of most men to the educational processes of new experience and new ideas, remembering at the same time that this responsiveness is usually slow, since democracy is fundamentally conservative. Ideas must win their way to real acceptance in a democracy; they cannot be imposed by a blindly logical radicalism. The atmosphere of freedom in which this acceptance of ideas takes place is precious both to individuals and to society. By protecting individual differences it promotes individual happiness. By protecting the development of new inventions in ideas, it promotes the kind of adaptive change which is vital for the survival of a complex society.

This thesis emphasizes the need for new kinds of public understanding, rather than the development of a better class of leaders. It is an achievement to expand an élite successfully. It is important for any society to develop the kind of leadership which can be trusted. But the new kind of society which democracy wants and technology needs is also a society of widely distributed personal capacity.

—RICHARD DYER MACCANN.

University of Iowa
January, 1973

ACKNOWLEDGMENTS

Apart from indirect debts to Walter Lippmann and to John Grierson for some of the concepts presented in the early chapters, the chief additions to the following list of sources are:

George Stevens Jr., director, and Anthony Guarco, deputy director, of the USIA Motion Picture Service, 1962–67.

Ronald Capalaces and Anne Michaels, motion picture service, Office of Economic Opportunity, 1970.

My thanks, as of 1951, to:

Pare Lorentz, Lowell Mellett, Arch Mercey, Roy Stryker, John Fischer, Willard Van Dyke, and John Franklin Carter for thinking back and talking over old days in the Resettlement Administration, Farm Security Administration, and U.S. Film Service.

Philip Brown of Farmers Home Administration for digging up what RA files were left. Allyn Walters and Edwin Locke for going over some Rural Electrification Administration film history. Chester Lindstrom, R. L. Webster, and Walter Scott for facts about the Department of Agriculture Motion Picture Service.

Colonel R. C. Barrett, Major Griffin L. Davis, James Gibson, and Paul Murdock of the Army Signal Corps; Dewlaney Terrett of the Defense Department historical staff; Thomas Orchard and Walter Evans for information about Navy films.

Herbert Edwards and John Devine for background about the State Department's motion picture problems. Lothar Wolff for a direct

report on Economic Cooperation Administration films. Kenneth
Macgowan and Alan Fisher for insights into the story of the Coordinator of InterAmerican Affairs.

Robert Sherwood, Archibald MacLeish, and Louis de Rochemont
for general encouragement and specific advice. Francis Keppel,
Charles Siepmann, Alice Keliher, Gloria Waldron, Raymond Spottiswoode, Florence Anderson, and Richard Griffith for helpful talks
along the way.

Frame enlargements from U.S. Government films were prepared by
William Murray and the staff of the motion picture section of the
National Archives.

Dr. Bruce Linton, chairman of Radio-Television-Film at the University
of Kansas, provided funds for typing the major portion of the manuscript,
during the time I was a member of his department (1965–1970). As she
has for earlier books, my wife (who is also an author) has encouraged me
during delays and difficulties, and her critical reading has kept me aware
of the everpresent need for clarity, conscience, and correctness.

This book is dedicated to two professors of political science whose
high standards of humanity, intellect, and commitment guided and supported me at crucial times: John Gaus, now deceased, of Harvard University, who was the adviser on the original dissertation, and Walter
Sandelius, now retired, who was my teacher at the University of Kansas.

R.D.M.

Portions of Chapter 7, "World War II: Armed Forces Documentary," appeared in Lewis Jacobs, The Documentary Tradition © 1971
by Lewis Jacobs, published by Hopkinson and Blake; reprinted by
permission.

A shorter version of Chapter 8, "Film and Foreign Policy: The USIA,
1962–1967," was published in Volume IX, Number 1, Fall 1969,
Cinema Journal and appears here by permission of its editor.

Part of the last section of Chapter 10, "The Democratic Dialogue,"
was included in a talk for the Voice of America, "The Documentary
Film in the U.S. Government" (1972). It has also appeared in Arts
in Society, Volume 9, Number 2, Summer-Fall 1972.

INTRODUCTION

It is regrettable that a few *cognoscenti* in the realm of communications theory continue to support the notion that what the new sight-sound media contribute to the political process is ephemeral and hence irrelevant, if not downright harmful, to the free society. Those who should know better still maintain that the political effects of film and television communication are less significant than messages transmitted to us by courtesy of Gutenberg's invention. Such a narrow view not only suggests ignorance of the central facts of socio-political communication in our time, but of the entire historical evolution of *homo communicatus*.

In truth, the print-versus-non-print argument no longer has a real point of focus, and is kept alive only in a running dialogue-of-the-deaf between defenders of print vested interests and zealous audio-visual technicians. It is far more sensible simply to recognize that all of man's communications throughout history have been cast within two broad media-systems, the "platform" and the "parchment"—both of which are very much alive and well today.

We must look upon the new media of radio, television and motion pictures as nothing more than extensions of the ancient platform tradition, and it is as foolish to deny their impact upon our political institutions today as it is to deny the "influence" of every great political figure in history. Man's political history has been shaped not so much by words on paper as by human personalities in public verbal interaction, and as the extensions of this interaction dominate our experience, so the influence of the parchment tradition must continue to wane.

It is too easy to despair, however, of the exponential growth in political thrust of the new media. It may well be that we are, as McLuhan warns, within the gates of the electric culture, where we are struck dumb. But it is quite possible that we can come to a full comprehension of the situation to which these dynamic extensions of the platform have brought us. Certainly it is in the search for such comprehension that the parchment tradition may yet enjoy its finest hour. If print, quite truthfully, is "dead" it is only in the sense that Thomas Altizer once described the "death of God." What theologians intended by their dramatic formulation, Altizer observed, was to call attention not to the *absence* of the *experience* of God, but to the *experience* of the *absence* of God. Similarly, it may well be that the social dislocation being felt in our time results not from *absence* of the *experience* of print, but the *experience* of the *absence* of print. More and more, as waves of aural-visual kinetic transmission of reality wash over us, we seek a reassuring psychic distance between ourselves and life around us—a distance which print once could provide.

This need for surcease has led those of little faith either to that cynical despair reflected in 1984, or to an illogical effort to suppress or ignore the impact of the new media upon human experience in the electric age. Those who understand, however, how essential both traditions are have abandoned these positions and are engaged in positive effort to support that thought and reflection which enables us to prevail in the time of "maximum media" by giving direction to them.

In this connection, Richard· Dyer MacCann has provided a useful point of departure. Throughout his distinguished career as scholar, reporter, writer and teacher, Dr. MacCann has demonstrated a profound grasp of how the motion picture interfaces with our system of political communication. *Studies in Public Communication* welcomes his scholarly history of the crucial effort by political leaders of good will and high purpose to seek broad public support by employing the art and technology of the motion picture.

A. WILLIAM BLUEM, PH.D.
Professor of Media Studies
Syracuse University

THE PEOPLE'S FILMS

Democracy's
Public Relations

The range of attention is the main premise of political science.
                                                    —Walter Lippmann [1]

It is argued, the mass of the reading public is not interested. . . . Presentation is fundamentally important, and presentation is a question of art. . . . The function of art has always been to break through the crust of conventionalized and routine consciousness.

                                                    —John Dewey [2]

THE FREE marketplace of ideas proposed by John Stuart Mill may theoretically have existed at some moment in time. But in practice, there are too many people talking. The competition for attention has led to a surplus of communication, and the marketplace is dominated by the loudest shouters. Every communicator must seek to be coercive—must demand and hold attention long enough to persuade. It is not a quiet world we live in.

In this pluralism of publication, government has its own problems in being heard. Mass media and politics have become inseparable. Furthermore, men in public life are beginning to see that the most important public messages can no longer be merely neutral or informational. They have to reach the citizen, stir his sympathy, focus his decision, encourage him to act.

[1] *Public Opinion*, p. 198 (Penguin edition). This remarkable statement, made in 1922, has been little noticed by political scientists.
[2] *The Public and Its Problems*, pp. 183–184.

3

How can this be done without taking away the citizen's power of choice, without violating his right to pay no attention?

The history of the documentary film shows that the U.S. government has tried, from time to time, to enter the marketplace of opinion with all the energies of art. The chapters that follow are concerned with the content and method—and to some extent the effectiveness—of these attempts to dramatize public policy. The present chapter inquires into the purposes and the propriety of such public relations activity by a government which seeks to express, rather than to direct, the popular will.

What Should the Public Know?

Communication is the effective transmission of ideas from one person to another. It is the achieving of some degree of impact, of comprehension, of memory. It becomes public communication when it is directed through mass media toward the general public.

Public communication is to social science as technology is to science. It is the process by which social values are constructed and changed. The modern public relations campaign, in government or outside, is a formal attempt to build a new addition on the structure of our attitudes toward the world. When it takes place in government, it means that Congress has passed a law establishing an agency with a particular mission. That mission includes an information process—to make its service better known or its regulation more understandable.

The power of publicity in government is a two-edged problem. It is at once indispensable and irritating. For want of clear communication, the public may become confused and miss the whole point of a new public policy. And yet if the thing is hammered too hard, the public and its representatives may feel strongly that propaganda is outrunning policy—that administrators are not being mindful of the primacy of Congress in determining the scope of administrative action. This was the usual reaction to the social action programs of the New Deal.

Should the government warn its citizens not to leave burning matches in national forests?

Should the government urge its citizens to use public health facilities—national, state, and local?

Should the government actively advertise to farmers its credit facilities—and perhaps advise them on how to spend the money they borrow?

Should the government give well-worded advice to industrial executives about the intricacies of social security taxation—and at the same time point out why it is important in a democratic society?

Should the government persuade the people of the value of certain administrative programs by dramatizing the problems that need solving and how these programs came to be voted for in Congress?

Should the government issue dramatic explanations of the reasons for war preparations and forceful appeals for cooperation with emergency executive controls?

The answers to these questions, of course, are progressively more difficult. All but the first one, perhaps, would make a large segment of the public somewhat uneasy. On the one hand, the conservative will usually say that the government hasn't any business in the advertising business: it is undignified and tends toward dangerous monopoly, and anyway the newspapers ought to do the job. On the other hand, the apostle of social change will say that a broad concept of public relations is part of the American way of life—that every means of persuasion should be placed at the service of the elected leaders of the people.

In the 1960's, in the face of an increasingly unpopular war in Viet Nam, that last question began to divide the articulate populace in quite another way. Those who were against the war found the use of publicity —and the complementary misuse of secrecy—inimical to the public good. "The Selling of the Pentagon," an inquiry by CBS-TV into the public relations activities of the Defense Department, became an attack on the Nixon administration and the conduct of the war.

The issues of government information, like the issues of politics, will always be fought out in an arena of specific conflicting attitudes and forces. It should be clear that every government agency, whether we like it or not, has public relations. For realistic decision-making, officials must know what the public is thinking. This will temper and change, to some extent, the decisions being made. After that, the decisions themselves must be explained, in all their ramifications, to those whom it affects— and sometimes to the rest of the people as well.

That explanation involves technical problems. Understanding is not achieved by simple publication. In the first place, at different educational levels, different language is required to accomplish understanding. Hence the need for many different kinds of specialized and mass media to reach different clienteles. In the second place, publication alone does not necessarily achieve attention. If the enlistment of public support for a government program is desired at all, then gray press releases are a waste of money if the program could be promoted instead with drama and color and originality. It makes no sense for the Budget Bureau to accept radio but not movies, or pamphlets but not color slides, since the Defense Department has widely differing needs and the Social Security program is still another matter. Drama and humor may be needed. Direct-mail appeals may not be as effective as cartridge films and portable projectors. Democracy does not have to be behind the times.

Should government publicity be restricted to programs which are not controversial? How can controversy ever be avoided? [3] The more controversial a new public program is—and the more difficulty it has encountered in getting through Congress—the more it will need the aid of publicity to explain its aims and procedures to the public. Very often in practical politics the losing minority in Congress attacks the information service of the agency as a way of attacking the program. This happened over and over again with New Deal agencies in the 1930's. But the suppression of the appeal for public understanding is no more fair than it would be to suppress the opposition to the program after it gets under way.

What, then, are the limits of government "propaganda"?

The most obvious requirement for the federal publicity man is that he should stick to his mission. He should not go far afield from his responsibilities and give opinions on irrelevant matters, and he should discourage such activities by other civil service employees. Generals should not be selling a particular kind of foreign policy; in "The Selling of the Pentagon" they were caught doing so. Labor Department officials should not go around making pronouncements on tax policy. Housing people should not interfere in transportation issues. These are matters for top political appointees to fret about, discuss and decide—or recommend to Congress.

More important, the publicity staff should avoid any appearance of seeking new worlds to conquer. There is a big difference between explaining the present program and proposing a new, expanded one. If the agency head and his assistants want to ask for new authority in a new area, this is a political matter. A cabinet member may properly make speeches and give out promotional statements before Congressional committees. But if he tries to use the resources of his permanent staff to stir up the voters to lobby for an expanded program, he will find hostile Congressmen awaiting him at budget time.

It may be impossible for the agency publicity man to avoid being partisan, since he is telling the story of a program for the direct benefit of the party in power. But it is possible to avoid prospective zeal for power. He has a big enough job promoting understanding of the current program without promoting new fields to promote.

Obviously there is an almost indistinguishable line between praising present practices and proposing future policy. The distinction is important, however, and being procedural rather than substantive, it can be enforced. The difference is illustrated by the public sale of General George

[3] Zechariah Chafee, Government and Mass Communications, Vol. II, p. 762: Controversy as a line of distinction is "far from being a bright line." After an interview with John Grierson for the Commission on Freedom of the Press in 1946, he questioned the assumption that an information service will not be an instrument of the party in power. "It is unlikely that the information service will always stick to matters of 'general consent' and stay away from controversial subjects."

C. Marshall's report on World War II. Zechariah Chafee has pointed out that it contained a plea for universal military training. But this was a report to Congress by a responsible administrative official, a chief of staff noted for his meticulous understanding of political protocol. If Marshall had sent it down the line to be dramatized and advertised by the PR staff, it would have been a campaign for public support for a future decision.[4]

From 1936, when the chief educational officer of the Food and Drug Administration lobbied with the public for stronger controls, to 1958, when the foreign aid program was promoted by a White House conference intended to bring public pressure to bear on Congress, the line has often been crossed.[5] Modern methods of getting attention—such as creating an event which must in turn be publicized—are enough to keep any serious public servant in doubt about his position. But the main issue is the future tense. If bigger and better appropriations are the goal, the publicity man should limit his persuasive tactics to the meetings of Congressional committees. Speeches, periodicals, movies, and other public communication media can be used to strengthen the present program. If this is well and truly done, the future will take care of itself.

There is a substantive question which must also be considered. John Grierson's affirmation of the wide scope of educational activity by government is eloquent, and the public life of this documentary film-maker was largely devoted to its attainment in England:

> We have worked in a dozen very different areas, and made a first tentative shot at picturing the worlds of communication and science, public administration, and social welfare. . . .
>
> There are, in fact a thousand other gaps to bridge between, shall we say, the farmer and the research station, between the citizen and better practice. Our system of communications must provide for a rich flow of living records from which each of us, in our own separate interest, learns what the other fellow is doing and is thereby enabled to pull up our own standards.[6]

This kind of general education is a richly rewarding enterprise for society, and is particularly adapted to the medium of film. It is not necessarily a job for government.

There might be a real danger of informational monopoly if the U.S. government were to undertake an educational project of such indefinite

---

[4] Chafee, p. 763. A film was made on this subject two years after Marshall's departure from office as chief of staff; it was called *Plan for Peace* (M-1324, released 1947) and Selective Service in peacetime began the following year.

[5] See James McCamy, *Government Publicity*, p. 26. Also James N. Rosenau, *Public Opinion and Foreign Policy*, reviewed by David Berg in *Quarterly Journal of Speech* together with other related books, October 1971, especially p. 355.

[6] Forsyth Hardy (ed.), *Grierson on Documentary*, p. 199.

magnitude. Here another line needs to be drawn. The proper subject of governmental information is government. If social problems and special interests are to be studied on film, they should be only those about which the government has taken action. It is a large enough field. No documentary director need fear he will lack for subjects within the broad arena of governmental concerns.

The processes of decision-making in government, however, are rarely the subject for dramatic analysis. Anything approaching an educational or documentary presentation of government in action is almost completely lacking in American mass media. The snippets of news each day, the enormous engine of convention coverage every four years, an occasional issue-oriented program featuring contradictory statements by public figures —this is approximately the gamut. The process of government is largely a mystery for anyone who confines his attention to the television tube.

It should be part of the business of government to tell its own story. There are dangers of partisanship, of course, and of suppression of facts. There are far greater dangers of dullness. But it should be constantly undertaken, and with the highest sponsorship—the President and the Congress.

The underlying difficulty in undertaking a broader program of public information about government is the multiplying complexity of government itself. Not only are the subordinate decisions of the general bureaucracy hard to explain; the most sweeping legislative actions are of baffling variety and entangled with many conflicting interests. Why should anybody try to simplify all this so that voters can understand? Isn't it enough to ask them to vote every couple of years?

Walter Lippmann has long since told us (in *Public Opinion*, published in 1922) how limited is man's capacity for absorbing facts. The information available fails to reach us, not only because of our lack of time, our lack of close contact with events, and our short span of attention, but also because of the stereotypes in our minds which "intercept information on its way to consciousness." Ordinary men are not "omnicompetent citizens" who can figure out the complexities of great issues. They can only be expected to say "yes" or "no"—like a computer—to a general program. Lippmann makes an important assumption:

> In the absence of institutions and education by which the environment is so successfully reported that the realities of public life stand out sharply against self-centered opinion, the common interests very largely elude public opinion entirely, and can be managed only by a specialized class whose personal interests reach beyond the locality.

If reporting is unsuccessful, then more and more of the public's decisions must be made by administrators. We can accept this as a fact of life in many directions, without accepting his corollary thesis of the role of the public in all decisions:

> The necessary simplicity of any mass decision is a very important fact in view of the inevitable complexity of the world in which these decisions operate.[7]

Is a mass decision actually so simple? Nobody can deny that the way the public thinks can sometimes be pretty unprofessional and non-rational. That is in the nature of the broad, sweeping decisions—not simple decisions—the public is so often called upon to make. And it reflects the real and complicated feelings of the citizens who will be affected by those decisions. These feelings can be dismissed easily enough as "emotions," just as the specialists' materials (on which Lippmann was so sure the administrators would apply objectivity) can be dismissed as dry and disembodied facts. But the specialist, however gifted he may be with a bland and quantitative grasp, is the very man who cannot know the qualitative complexity of the lives of the mass of men. The citizen is the only one who knows "where the shoes pinch": he has knowledge about the common life and the impact of law and taxes and prices that the specialist can never have. The citizen knows the way things are—and the way they ought to be.[8]

Public decisions, so deeply rooted in feelings and values, cannot be predigested, simplified, or quantified. They can, however, be illumined and enriched and made more fully informed. The public deserves to be given the kind of information and the kind of shared experience that will actually help.

This does not mean the public must be lectured at, or made to memorize a few carefully selected facts that "really matter." The stereotyped notion about citizen stereotypes which proposes to "Simplify! Simplify!" is all right for selling government bonds. It will not help very much on the large issues, and it will never make the citizen feel at home with his government.

Why assume that all things must be simplified so that the public may forever deal with simple things? Why not assume that the public understanding can be made more complex? What about some new inventions in public reporting that might make "the realities of public life stand out sharply"? Why should "the common interests very largely elude public opinion"?

---

[7] Pp. 93–94, 176.

[8] See John Dewey, p. 206: "The man who wears the shoe knows best that it pinches and where it pinches, even if the expert shoemaker is the best judge of how the trouble is to be remedied." See also A. D. Lindsay, *The Modern Democratic State*, p. 270: "The argument about the shoes pinching is the argument which justifies adult suffrage. If government needs for its task an understanding of the common life it exists to serve, it must have access to all the aspects of that common life."

The ideal way to understand government, no doubt, is to take part in it. Only those who participate in politics or in pressure groups can really feel the cross-currents of modern political life. The Democratic convention of 1972 demonstrated that a lot more could be done with this than anybody expected. But the vast majority of citizens must depend on other ways of seeing. What is most needed is some new way of getting "inside" the process of decision-making itself—inside the currents of thought and influence and action which come to a climax in a law or an administrative order or a new policy.

The administrator himself is not very often able to tell anyone in any interesting way what it is he goes through. It is seldom possible for a man of action, even if he has a strong ego, to reconstruct the story of his actions effectively. To attract and hold attention, to reach the consciousness of the average man, he must call for the intervention of artists and editors, dramatists and photographers. His story must fit the facts, but it must reach the emotions, too.

The documentary film is one way of achieving a kind of popular experience "inside" difficult public problems. Both the problems and the decision-making process can be dramatized—although history shows that the problems, not the solutions, have more often been brought to the screen. To dramatize the politician's hard choices among facts and opinions—perhaps even the hazardous and delicate elements of conflicting personalities—will be to show ordinary citizens how their elected and appointed leaders do their work.

This kind of communication is as salutary for government officials as it is for citizens. Every attempt to explain what he does gives an administrator a clearer view of his goals and methods. Every attempt to communicate honestly with his constituents makes the public man—whether bureaucrat or politician—more aware of the men and women he serves. The people will be gaining a real understanding—a knowledge-of-acquaintance—not merely with the tiresome *pro* and *con* of specific issues, but with the way government works.[9]

The process of government is the heart of the matter. Democracy is not an abstraction but a process, a hardworking means to ideal ends which are constantly reshaped by new needs and interpretations. Anybody can talk grandly of goals. Goals are far-off, indistinct. Methods are what we live with. If American voters are mystified by the machinery of means, they are shut out from the most essential understanding of their own self-government.

[9] Elton Mayo took from William James a "simple distinction" about learning (*The Social Problems of an Industrial Civilization*, p. 16): "Almost every civilized language except English has two commonplace words for knowledge. . . . This distinction, simple as it is, nevertheless is exceedingly important; *knowledge-of-acquaintance* comes from direct experience of fact and situation, *knowledge-about* is the product of reflective and abstract thinking."

The Documentary: Creative and Persuasive

The documentary film, like most valuable things, is difficult to define. The nonfiction film is somewhat easier: we can call it a way of reporting on a person, place, or event which does not depend on an invented story line. But the tradition of the documentary has led us to expect something more special than straight reporting, something unique and rather wonderful—factual, yet artistically arranged. John Grierson, the leader of the British documentary movement of the 1930's, called it "the creative treatment of actuality."

How creative should it be?

The makers of social action documentaries in the 1930's tended to cling to the belief that only "real people" ought to be photographed in their films. This concept came out of an era of realism in still photography, when the man at the machine or the plow had to be real in order to seem real. As long as the daily routines of farm or factory are the central concern of the film, an amateur can easily enough duplicate those routines. He cannot ordinarily duplicate an emotional crisis. Therefore a whole range of realistic experiences, requiring the services of actors, must be left to the fiction film.

The important thing is not the authenticity of the materials, but the authenticity of the result. Robert Flaherty was perfectly willing to "fake" a scene so long as the total impression was true to life as he saw it. He photographed the Eskimo Nanook in half an igloo—open to the sky and to the camera. He reenacted older traditions of tattooing in *Moana* and sent the islanders of Aran on a dangerous search for the basking shark, because he wanted to recapture a way of life that was past.

The American newsreel invention called *The March of Time*, founded by Louis de Rochemont in 1935, even used the studio and actors occasionally, as well as specially filmed interviews; this supplemented material the news cameraman was lucky enough to catch on the spot. Impersonations would certainly not be acceptable today, but *The March of Time* was a historic step toward a fuller, more truthful kind of reporting in depth.

The makers of a film about the Viet Nam war ran into a storm of disapproval when a wire service reporter discovered one day that they were "setting up" some battle close-ups, as newsreel photographers had done for years. The reality of the final film was considerably restricted when the USIA had to bow to pressure and forbid any further connecting shots of this sort.[10]

Certainly a scrupulous concern for real locations and the use of non-professional performers can have a great deal to do with the truthfulness of a film. The studio-trained director is the one most likely to miss the feeling of authenticity. Yet a lot of meticulous factual details can hardly make a film true in its essence. California movie executives made newsreels in 1934 purporting to show that thousands of hoboes were flocking to the west coast to cash in on Upton Sinclair's possible victory in the race for governor. The question about such a "newsreel" is not whether the few hoboes depicted were real, but whether the over-all implication of the film was false.[11]

The Canadian National Film Board, in its catalog for 1948, *Canadian Image*, made a helpful distinction on the basis of "story," using that word as a newspaper reporter or a writer of magazine articles would use it:

> A documentary cannot be dreamed up by a script writer spinning a story web out of his personal contemplation. He must go to the actual. There he may select and compress in order to get his story on the screen in 20 minutes running time. He may reenact something that happened yesterday. But he may not do violence to reality. If the facts provide no happy ending, neither may he do so. But he may indicate how a happy ending might be achieved. For if the documentary dealt with all the facts it would be like life itself: long periods of boredom punctuated with moments of intense excitement or crisis. It is the documentary film-maker's job to isolate and then synthesize these moments of excitement or crisis, since in their understanding often lies the essence of reality.

In the 1960's, new technical advancements in the reporting of reality brought new issues of style and responsibility.

Cinéma vérité (or direct cinema) came in with the invention of cheaper synchronized sound for 16mm film. A light-weight shoulder-mounted camera plus a fully portable microphone and recorder meant that two men working together could reproduce the faces and voices of people talking as they naturally do. No studio set-ups or prepared scripts were necessary or suitable for this kind of film-making. Under the old newsreel "single system" of sound recording, editing or rearrangement of sound was possible (by substituting narration for the speaker's voice) but this was not the usual handling. The traditional documentary method had been silent shooting with narration added afterward; this meant a less

10 January 13, 1965. See Chapter 8.
11 See Henry Pringle, "The Movies Swing an Election," *New Yorker*, April 4, 1936; Bosley Crowther, *Hollywood Rajah*, 225–228; Upton Sinclair, "The Movies and Political Propaganda," *The Movies on Trial*; Raymond Fielding, *The American Newsreel*, 1911–1967, pp. 268–269.

realistic effect but much more flexible handling in the editing room. Now the film maker can have all the real sound, if he wants it, and he can edit any way he chooses, with sound or without, with narration or without. The only thing he cannot ordinarily do is to unmix the recorded sound effects and voices on the track.

Yet *cinéma vérité*, for all its new technical advantages, tends to revert to the worst disadvantages of the primitive newsreel. In the first place, some of its more doctrinaire practitioners stoutly maintain that they are more "truthful" if they simply shoot what they happen to see, without doing any kind of research beforehand. In such a view, ignorance is bliss, and the audience is apparently encouraged to remain in the same state of ignorance as the film-makers. In the second place, the very "sync-sound" nature of the *cinéma vérité* technique tempts the film-maker to seek out the most exciting events and the most conflict-ridden situations—elements that grab attention, shock or entertain. Finally, because sound and picture arrive in the cutting room in exactly equal lengths, *cinéma vérité* tempts the film editor to do little more than splice the footage together without change or interpretation and call the result a work of untouchable art.

The remedy for these primitivisms—as in most other departments of life—is the application of some knowledge, effort, experience and intelligence. As practiced by Richard Leacock or William Jersey, documentary film-making is still understood to be a part of the tradition of public enlightenment. *Cinéma vérité* is simply a way of getting closer to the emotional or decision-making fabric of life. It does not absolve the film-maker of certain obvious responsibilities—to select subjects for their significance, research them thoroughly, and apply in the editing room the rational balancing of narration.

It is real concern with subject matter, not with method, which counts most heavily in bringing a documentary film-maker close to the truth. It is integrity of purpose, bent upon authenticity of content, which brings with it the desire to seek out real places and real people as means.

The documentary is concerned with man—his history, his problems of living in society, his means of livelihood, his politics, his changing attitudes toward himself. If this is the case, it need hardly be added that the documentary often deals with controversial subjects. A subject about which there is no controversy usually falls under the heading of science, or else it is a subject so widely accepted that a film about it can be called primarily an instructional or training film.

The documentary teaches. But it often does so by giving strange new information, or old information from new viewpoints. It appeals primarily to man's faculty of judgment. Like a nonfiction book which achieves popular or critical success, it may be nostalgic or informative, reassuring or disturbing, but its editing and narration will be held together by a central idea. Its commitment may be passionate, its method emotional and its style a triumph of art. The effect of the film may be to change the basis of judgment and eventually to change men's minds.

How persuasive should it be? Can it be called documentary if it is one-sided, propagandist?

It might seem logical to try to limit the documentary to the requirements of objectivity, but these requirements could never be adequately defined. And to say that a film with an editorial point of view cannot be documentary in nature and educational in effect would be to rule out much of the best nonfiction now in existence and much that will be filmed in future. The value of the balanced, objective report is unquestionable. The value of liveliness, of attention-getting excitement, which lies in the convinced propagandist presentation, is also very great— especially in an age of excessive communication.

At its best, the documentary film—like democracy, like education— is an expression of faith in man's ability to understand himself and to improve his lot. Therefore many of the most vital American documentaries have been critical of the existing order. Even Robert Flaherty, who was rarely an activist, made a questioning kind of film called *The Land*. Pare Lorentz would have had little to say if he had been denied by his government the opportunity to be indignant about man-made dust storms and floods. The great tradition, including the work of Edward R. Murrow and his successors on network television, has not been self-praise but self-questioning, the familiar American muckraking tradition which says, "We aren't living up to our ideals. There must be some better way."

The documentary film may, and almost always does, use unscripted situations, natural backgrounds, and untrained performers, but this is not as important as the requirement that its action must be action which has happened. Content, not method, is what matters most. The documentary's content—often controversial—is primarily concerned with public affairs and social studies, presenting facts selected for relevance from thorough research, edited by artists in terms of a central idea, usually taking account of more than one viewpoint but not necessarily refusing to offer a conclusion. It is a combination of science and art, of research and insight, focused on man.

As such, the documentary is well suited to an age which needs the heart of its public problems made meaningful to the public. These problems—now so often concerned with the crowding of cities and the pressures of living in a technological age—are increasingly emotional in tone. The merely informational or news film seldom touches the deep feelings behind such issues. The documentary can reach the depths of human concern, appealing not only to the mind but to the heart.[12]

[12] Cf. Chafee, pp. 781–782: "Should an information service merely distribute what is commonly known as news, or should it also deal with 'pre-news,' that is,

It is, of course, a dangerous thing to turn loose the creative and persuasive force of the documentary film at the beck and call of ambitious bureaucrats. They may use it to flood the marketplace of communication with dramatized half-truths and misstatements of fact. But the more important danger is that the great public problems and the increasing complexities of government decision-making will never be reported by the effective communication of film, and that a very large part of the busy public will therefore never know about them at all—will never even begin to understand them.

---

questions of principle and decision—the considerations on which policy is based? The broader scope has much more effect on national morale. . . . Much more than facts is needed by us citizens if we are to become conscious that we are partners and not just passengers in the difficult enterprise of government."

The government documentary, in other words, must concern itself with more than reports of decisions; here the documentary's *content* should be the *methods* of government, both executive and legislative—the characteristic machinery of means plus the varied personal wills which are assumed to express some part of the will of the people.

2

Documentary in England and Canada

THE STORY of the documentary film in England is almost literally the story of one man—John Grierson. No other individual has had comparable influence or occupied so commanding a position in the history of the documentary movement. Not even Robert Flaherty, who can properly be called the father of documentary, reached the kind of continuing personal influence which Grierson built up by his writing and by his training of a whole corps of new directors. Sergei Eisenstein, whose influence on the techniques and the political awareness of film-makers has certainly been great, was increasingly limited by the framework of his ideology; in later years the changing demands of Soviet nationalism and political criticism as well as the advent of the sound film served to limit his mastery of the medium and his international influence.

Grierson was influenced by both of these men. But after he was well under way, he began to reject what he called "aestheticky" approaches to film, and also found less and less interest in Flaherty's explorations to the far corners of the earth—keen-eyed researches into strange customs which nevertheless seemed to Grierson unrelated to the social and economic problems of his own society. He wanted to show the turning of wheels and the whir of machinery in contemporary civilization, not because of the "symphony" of sound and pattern which could be evoked, but for the hard thinking which might be aroused. He was fond of saying, as Paul Rotha has said more emphatically, that the documentary must be propagandist. Behind this sense of the role of film in the social order there was a strong sense of the vastness of the forces which modern science had unleashed upon mankind, and the urgent necessity for men to use these great forces freely for good, not secretly for evil.

Politically he cannot be said to have found peace in any dogma, but he was greatly influenced by Walter Lippmann and by the three years he spent studying the press and the film in the United States. Far more important than the dramatic impact of Eisenstein's ideas or the dramatic onrush of collectivism in Soviet Russia was this realistic skepticism which pointed out the extremely limited reading habits, the narrowly structured stereotypes, characteristic of the average man. If he had any systematic political theory at all, which is doubtful, Grierson seems to have put primary emphasis upon the impersonal forces of science, engineering, collectivism, economic determinism. Men had to be shown that the role of the individual was nowadays at a minimum.

> For three hundred years we have had our focus on the individual. . . . We have built our State on the freedom of personal adventure. But discoveries have involved organization, greater and more complex organization. Individual adventure becomes less important than co-operation. In fact, the individual outlook becomes less and less valuable and more and more harmful unless it is transmuted into the corporate outlook.[1]

Grierson, of course, did not stop with pessimism. He wanted to do something about it, and he found his great hope in what Forsyth Hardy calls "selective dramatization of facts in terms of their human consequences." [2] The motion picture was to make individuals understand the irrevocable collectivization, mechanization, and complexity of modern life. It was to help in achieving common patterns of thought in the face of such changes.

Grierson's own life and work contradict his gloomy analysis. In whatever box one's estimate may be enclosed—film philosophy, governmental leadership, information activity—the presence of this one man of irrepressible vitality, combining analytical pessimism in theory with dynamic hope in practice, did change the social situation and affected history.

John Grierson and the Empire Marketing Board

Grierson was the son of a Scottish schoolmaster. Born in 1898 at Deanston, near Stirling, he was a hard-working student, and won a scholarship at Glasgow University for his college years. During the first World

[1] John Grierson, "Films and the Community," *Grierson on Documentary*, pp. 153–154 (first U.S. edition, 1947).
[2] Hardy, Introduction, *Grierson on Documentary*, p. 4.

War he spent three and a half years in the Navy, doing auxiliary patrol
work and mine-sweeping. He returned to Glasgow to graduate in philosophy and afterward lectured for a time at Durham University.

It was at this point of his development that the young veteran and
scholar took his trip to America. He studied public opinion and public
relations from 1924–1926 as a Rockefeller Research Fellow in Social
Science. Part of his work in political science at the University of Chicago
involved an inspection of the so-called yellow press and its effectiveness.
These newspapers, he saw, were selecting the news and hammering it
home. However one might view the correctness or social advantage of
their editorial judgments, the selection process was taking place, and
sensationalism of writing and headlining enlarged and dramatized the
stories which had been selected.[3]

In fact, it seemed to him that the mass media in general were taking
over the job of the schools and churches. They were being listened to,
where preachers and teachers found their exhortations falling on deaf
ears. Or more exactly, the indeterminate, unconscious effects of exposure
to mass communications were bound to be deeply embedded effects, however difficult it might be to extricate and rationally analyze them. Why
could not these media become channels for more mature thinking? Why
could they not be used, perhaps, by students of social science?

Grierson had already been reading a good deal of Walter Lippmann,
who had published by this time both *Public Opinion* and *The Phantom
Public*. He was impressed by Lippmann's notion that men build up for
themselves differing "pictures in their heads" of what goes on around
them—that this pictured "pseudo-environment," not the factual situation,
is the real basis for both attitude and action.

> The way in which the world is imagined determines at any particular
> moment what men will do. . . . What each man does is based not
> on direct and certain knowledge but on pictures made by himself or
> given to him.[4]

It is not surprising therefore, that the young British visitor early fixed
on the motion picture as probably the most powerful medium of public
information in our century. In fact, Lippmann personally encouraged him
to do so. Filled with the yeast of new ideas, he could hardly refrain from
taking an active part in discussions about them. He wrote guest columns
of film criticism for New York papers, including the New York *Sun*. He
turned up in Hollywood to study production and meet people like Chaplin and Stroheim. He wrote on film aesthetics and on audience measure-

[3] *Ibid.* Richard Griffith and Mary Losey, introductory notes, p. 97.
[4] *Public Opinion*, chapter I. Grierson says that Lippmann, when he met and talked
with him, pointed the younger man in the direction of the movies. *Grierson on Documentary*, pp. 260–261. See also Jack C. Ellis, "The Young Grierson in America,"
Cinema Journal, Vol. VIII, No. 1, Fall 1968.

ment. He met Robert Flaherty, who had already produced both *Nanook* and *Moana.* He helped to prepare the English version of Eisenstein's *Battleship Potemkin.*

These were some of the experiences Grierson took to England with him. Back in London, one of the first places he visited was the office of the secretary of the Empire Marketing Board.

In an article in the *Spectator,* Sir Stephen Tallents has told about his first meeting with Grierson in February 1927, and how he was "brimming with ideas." [5] That interview made quite an impression on the EMB secretary, and the young Scotsman got the job. This was a decision of historic importance for the development of the non-fiction film.

The EMB was supposed to encourage empire trade, and primarily the sales of empire goods in Great Britain. The job was therefore, as Tallents conceived it, largely an informational one. He had been appointed secretary in 1926. The Arts Enquiry report on *The Factual Film* thus evaluates the EMB's pioneering in the informational field:

> It became the first Government body in this country to undertake public relations work on a large scale and to make wide use of publicity media, including the film. It was the first official body to have its own film production unit.[6]

The attitude toward government publicity work in England at that time was not much more advanced than it was in the United States. One or two departments had public relations sections and there were also "press officers" (and others without such title who did the same work) to provide help for newspapermen. But all this was in large part a series of left-overs from the exigencies of wartime informational problems, not a response to new and growing social needs for communication. The British Council was not to be set up till 1934. Despite the widespread acceptance of advertising as a fact—as well as the now-familiar American merchandising practices of Selfridge's department store and the clear-cut presence of a "yellow press" related in kind to the press Grierson had studied in America—it could hardly be said that public relations as an over-all concept was much thought about in private or public business.[7]

As far as motion pictures were concerned, the British producers had not yet recovered from the Hollywood-flooded market of World War I. The proportion of British films being shown in Britain was only five per cent; American films took up 85 to 90 per cent of theater time. The situa-

[5] "British Documentary Films," November 19, 1937. See also Sir Stephen Tallents, "The Birth of British Documentary," in *Journal* of University Film Association, Vol. 20, No. 1, 2, and 3.

[6] P. 44.

[7] Political and Economic Planning Pamphlet No. 230, February 2, 1945, "Government Information Services," p. 4. See also PEP No. 14, "Government Public Relations," November 21, 1933: "Government public relations are as strange a subject now as broadcasting was a dozen years ago, or the cinema before 1914."

tion was so serious that the Government was about to pass a Cinemato-graph Act requiring annually increasing quotas of British-made films to be included in exhibitors' lists. Factual films, beyond the routine newsreel, were few and far between, although Bruce Woolfe had begun a series called *Secrets of Nature* in 1919 which had been used in school science courses. Gaumont-British Instructional did not begin important work in this field until 1934. The British Film Institute was still five years away.

Nevertheless, Tallents had from the first given some thought to the publicity role of the motion picture. Specific plans had already been made before Grierson arrived on the scene, and it was this very fact which kept the new recruit hovering in the wings for the time being. Tallents had had a talk with Rudyard Kipling in the summer of 1926, and Kipling had indicated he might be willing to advise on film-making. Naturally Tallents was delighted, and soon Walter Creighton was at work on a seven-reel epic depicting the intangible ties of imperial relationships "by a series of lavish pictures of imperial cavalcades bringing across the world the ingredients for the King's Christmas pudding." [8] This hopeful—and expensive—effort was shortly interred in the vaults of the EMB. *One Family* was not a success, critically or otherwise.

Apparently Tallents was not a man to be easily dismayed, though further film-making might have seemed to be jumping, so to speak, from the pudding into the porridge. The kind of realism Grierson had been urging upon him was certainly different enough from *One Family*, but seemed no more promising to the untutored and skeptical eyes of Treasury representatives.

Some tutoring had been brought to bear, however, on the members and associates of the Empire Marketing Board. Tallents had put Grierson to work temporarily on just this job.

> He wrote indefatigable memoranda about foreign cinematic exper-ience, and arranged after office hours a series of notable film displays at the Imperial Institute, which taught us and a few favored guests what other countries had done and were doing to put their achieve-ment, instead of their day-dreams, on the screen.[9]

Eisenstein, Pudovkin, Ruttmann, and Flaherty were prominent on these educational programs. Although he was later to criticize each of these directors in one way or another for their isolation from the common-places of the common life, he was learning from them now and using them to show others what films might do. The famous Odessa steps se-quence and the mutiny scene from *Potemkin* were worked overtime, and anybody with a prophetic cinematic eye could have seen what Grierson might do with a combination of Flaherty's *Nanook of the North* and Ruttmann's *Berlin*.

[8] *The Factual Film*, p. 46.
[9] *Spectator, op. cit.* Tallents remembered, among others, *The Covered Wagon*, *Turksib*, *Storm Over Asia*, *Earth*. See also *Grierson on Documentary*, p. 122.

The decision to give Grierson a free hand with the film did not come till April 27, 1928. In the office of the chairman of the EMB, a meeting was held which included three members of the board, the secretary (Tallents), Grierson, and Mr. Arthur Michael Samuel, the Financial Secretary to the Treasury. Mr. Samuel, it seems, was the greatest living authority on the British herring industry. He had gone so far as to write a book about it. Although he came to the meeting prepared to express his adamant opposition to the use of films for advertising Britain, he was met with a proposal to publicize the herring industry.

What was needed, the Board officials all sagely agreed, was a film which would offer some of the authentic flavor of English character and enterprise, but limited enough in scope to be immediately meaningful and informative to an English audience. Grierson had worked with minesweepers during the war and could be expected to turn up something interesting in the way of a nonfiction sea story. The meeting ended with considerable enthusiasm all around, Mr. Samuel offering his specialized knowledge if needed, and the Board members gladly accepting it. Tallents describes the results as follows:

> The decision to embark, you will have noted, involved two top-ranking Cabinet Ministers, and the making of the film created, I am sure, agonies as sharp as ever attended the making of say, Eisenstein's Mexican film or *Caesar and Cleopatra*. A drifter, the "Maid of Thule," was hired at Stornoway, chiefly on the strength of her crew's supposed photogenic quality. John Skeaping designed a cabin set, which was erected near the harbour. A fisheries protection cruiser obliged with power for the lighting. The underwater scenes were supplied by dogfish chivvying small roach about a tank on the Plymouth Marine Biological Station. Then the "Maid of Thule" couldn't find the herrings, and operations had to be transferred to another drifter at Lowestoft. Next the chairman of the company, with whom a contract had been made for the film's production, turned up in my room one evening with a long face to declare that it was a predestined flop and had better be abandoned. That was one of the real crises of my official life. But I left Grierson to deal with him. Production was resumed. On November 10th, 1929, the Film Society put on *Drifters* in a programme with *Potemkin*, and it won much applause in the theatre and praise thereafter from a number of critics.[10]

The success of this small and simple movie depicting the toil and courage of fishermen contrasts obviously enough with the unsuccessful pretentiousness of the feature-length Imperial Pudding. The significance of *Drifters*, however, lies not in its individual success but in the fact that it started something.

[10] "The First Days of Documentary," *Documentary News Letter*, January–February, 1947. Reprint of parts of Cobb Lecture, delivered at Royal Society of Arts, November 1946, as first printed in *Journal* of the Society, December 20, 1946. *Drifters* was made by the New Era Studios (*Grierson on Documentary*, p. 122).

This was the first and last film that Grierson himself was responsible for, as director. Not long after, he did bring in Robert Flaherty to do a much-praised survey called *Industrial Britain,* and both shared in the direction. But the new films officer of the Empire Marketing Board had something bigger in mind than a career as a man behind the megaphone. He might single-handedly have produced three or four films a year, interpreting, as *Drifters* did, one segment of the British community to the rest of the community. However much this might have brought him in the way of artistic reputation, he chose instead to be a director of directors— that is, in motion picture terms, a producer. And he gradually brought together a unique aggregation of bright young men, instilled them with his purposes, and gave them free range for their skills.

> Because the job was new and because it was too humble to appeal to studio directors, it was also a question of taking young people and giving them their heads.

> That was in 1930. In the three years that followed, we gathered together, and in a sense created, Basil Wright, Arthur Elton, Stuart Legg, and half a dozen others. Wright was the best all-rounder. One or two others, it seemed, would presently be heard from.[11]

Among the early films, all short and all made without lip-synchronized sound because of lack of money and equipment, Roger Manvell selected for special mention six besides *Drifters* and *Industrial Britain:*

The Country Comes to Town
        (London's market services, directed by Basil Wright, 1931–2)
O'er Hill and Dale
        (A day in the life of a border shepherd, Basil Wright, 1932)
Windmill in Barbados (Basil Wright, 1933)
Cargo from Jamaica (Basil Wright, 1933)
Granton Trawler (Edgar Anstey, 1934)
Aero-Engine (Arthur Elton, 1934) [12]

Writing in the summer of 1933, Grierson included in his own assessment, besides a third Wright picture from the West Indies, *Upstream* (about salmon fishing in Scotland), *Big Timber, Shadow on the Mountain* (pasture experiments at Aberystwyth), *The New Generation,* and various films for the Ministry of Agriculture and for the schools. Edgar Anstey was also responsible for *Uncharted Waters,* a film about Labrador. Experimentation was well under way, too, in various directions—*Hen Woman* was a story documentary; Paul Rotha was already interested in abstract films. The pattern of outside sponsorship was beginning. *Lancashire at Work and Play* was being made for the Travel Association; the

[11] Grierson, "The EMB Film Unit," *Grierson on Documentary,* p. 123, written originally for the *Cinema Quarterly,* Summer 1933.
        [12] *Film,* p. 95.

Gramophone Company hired Grierson on a private basis to produce and Elton to direct *Voice of the World;* and it is significant that Stuart Legg was already working on two films for the Post Office. In all, the EMB Film Unit produced about a hundred original motion pictures.[13]

Grierson himself, besides his responsibility as producer, was busy giving lectures about documentaries and education and the community, and wrote countless articles on documentary theory. He was instrumental in establishing the Empire Film Library at the Imperial Institute, where schools and private groups could procure nonfiction films. His energy was prodigious and his influence growing.

In 1933, the Empire Marketing Board was dissolved by an "economy campaign," but the documentary film was in England to stay. However experimental they were, however coldly received by theatrical cinema distributors, the nonfictional products of the EMB determination to "bring the Empire alive to itself" had met with considerable public applause. The Grierson crew had brought film itself alive for new purposes. And it began to be apparent that the comprehensive concept of public relations sponsored by the EMB was destined to be influential in British administration.

The General Post Office and Film Centre

Later in 1933, Sir Stephen Tallents was appointed the first public relations officer of the General Post Office. Sir Kingsley Wood, the Postmaster General, was reorganizing inside and out, and he had a three-fold publicity goal: To develop the business of the GPO, to secure the cooperation of the public in the details of that business, and to make members of the staff feel that their work was understood by the public.[14] In an article in the *Spectator*, he linked the publicity process integrally with departmental functions themselves:

> The public need is not met by the mere provision of . . . services.
> . . . The old "take it or leave it" attitude . . . was like building a house and providing no access to it. At this point we approach a basic theory of advertising—namely, that you must believe that a thing is useful before you *will* use it, and you must know that a thing exists before you *can* use it.[15]

[13] "The EMB Film Unit." Hardy, Introduction, p. 11.
[14] See PEP No. 228, "British Documentary Films," December 8, 1944.
[15] "Government Publicity," November 19, 1937.

Radio and telegraph are part of the Post Office responsibility in Great Britain, and when the Film Unit moved to the GPO with Sir Stephen Tallents, it would seem to have been a particularly stimulating opportunity. To extol the successes of communication itself surely must be a job fit for trained communicators. There were drawbacks:

> One remembers looking at a sorting office for the first time and thinking that when you had seen one letter you had seen the lot. . . . We gradually began to see, behind the infernal penny-in-the-slot detail in which the Post Office is so symbolic of our metropolitan civilization, something of the magic of modern communication. We saw the gale warning behind the Central Telegraph Office, the paradox of nationalism and internationalism behind the cable service, the choral beauty of the night mail, and the drama tucked away in the files of the ship-to-shore radio service.[16]

This, of course, was openly publicity for a Government department, not merely trimmings for the generally agreed advantages of international trade. It was put on the most forthright advertising basis, but used fully the powerful tools of drama, poetry, music and montage.

The GPO period was the time of ripest experiment for Grierson both in poetic imagery and social documentation. For *Night Mail*, directed by Harry Watt and Basil Wright, Benjamin Britten wrote the music and W. H. Auden wrote part of the commentary.

> Past cotton grass and moorland boulder,
> Shoveling white steam over her shoulder,
> Snorting noisily as she passes
> Silent miles of wind-bent grasses,

the night train carrying letters for Britons became also a symbol of what Manvell calls "industrial romanticism." *Coalface* was about mining, but it had another Auden background, and the commentary was spoken in part by a recitative chorus.

Less self-explanatory than these titles, perhaps, is *The Saving of Bill Blewitt*, which, like the story of ship-to-shore radio service in *North Sea*, dramatized a story about real people. In this case the purpose was to "bring alive" a Post Office Savings Bank in a Cornish fishing village. Some other films made by the GPO were:

6:30 *Collection* (Edgar Anstey, 1934)
Under the City (Arthur Elton, Alexander Shaw, 1934)
Weather Forecast (Evelyn Spice, 1934)
Airmail (Arthur Elton, Alexander Shaw, 1935)
BBC—Voice of Britain (Stuart Legg, 1935) [17]

[16] Grierson in the *Fortnightly Review*, August 1939.
[17] Manvell, *Film*, p. 97. *Coalface* was directed by Alberto Cavalcanti, *North Sea* by Harry Watt. The important contributions of Cavalcanti to the GPO days have not yet been adequately assessed.

Neither the weather nor the BBC could escape the poetic trend and there was plenty of specially composed music, too. This is not to say that there was a distinct aesthetic pattern in all the films produced. Certainly the emphasis was on message, and on a technique to fit the message. But this period does contrast markedly with the later days of the wartime Canadian National Film Board, when Grierson's demand was for terseness, directness, speed.

Probably the most remarkable development in the whole story of British documentary production was now beginning to take place along-side the GPO activities. Shortly after the Gramophone Company had hired Grierson and Elton to do *Voice of the World*, Paul Rotha (who had left the EMB Film Unit the year before) was asked to produce a film about Imperial Airways. It was called *Contact*, and ran to four reels instead of the usual two or three; its success was considerable, in that it got a large number of theatrical showings. Rotha did some other documentaries for industrial sponsorship, notably *Shipyard*, for Vickers-Armstrong and the Orient Line. He made *The Face of Britain* for Gaumont-British Instructional, which was then beginning its entry into the factual film business.[18]

In 1934 Shell Marketing and Refining Company formed the Shell Film Unit, and Edgar Anstey was invited to take charge. *Power Unit* (1936), *Transfer of Power* (1939), *Distillation* (1940), *Hydraulics* (1941), are examples of the difficult scientific subjects dealt with in this experiment in educational public service. They were much used in the schools, and along with other scientific films in the Shell Library, were distributed to subsidiary companies all over the world. Statement of sponsorship appeared only in the credit titles.

Another offspring of the GPO unit was the Strand Film Company, set up for documentary production by Donald Taylor and Ralph Keene, with Rotha in charge of production at first and Stuart Legg later. From 1936 through 1939, about 80 films were produced for such varied sponsors as the National Council of Social Service, the National Book Council, and the Royal National Lifeboat Institution, as well as for government departments.[19] The Realist Film Unit was established in 1937 by Basil Wright, and did films for *The Times* Publishing Company (*The Fourth Estate*, 1939), the League of Nations, the British Commercial Gas Association, and other national groups.

It was the work of the Commercial Gas Association which resulted in the most extraordinary statements, among all these films, of the need for social change. Manvell described this organization as "the most liberal of commercial producers in the range of social problems that were dis-

[18] *The Factual Film*, p. 53.
[19] *Cover to Cover* (1936) on books and their history; *Men of Africa* (1938) on colonial administration; *Future's in the Air* (1937) on empire air routes.

cussed in its films." [20] Beginning with a prescribed program of five films, the Association called in Elton and Anstey to talk about subjects and treatment. This was in 1935. *Housing Problems* was one of these early ones. By means of on-the-spot interviews and unplanned shots of slums in Stepney, documentary support was built up for the case against unplanned housing. Later examples of this kind of public service by the gas industry were *Enough to Eat?* (1936), *Smoke Menace* (1937), and *The Londoners* (1938). *Children at School* (1937) was particularly notable for its contrast between the possibilities and the realities of school environment.

It is not without interest that the most important film contributions to public thinking about social problems, social change, and planning, were made by private industry, not by Government departments. The early experimenting—the demonstration of what could be done in the way of public reporting—was done by enterprising young men in the bureaucracy. Then some of these same men were hired from outside to do a broader job, a public service job, exploring the problems of choice that lie behind social ills, as a feature of industry public relations.

This was one kind of response to the Grierson activities. There were others. In hearings before the 1934 Select Committee on Estimates, the Film Industries Department of the Federation of British Industries objected to government production and distribution of films. The report went so far as to recommend that the GPO Film Unit confine itself to straight advertising and intra-office instruction.[21]

These differing responses interacted, of course, and the result of criticism, in part, was the establishment of the outside production agencies. Such films could not be criticized simply on the basis that government had produced them, and that therefore something must be wrong with them. In June, 1937, Grierson resigned. It seemed a good time to get out and start something independent of government and of industry which would provide continuing stimulation and encouragement for the documentary idea.

The result was Film Centre, set up in association with Arthur Elton, Stuart Legg, and J. P. R. Golightly, as a headquarters for research, consultation, planning and contact.[22] It was not a production company, but its members were available for producing jobs. Emphasis was placed on nontheatrical distribution and the expansion of such audiences as well as theatrical programs. A typical example of Film Centre's coordinating work was the production of seven films comprehensively presenting a screen survey of Scotland, planned for release just before the Empire Exhibition

[20] *Film*, p. 102.

[21] *The Factual Film*, pp. 51–52.

[22] In 1935 the Association of Realist Film Producers had been formed by a dozen of the well known people in the production field, and had been acting as a kind of trade association and public relations body.

in Glasgow. Grierson drew up the program, and production was shared among such groups as Strand, Realist, Gaumont-British Instructional, and Pathé. The Films of Scotland Committee, set up by the Scottish Development Council in consultation with the Secretary of State for Scotland, was the sponsor. Financing was accomplished by a combination of industry, government, and other interested groups, a combination which deserves special study in its own right as a precedent for public relations films.

Wartime Films

J. B. Holmes and Alberto Cavalcanti stayed on as producers at the GPO Film Unit until 1940, when the war brought a hiatus which almost overturned the governmental documentary movement altogether. In September, 1939, with the establishment of the Ministry of Information, a Films Division was also created. But by April of the following year, it had had three different directors, and the GPO Unit—although it had produced *The First Days* and *Squadron 992*—was not being used by the MOI and was uncertain of its role in the new state of things. The third director, J. L. Beddington, formerly director of publicity for Shell-Mex, asked for a memorandum on the situation from Film Centre, and from that point on, wartime documentary continued in the spirit and pattern of the EMB–GPO experiences. The GPO Unit was brought into the Film Division bodily as the Crown Film Unit.[23]

There were changes, of course, but chiefly in emphasis and in quantity. The clear-cut purpose of winning the war superseded all other objectives. Production expanded enormously, and in addition to the establishment of a Colonial Film Unit, many outside documentary producers were called in for assistance. By the end of 1945, 726 films were completed, of which 90 per cent was contract work by independent companies. These companies were allotted a small profit—which might more properly be called a fee—and were subject to the accounting procedures of the Division. Decisions about film topics were made with the collaboration of Ministry representatives even when the films were made for the specific needs of other government departments.

At first there was extensive experimentation with weekly five-minute films for use in the motion picture theaters. They were distributed free to assist in specific campaigns—salvage, blackout, recruiting—or else for morale purposes, or to give information about the strategy and progress

23 *The Factual Film*, p. 64.

of the war. These trailers used straight reporting, drama, comedy and cartoons. The idea was discarded, after nearly a hundred had been made and used, in favor of monthly fifteen-minute reports. Thirty-seven of these were produced up to the end of 1945, and their titles illustrate the extent to which more or less "non-war" subjectmatter became logically necessary for programmatic balance:

> *War in the Pacific* (1943), with newsreel extracts, maps and diagrams; *Conquest of a Germ* (1944) a tribute to the doctors and research workers who discovered the sulphonamide drugs; the *Crown of the Year* (1942) on farming; *Power for the Highlands* (1943) on the Scottish hydro-electric scheme; *Subject for Discussion* (1943) on the symptoms, effects, and treatment of venereal disease; *Tyneside Story* (1943) depicting the wartime revival of shipbuilding on the Tyne; and *Broken Dykes, French Town,* and *Stricken Peninsula* (all 1945).[24]

Additional titles, using techniques which were more factual, more to-the-point, or for more specialized audiences, were produced strictly for non-theatrical use. There were 153 of these.

One of the spectacular developments in wartime was the expansion of nontheatrical distribution. Under the necessity of getting out government messages of various general and specialized kinds, the Ministry of Information was able to go far beyond the tentative experiments of the EMB and GPO. The EMB had organized a library of Empire films and had given regular shows in the cinema hall of the Imperial Institute. The GPO continued this local exhibition and national distribution, adding a few motorized units as an experiment, to carry films to small groups on irregular schedules.

The Ministry of Information, besides sending productions—especially the feature-length ones—through regular commercial channels, stepped up this direct appeal to private groups. In 1940–41 there were 50 mobile units in operation. By 1943–44 these had increased to 144, operated on a regional basis. Traveling shows were supplemented by programs in public libraries and in regular moving picture theaters out of regular hours. The total audience for the year 1943–44 was estimated to be 18,500,000.[25]

The most important achievements were the documentaries about the war, beginning with *Target for Tonight* in 1941.

> Exhibitors paid this film the supreme compliment of criticizing the distribution agreement between the Ministry and the Exhibitors' Association. Here at last was a documentary they and the public asked to see because it had the star value of being about the RAF. It

[24] *Ibid.,* pp. 66–67.
[25] *Ibid.,* pp. 59, 77.

illustrated processes (in this case how a raid over German territory was actually carried out) and at the same time showed us people. . . . It did not forget to dramatize the personalities of its human material who speak and act like real people in the middle of a real job with the RAF's flair for understatement.[26]

This proved to be the main job of the Crown Film Unit during the war. *Coastal Command* (1942), *Close Quarters* (1943), *Desert Victory* (1943), and *Western Approaches* (1944) were also successful with theater audiences.

All these films were widely shown in the cinemas and were of the dramatized type with servicemen playing themselves under the superb direction of the Crown tradition, with no self-consciousness, no pose. All these films were in their way masterpieces. They did not, of course, deal with social problems like the documentary of the pre-war period. They dealt with the typical life and typical duties of the services concerned, and they illustrated their stories by the selection of men who by personality and photogenic quality epitomized the personnel who were fighting the war.[27]

Caught up in the intense activity and simplified goals of wartime film-making was a young director of unusual gifts. Humphrey Jennings joined other Cambridge graduates (Stuart Legg, Arthur Elton, Basil Wright) at the GPO in 1934, left again after a year or two, came back in 1938 and continued throughout the war with the Crown Film Unit. A painter and poet who had worked in theater and studied under I. A. Richards, he represented a quite different turn of mind from the social and educational enthusiasms central to Grierson's mission. Furthermore, he was only briefly influenced by Grierson, since Grierson was in Canada during the war. Yet he accepted with steady enthusiasm the task of presenting on film the essence of British character and the response of the British people to the war. It was a clear case of the coincidence of artistic commitment with a public need.[28]

Jennings' ability to reveal the common life was early shown in a brief but influential study of miners, school children, and others, *Spare Time* (1939). The GPO unit's fervor and experience seemed to draw out of him what he felt about humanity, and soon he was set on the course that was so bright and so brief.

[26] Manvell, *Film*, p. 110.
[27] *Ibid.*
[28] See Lindsay Anderson, "Only Connect: Some Aspects of the Work of Humphrey Jennings," *Sight and Sound*, April–May, 1954 (reprinted in *Film Quarterly*, Winter, 1961–62). Also in *Film Quarterly*, same issue: Gerald Noxon, "How Humphrey Jennings Came to Film"; William Sansom, "The Making of Fires Were Started." A tribute pamphlet, *Humphrey Jennings*, was published by a special memorial committee in 1950, with articles by John Grierson, Kathleen Raine, Basil Wright, Dilys Powell, Ian Dalrymple, and John Greenwood (Olen Press).

In *Fires Were Started* (1943), Jennings achieved through a combination of actuality filming and dramatic reenactment an evocation of
the dangers of fire-fighting in London during the blitz. It was a remarkable
sharing of experience, a combination of casualness and tension which
reminds one forcibly of Flaherty. In fact, he seemed to be able to draw
from his nonprofessional actors the same kind of fierce devotion to the
needs of the film that Flaherty did in *Man of Aran*.

The Jennings style was more characteristically seen in two shorter
films, *Listen to Britain* (1941) and *A Diary for Timothy* (1945). Constructed almost like photo-albums, with the most limited kinds of action
and scene, they were nevertheless subtle in their simplicity, moment
gliding into moment, as natural sounds, echoing into the preceding shot,
linked shots into sequences and idea to picture. *Listen to Britain* was not
so much about war itself as it was about waiting and watching. James
Merralls, in an article in *Film Quarterly*, says:

> In *Listen to Britain* there is no narration. The dialogue consists of
> scraps of conversations overheard in passing. The theme of the film is
> the oneness of the British people at war, and we see shopgirls and
> factory workers, the Queen at a Gallery concert, engine-drivers and
> airmen, soldiers on leave, Flanagan and Allen at a lunch-time concert
> in a factory canteen, all seen as part of the fabric of British life in a
> time of stress. One sequence in particular is a memorable example of
> the oblique method Humphrey Jennings was developing in his later
> film essays. It is the concert at the National Gallery; as in *A Diary for
> Timothy* Dame Myra Hess is playing. During the concert the camera
> glides away from the pianist, first lingering on the audience, entranced
> by a Mozart concerto, then gliding around the Gallery, along the sand-
> bagged walls where the paintings ought to be hanging, then outside
> to the noble classical portico, out into a bright London spring day
> until the rumble of the traffic drowns the music and the image fades
> into one of a factory, the roar dissolves into the music of a brass band.
> It is a sequence which stays in the mind's eye, for it is one of the
> loveliest in English cinema.[29]

Jennings' films formed a fitting climax for the documentary movement in England, attesting the vitality of the creative atmosphere Grierson had established. His career, unfortunately, was cut short at the age of
43: he died in an accident in Greece in 1950.

Documentary production, in any qualitative sense, did not survive the
war in England. The Labor government, strangely enough, did not see the
use of communicating either goals or methods through the moving image.
The British Information Service made all sorts of travelogs and ceremonial
subjects available to embassies overseas, plus a few of the old Crown Unit
wartime films, but the troubled inquiries central to the documentary

[29] "Humphrey Jennings: A Biographical Sketch," Winter 1961–62.

spirit were shelved. The Colonial Film Unit continued for several years to encourage basic education in the African colonies, turning over some of its facilities and personnel to the new countries as they became independent.

Sight and Sound published puzzled articles asking why the documentary was in the doldrums: Did it need government subsidy? Did it need crisis or poverty or public anguish in order to flourish? Was there a cycle in such things? John Grierson, back from his adventures in Canada and a brief attempt to set up a company in New York, found little to do in England. Eventually he moved to Wales, where he prepared a weekly television show, broadcast from Scotland, introducing and commenting on short subjects, new and old, as examples of the art of the cinema.

Subsidy did result in a new "wave" of documentary work in the late 1950's. The money came primarily from the Ford Motor Company and from the British Film Institute Experimental Film Production Fund. The impulse, however, was brief, perhaps because the young directors who accepted the assistance seemed to be looking beyond it to feature filmmaking.

The Free Cinema group announced themselves at their first public showing as concerned with "a belief in freedom, in the importance of the individual, and in the significance of the everyday." Lindsay Anderson's encounter with a school for the deaf resulted in one of the finest examples of the documentary art, *Thursday's Children* (co-directed by Guy Brenton). He also made (the same year, 1953) *O Dreamland*, a sardonic view of a carnival after hours, and *Every Day Except Christmas* (1957), a surface probe of the daily doings at Covent Garden market.

Karel Reisz and Tony Richardson co-directed a jazz club picture called *Momma Don't Allow* (1955). But it was Reisz who created the centerpiece of the collection. He was able to expand on the content and method of that earlier collaboration in his study of a boys' club on the "wrong side" of London. *We Are the Lambeth Boys* was a remarkable preview of *cinéma vérité* methods, as he listened in on club discussions and dances, sought out both boys and girls at their humdrum daily jobs, and went along on the boys' sad, surrealistic encounter with a wealthy public school in an annual cricket game.

Thus a small amount of government money did give a few filmmakers helpful training. It may be doubted, however, if these shorter films were the main impetus for the realist films of the 1960's—new writers and a new generation of actors were at least equally important. Anderson, Richardson and Reisz began as critics for the film magazines *Sequence* and *Sight and Sound*. They were not Grierson men. They did not linger long in the documentary pulpit, but moved out as fast as they could to the world of feature entertainment.

In England, as in the United States, the documentary concept was taken over by television. It has had a rich and varied development under the public subsidy of the British Broadcasting Corporation.

It was in Canada that the Grierson philosophy and energy reached full fruition. Here there was a bigger job to do. Documentary developed astonishing variety and vigor and carried with it into peacetime increasingly a promise of permanence.

The National Film Board of Canada

In 1938, Grierson was asked to visit Canada and make proposals for legislation coordinating film activities in that country. The situation in Canada was unusual in that almost no private motion picture production was on the scene. Three small independent units in Montreal, Ottawa and Vancouver provided little competition for Hollywood output. There was a government motion picture bureau, but it was mostly concerned with attracting tourists.

The National Film Act of May, 1939, provided for a seven-man National Film Board, linked to the cabinet by its chairman, who was in the beginning the Minister of Trade and Commerce.[30] The first Film Commissioner, executive officer of the Board, was John Grierson, and he stayed till the end of the war. All departments of the government were directed to consult with him before initiating the production of any film. Except when he agreed to let the work be done outside, all of the production and processing was to be done by the Board and its subsidiary agencies.

The NFB became a big producer—as many as 300 films a year by the end of the war—and a big distributor.[31] Grierson insisted on a straightforward news approach, with overtones of *The March of Time.*[32] *Canada Carries On* told Canadians what other Canadians were doing. *World in Action* posed the problems of war, peace and international relations.

A spectacular side of the story was the distribution network Grierson immediately created. He wanted to reach the scattered population of the western territories as well as the city people who had theaters easily at hand. As soon as the Act was passed, he made telephone calls to univer-

[30] For the "Act to Create a National Film Board" passed May 2, 1939, see Appendix D of Arts Enquiry, *The Factual Film.*
[31] "Presenting NFB of Canada," leaflet published by the National Film Board, Ottawa, 1949.
[32] In fact he hired "The March of Time" to do a study of Canada's economic contribution to the war before the Board was ready to do its own production.

sities and provincial departments and had regional agents appointed. These in turn found projectionists and planned for showings.

In less than a month there were 30 mobile units on the road, and these more than tripled by the end of the war. Villages on the route were visited once a month by auto, train or sleigh and in Quebec "whole parishes reported that these were the first talking movies they had ever attended." Farm women planned social hours and suppers afterward, and university extension services had forums in connection with the shows. In British Columbia one group came 40 miles by canoe. In North Battleford, Saskatchewan, an isolated widower, accustomed to making trips to town only for supplies, changed his habits and started walking in seven miles to see the pictures, his only worry being that "he may get the wrong date for the next showing fixed in his mind." [33]

At the start, Grierson brought in people from England who knew his way of working—Stanley Hawes, Raymond Spottiswoode, and Stuart Legg—who became, in effect, executive producers.[34] Legg, a widely published poet, was especially assigned to films for theatrical distribution. After that, as he had done in England, Grierson began interviewing new, untried young men, looking first for graduates in political economy or history but also for special attributes of curiosity, literacy and willingness to work.

Among the hundreds he hired was a graduate in English language and literature from the University of Toronto. Tom Daly has since reported that he felt he knew nothing about anything by the time he was through being interviewed. Grierson was sick in bed at home but hard at work receiving a stream of visitors. He gave Daly a trial assignment, to do a script about Toronto. The script wasn't much good, according to Legg, but the research showed promise. Daly was put to work in the stock footage library and became an expert on what film was available. Later he worked in the editing rooms, and after the war he emerged as the leader of a unit and executive producer of some of the best films made by the Board.[35]

Other Canadians who signed on with Grierson were Evelyn Spice (later Mrs. Lawrence Cherry), Julian Roffman, Donald Fraser, James Beveridge, Guy Clover, F. R. Crawley, and Ross McLean. From Holland for a short time came Joris Ivens and John Ferno; from France the cameraman Boris Kaufman and the animator Alexander Alexeieff; from

[33] Zechariah Chafee, *Government and Mass Communications*, Vol. II, p. 741. Donald Buchanan, "Canadian Movies Promote Citizenship," *Canadian Geographical Journal*, March 1944.

[34] *Grierson on Documentary*, pp. 17–18, 185–186.

[35] A history of the NFB was prepared sometime in the 1960's but never released for publication. Some of the material in this paragraph and in others is drawn from that confidential document. An extensive history has been prepared by Rodney James as a Ph.D. dissertation at Ohio State University (1970).

the U.S., Irving Jacoby, Roger Barlow, Nicholas Read, Leo Seltzer, the Negro novelist Richard Wright, and even Robert Flaherty for some camera work. From England, very soon, came Norman McLaren, who was to stay and carve out a special niche for himself as a world-famous animator—a far cry from the no-nonsense straight news Grierson claimed he was after.

Subjects ranged from *Women in the War* (Hawes) and *Action Stations!* (Ivens), the latter about the merchant marine coping with submarines in the Atlantic, to *High Over the Borders* (Irving Jacoby and John Ferno), which Jack Ellis describes as "a beautifully-made film on the facts and mysteries of bird migration in the western hemisphere, the cost of which Grierson, in a feat of persuasiveness, managed to charge to the Royal Canadian Air Force." [36]

Other titles in the *Canada Carries On* series were *Farm Front, People's Bank, Hands to the Harvest, Ottawa on the River, Thought for Food, Peoples of Canada.* Others in the *World in Action* series were *The Mask of Nippon, Our Russian Ally, Ukrainian Christmas Holiday.*[37]

At war's end, Grierson left the Board in the hands of Ross McLean and went to New York to plan some international documentary projects. The new Films Commissioner presided over all sorts of useful films made for various departments, such as *Rural Health, Just Weeds, Vegetable Insects, Know Your Baby, Accidents Don't Happen.* For 16mm audiences a little entertainment, too, was in order, to make the others go down easier—sports, music, cartoons, *Birds of Canada No. 2.* The 1948 catalog gave 30 titles in agriculture, 14 under "children," 29 on citizenship and the community, 46 on creative arts, 22 on geography and travel, 21 on health and welfare, 19 on world affairs. *Canada Carries On* continued under the heading of "citizenship and community" with such titles as *The Challenge of Housing* (1946), *The Home Town Paper* (1948) and *Johnny at the Fair* (1947). *People with a Purpose* was produced by the Manitoba Federation of Agriculture and Cooperatives, and for the Mounted Police there was *RCMP File 1365—The Connors Case.*

By 1949, McLean was confidently preparing expanded activities for the NFB, under a new organization with even more independence, along the lines of the Canadian Broadcasting Corporation. His bigger budget came up against a convergence of attacks on the Board.

The attacks came not only from the growing ranks of commercial 16mm producers, who claimed that they were being discriminated against, but also from government departments which were being served

[36] Dr. Ellis, professor of film at Northwestern University, is preparing a biography of Grierson. Extracts have appeared in *Cinema Journal*, Fall 1968, and Fall 1970. See the latter for data on personnel as summarized in the preceding paragraph: "John Grierson's First Years at the National Film Board." See also Note 4, above.

[37] Manny Farber, "Wartime Documentaries," *New Republic*, February 15, 1943.

by the NFB. It seemed to these departments that they were getting very slow service, with high prices and special charges, and that they were being allowed very little control over the film product they paid for. Others were harsher: they said the Board was using its monopoly position to slant labor movies in favor of Communist-dominated unions. There were newspaper stories about the RCMP investigating all NFB personnel and it was claimed that the ministry of defense would no longer trust the Board with secret subjects.[38]

The upshot was a minor reorganization of the Board (including a tighter system of financing), a few resignations, and the replacement of McLean, at the end of his term, by W. Arthur Irwin, editor of *Maclean's* Magazine. There was no change in the basic power position of the Board in deciding who would make pictures, but it was evident that the new Commissioner was expected to bring a less rigid approach to outside contracts.[39]

Without attempting any full analysis of the facts at the crisis point of 1949–50, it seems fairly clear that the first decade of the Board brought into view the basic problem of any central government information program. One agency in a great national capital cannot presume to tell all others what publicity is best for that agency, and this seems to be what the Film Board was increasingly doing. In Washington and London, central information services had been cut back drastically in 1946. In Ottawa, the National Film Board survived. This was fortunate not only for Canada but for the world.

Beyond the questions of administrative relationship and political climate there was the broader issue of government power over the thinking of its citizens. Zechariah Chafee was justified in finding cause for alarm in the Film Board's monopoly position.[40] In Grierson's hands, no doubt there was a healthy freedom and even conflict of ideas within the Board. But after his departure it became a question to many observers whether the content of Canada's films should be dictated by a small group of writers, with community film forums controlled to a great extent by officials sent out by this same group. It seemed likely that under such

---

[38] "Film Board Monopoly Facing Major Test?" *Financial Post*, Toronto, November 19, 1949. *New York Times*, same date. Gerald Pratley, in "Canada's National Film Board," *Quarterly of Film, Radio, and Television*, Fall 1953, pp. 20–21, indicates that the *Ottawa Citizen* countered the attacks by the *Financial Post* by connecting them with a "long-planned scheme devised by Canada's commercial film industry, and encouraged by American interests, to eliminate the Board."

[39] "At Least Three Employees Quit in Film Board Screening," *Montreal Standard*, March 25, 1950. See House of Commons Debates, Vol. 90, No. 30, March 29, 1950, p. 1343. See Bill 317, Second Session, 21st Parliament, 14 George VI 1950, as passed by the House of Commons June 23, 1950.

[40] *Government and Mass Communications*, Vol. II, pp. 746–748. See also Commons debates: one member had been carrying on a running battle against the NFB, declaring, among other things, that the public was sick of seeing the *Canada Carries On* series in the theaters.

circumstances information was eventually going to be misused by somebody. A similar issue was to come up again two decades later.

It was this very independence and vitality, of course, that helped to
make the NFB the world's best source of nonfiction films. The 1950's
may well be remembered as the Film Board's golden age, at least for
English language films.[41] Many of the subjects produced in this period
didn't quite fit the Grierson categories. They were clearly inheritors of
the Grierson search for focus in a postwar age. But they were not always
clearly propagandist, or even conscious of social problems. They did speak
eloquently of humanity. They influenced the style and content of documentary directors all over the world and seemed destined to be seen and
loved for years to come.

The decade began familiarly enough with a series on mental health—
the first such series to be extensively used and approved in the United
States. *The Feeling of Rejection, The Feeling of Hostility, The Feeling
of Dependency* were all dramatized case studies which helped clinician
and patient alike to see how childhood relationships might affect personality later on. *Shyness*, perhaps the best of the group, examined three
children who seemed to offer problems of maladjustment. One quiet little
boy turned out to be perfectly all right: he liked being by himself and
his life was full of reading and other pleasures.

Then something began to break loose in the Tom Daly unit, as
Roman Kroitor and Wolf Koenig set out to do a study of a simple work-
man in Winnipeg. It was part of a series to be called *Faces of Canada*.
Paul Tomkowicz, Street Railway Switchman, is a title hardly to be fitted
on a marquee or accommodated in a classroom, and streetcars were already
beginning to be subjects for nostalgia by 1954. The film nevertheless
carries a warmth and understanding rarely seen in documentaries—an
infusion of the Flaherty spirit into the Grierson tradition.

An immigrant from Poland, Paul Tomkowicz is a rugged old man
who looks after trolleys and the people who ride them. They take no
notice of him, and his view of them is also rather impassive. Yet he
represents something of the cement of civilization. He does his work, so
others can do theirs. He has a history: his narration tells us of happy memories in Paris and relatives brutally treated in Poland. The film combines
(somewhat uneasily) high-angle night-time shots of "man at work" and
the simplicity of the man himself, who has six boiled eggs in the morning. More than ten minutes might be excessive for a film like this, but it
is a model of its kind, reaching for points of contact between one human
being and the rest of us.

[41] Important retrospective articles on the NFB have appeared in *Sight and
Sound* (Peter Harcourt, "The Innocent Eye," Winter 1964–65) and *Film Quarterly*
(Howard Junker, "The National Film Board of Canada: After a Quarter Century,"
Winter, 1964–65).

City of Gold. **National Film Board of Canada, 1957**

Meanwhile somebody had discovered a huge collection of glass plate photographs in an old house in Dawson City, where the gold rush had once transformed the Yukon and changed the lives of thousands of men. Daly, Kroitor and Koenig determined to use this material to illuminate a moment in history. Colin Low moved out of the animation department to help them.

City of Gold (1957), winner of 28 different awards, has become a prototype for all films based on still photographs. It is also an outstanding achievement in the art of the documentary. The narration, written by Roman Kroitor and spoken by Pierre Berton (whose father lived through the wildest days of Dawson City) combines so felicitously with the pictures and music that the whole subject seems to take on a mysterious social importance. The theme emerges in a single picture—a crowd of Americans and Canadians simultaneously celebrating Dominion Day and the Fourth of July. By isolating and commenting on a few sober faces turned aside within the crowd, the film makes poignant their presence in that isolated place at that long-ago time:

> They had very little to celebrate. Only a few had got any gold and very few of these were able to hang onto it. Yet after the long months on the passes and the lakes and the rivers, they found themselves seized by a curious mixture of feelings, not the least of which was a strange elation.
>
> It's hard to believe, but after coming all this way, many of them never bothered to look for gold at all. It was as if somehow they had already found what they were seeking.

Read by itself, the narration for *City of Gold* has an unnerving simplicity which contrasts with the narration of *Night Mail* or *The River*. It is fully subordinated to the visuals, or more precisely, to the total effect of the film. When the words "little to celebrate" and "elation" come to rest on particular faces, the untrained observer feels an inexplicable sense of rightness and the student of film feels an inheritance from Pudovkin, Chaplin and Dreyer.

After these careful and delicate disciplines, the Daly group was somewhat reluctant to confront the demands of television. Colin Low was on the way to becoming a notable interpreter of the west, with *Corral* (a narration-less film about the breaking of a wild horse), *The Days of Whisky Gap* (using still picture techniques) and *Circle of the Sun* (about Indian customs). But Kroitor and Koenig set to work on a TV series about the city and its characters. In *Blood and Fire*, the Salvation Army showed its mettle. In *The Days Before Christmas*, the commercializing of religious holidays became pitilessly visual. In *I Was a 90-Pound Weakling*, physical "culture" confronted the camera. And in *Lonely Boy*, the hectic life of a Canadian pop singer, Paul Anka, became a contrasting counterpart for the old-age vignette of Paul Tomkowicz.

In an interview with Gideon Bachmann, Tom Daly has expressed the challenge always facing the documentary film-maker:

> I think most people have far too much knowledge as it is—far more than they know how to organize and make into some kind of mental order. But if one can really bring an experience to someone in the audience with an emotional realization of something, then this really could make a difference. He really could understand something differently. He really could have a new attitude as the result. He could begin to care about something he never cared about before.[42]

There have been many films of this sort. Guy Coté, in a series later listed under "social geography," reported on *Roughnecks* (about the oil fields), *Railroaders*, *Fishermen*, *Cattle Ranch*. Terry Filgate examined tobacco-raising in Canada in *The Back-Breaking Leaf*. Julian Biggs directed the best known of the Board's films for children, *Paddle to the Sea*, and after two years as director of production, made the NFB's most political film, a biographical study of Premier Smallwood of Newfoundland, *A Little Fellow from Gambo*. There was a series about cities, with Lewis Mumford as consultant. There was a group of films about young people's problems: *Phoebe* (teen-age pregnancy), *The Game*, *The Merry-Go-Round*, *Little White Crimes* (about young executives).

The Board has not been without pretensions, in the light of its growing worldwide reputation, for which its reach may have exceeded its grasp. One series attempted to show different styles of courtship in four parts

---

[42] Transcribed from radio interview on WBAI, New York City, 1962.

of the globe. A series about physics in cooperation with Harvard University was plagued with distribution problems. *Morning on the Lievre* turned out to be a bit vague in its attempts to be poetic. *Universe,* showing how far the Film Board had come since 1939 in its mastery of special effects, duplicated the visual feeling of travel among the stars but failed to be as interesting as it was impressive. And from 1964 to 1967, Kroitor supervised the building of Labyrinth for the Montreal exposition, a top-heavy $4,500,000 monument, sad to say, of technical overstatement and thematic confusion.[43]

Short films from the English-language units in the 1960's upheld the older tradition in the face of jarring new trends. Donald Brittain's *Memorandum* was a serious attempt to show how it felt to revisit concentration camps in Europe. *Fields of Sacrifice,* a lavish travelogue of World War II cemeteries, and *High Steel,* a Tomkowicz-style color film about an Indian construction worker, seemed to reflect a groping for respectable subjects. *Helicopter Canada,* a lengthy tour of the country shot entirely from the air, drew a saving lightheartedness from a script by Stanley Jackson. *The Rise and Fall of the Great Lakes* offered a bright new wrinkle for the classroom, as movie magic showed how the land was built up and worn down through the ages—and finally has been oppressed by man's junkheaps.

From about 1960, the NFB was torn by conflicting demands, and its survival as a public agency was almost as much in question by 1970 as it was in 1950. Various reports and recommendations were made by official and unofficial commissions, some having to do with the growth of bureaucracy within the Board, some concerned with the freedom of film-

---

[43] The author has seen many of these films (especially the ones he comments on) under such circumstances as (a) rental for college classroom use (b) a visit to Expo and the NFB in Montreal (c) meetings of the University Film Association. Most of them are available through 16mm rental agencies in the U.S. Various articles appeared at the time of Expo, including one in *Popular Photography,* June 1967 (John Durniak, "The National Film Board of Canada Is People, Darn Good People!"). A series of articles appeared in *Industrial Photography,* May 1963.

Labyrinth marched Expo-goers first onto five tiers or balconies overlooking two screens, one an up-ended CinemaScope on the wall, the other on the floor. In one scene a little girl threw something from the upper screen and it plopped into a pool below, but for the most part the two screens were not related in content. Apart from some wonderful overhead shots of trains, the rest seemed to be a headshaking, handwringing critique of modern life—racing cars, football, boxing, drinking and freeways. The sound track actually intoned at one point, "We haven't done so well." It was hard to get much out of this vague moralizing. (For a reverent and detailed description of Labyrinth, see *Film Quarterly* for Fall, 1967: Judith Shatnoff, "Expo '67—A Multiple Vision.")

After that, everybody had to troop into another auditorium to see a five-screen cruciform projection system which sounded as lugubrious as an early *March of Time.* It was all about death and fear and old people, garnished with a terrifying crocodile hunt, a batch of leering death masks, and close-ups of grisly tree roots. Perhaps this was Roman Kroitor's pessimistic answer to the hit of the New York World's Fair, *To Be Alive!*

makers to express themselves as artists. The latter proposition led to the
idea in some quarters that the Board could be transmuted into a semi-
private agency so that its employees could make films for any purpose,
including profit, entertainment and, perhaps, revolution. New trends
within the agency itself, so far as an outside observer could judge, might
well be aesthetically exciting; they seemed even more certainly to be
politically self-destructive.[44]

The most obvious crevasse was between British and French film-
makers, reflecting the bitterness of separatist movements in Quebec. As
a kind of balance for the Ontario base of the Canadian Broadcasting
Corporation in Toronto, the NFB was moved during the mid-1950's to
Montreal. Here the new quarters were magnificent compared to the converted sawmill of Ottawa days, but as so often happens in artistic ventures,
the creation of a comfortable environment signaled a kind of decline.
The French were determined to see it as merely the decline of "colonial-
ism" and British dominance. They entered enthusiastically into what
came to be called either the French renaissance or the French revolution
in Canadian film.

One of the beginnings was the appearance of a film called *Les
Raquetteurs*. The manner of its appearing was significant. Sent on a
routine newsreel chore to cover an annual competition of snowshoers in
a small town, Michel Brault and Gilles Groulx came back with what they
felt was a priceless picture of lower middle-class life. With the encouragement of Tom Daly and in the spirit of Humphrey Jennings' *Spare Time*,
they worked on their extra footage on nights and weekends. In due course
the Flaherty Seminar and other festivals acclaimed *The Snowshoers* as a
little masterpiece of human comedy. It was truthful without being cynical: the competitors who fell out of the race were shown to be more
natural and interesting than the winners.

After that came pictures like *Day After Day*, which did not have the
same spirit. A lifeless kind of disgust with life seemed to be the theme of
such *cinéma vérité*, and *A Saint Henri le 5 Septembre* carried it no farther.
The point seemed to be that the French film-makers really didn't want to
make documentaries. They wanted to make features. Perhaps more fundamentally, they did not feel comfortable within the prevailing theory of
public service. They wished to express themselves. Soon the argument
began to be heard that the government should give its own employed
artists freedom to attack all existing institutions and morality.

Features began to occur at the NFB, some of them stretched from

[44] See *New Canadian Film*, Montreal, January 15, 1970, p. 12, and reference
therein to *Parti Pris*, April 1964, in which Gilles Groulx called for the Board to encourage the "idea of a '*politique d'auteurs*' and have the strength to encourage freedom
of expression to the fullest extent" if it does not want to "become a pure propaganda
machine."

shorter projects in the manner of *Les Raquetteurs*.[45] Don Owen was to do a study of probation officers and ended up with *Nobody Waved Goodbye*, an English language feature about a boy's conflict with his parents. It was a compelling and rather gentle story, not unlike *The Four Hundred Blows*. Groulx made *Le Chat Dans le Sac*, about a writer who is put down by the establishment. There were others. There began to be features made outside the Board on an independent basis. There was pressure to create a government loan fund for features privately produced, similar to the Eady plan in England, and this Canadian Film Development Corporation was finally established by Parliament in 1967 with an initial fund of $10,000,000.

By 1970, there were features coming off the reels at the National Film Board which were destined to puzzle many taxpayers who had read in the National Film Act that the Board is to produce films "in the national interest." According to reports in New Canadian Cinema,[46] (published occasionally by *La Cinematheque Canadienne*) *Tout L'Temps, Tout L'Temps, Tout L'Temps* was about a rather drunken family reunion in Montreal in which "one by one each member of the family gets his and her miseries and disappointments off their chest and we discover their real unhappiness." *Entre Tu et Vous*, directed by Gilles Groulx, is a "story of everyday life in which seduction predominates. Seduction of woman with respect to man, seduction of society with respect to the individual. . . . By quiet presence, seduction, drugs, the argument, dialogue, contempt, repression and the rape of the human mind, the rape of man's conscience takes place. Reproducing fragments of our often cruel and absurd world, the film takes us into the lives of the couple and into collective life. While we attend a collective revolution, the couple is also revolting; they leave each other crying their disgust. . . ."

It is none too clear from these English translations, apparently prepared by French-speaking film-workers, what actually takes place in either film. But the affinity with Jean-Luc Godard and other contemporary European imagists of despair is clear enough. Surely it is a new concept of freedom which would turn over the public machinery of communication to artists, however brilliant and perceptive, whose basic philosophy is deeply pessimistic. One of the most jewel-like and jarring works of art produced at the NFB was Arthur Lipsett's *Very Nice Very Nice*, a ten-minute hymn to the futility of modern life. It is hardly surprising that this film-maker, having repeated his theme a time or two, has not done much else.

If a government film agency begins to say that life is a waste, it is only a step further to suppose that both government and film-making

[45] The first NFB feature had been made in 1951: the *Royal Journey* of Princess Elizabeth and the Duke of Edinburgh.
[46] March 15, 1970, pp. 14–15.

are useless. In such an atmosphere, can budget cuts be far behind? Austerity did indeed arrive, along with Prime Minister Trudeau, who was expected to be so enthusiastic about the arts. Furthermore, under Hugo McPherson, an English professor from the University of Western Ontario appointed as Film Commissioner in May, 1967, various reorganization plans had already been instituted which seemed even to the tradition-oriented film people arbitrary and unrelated to production goals. For a while it looked as if everybody of any importance might be leaving the Board and only the bureaucrats would remain.

Fortunately the time of trial did not last much longer than it did in 1950. The appointment in 1970 of Sidney Newman, a former employee of the Board who later worked for the BBC and for Independent Television in England, suggested a reasonable concern with the needs of creative people together with a working knowledge of the obligations of public service. In time, there would be a new decentralization, bringing filmmakers more in touch with the people in every province.

Closer to the traditions of the Board than traumatic dramatic features were the *Challenge for Change* program and the new short films for classroom use called *Loops for Learning*. The latter took its cue from the assumption that even poor learners can profit from repeated showings of visual material; within 8mm film or TV tapes, each pupil can proceed at his own pace. *Challenge for Change*, while essentially political and highly controversial, at least assumed that mankind can move ahead from their dissatisfactions, find ways out of poverty, and make life on earth as livable as modern material productivity makes possible. Initiated by Julian Biggs, directed for a two-year period by George Stoney, an experienced American documentary director, and later by Colin Low, the *Challenge* program used film not only to dramatize problems of poverty but to listen to individuals who were poor.[47] In *Up Against the System,* people on welfare poured out their bitterness toward rigid regulations and an unfeeling bureaucracy; a former case worker joined in condemning the petty spying required of her in her job. *Little Burgundy* recorded a small triumph of participation by the people during the planning of a vast housing project in Montreal.

The notion that poor people ought to swing some political weight is a chancy and exciting one for government agencies to cope with. But at least it is a public matter and its airing can be made the subject, eventually, of some sort of public policy. It would be hard to persuade any parliamentary body that a government agency's mission is to reveal the stresses and strains of private morality or to sell a "tragic view of life." The job of government film production is to rouse the creative and constructive energies of men for tasks on which a majority can agree.

[47] See Chapter 10 for further description of community action films made by the NFB.

3

U.S. Government Films:
The Early Period

THE EARLIEST of the stories about motion pictures in the U.S. Government is still told around the Agriculture Department.

Everybody knew how much Secretary James Wilson despised motion pictures. He openly regarded them as an invention of the devil. Some of his own departmental photographers were convinced, on the contrary, that films belonged in the governmental information process as certainly as did pamphlets and reports.

The year was 1908. David Wark Griffith was directing his first picture for Biograph. So far he was only a dabbler in films and had no intention of lending his real name to this questionable enterprise. The moving picture camera was itself more or less stationary as yet. The nickelodeon had turned up on the streets of American cities only three years before. The newspictures (and other more dubious matter) which had been shown in vaudeville houses and penny arcades since 1896 were hardly promising precedents for the dignity of public reporting.

Nevertheless these aforesaid Agriculture Department photographers were convinced, and staked their jobs on their conviction. Without bringing the matter to the Secretary's attention, they installed developing equipment for motion picture film in the Department of Agriculture laboratories. They took pictures of a flight by the Wright Brothers for the Army Signal Corps. Chiefly bent on scientific pursuits, they must have realized that they would eventually have to win over the Secretary. So after a good many months of attic-room experiments, they took a long shot, both literally and figuratively.

43

At a large meeting of corn club boys addressed by the Secretary himself, they placed the camera where he would not be likely to notice it and took motion pictures of the event. They developed and printed with care, and being satisfied with the results, took their courage in one hand and the film in the other, and invited Secretary Wilson to see himself on the screen. The firmly prejudiced department head was startled, but willing. And when he saw the pictures, he was delighted. Overnight the motion picture became something more than an invention of the devil. The clandestine film-makers no longer had to hide their celluloid.[1]

The Bureau of Reclamation in the Department of Interior had by this time taken up the challenge and made some pictures of large-scale farming practices, but lapsed into inactivity again shortly afterward, as far as films were concerned.[2]

It was not very long after this, too, that the Civil Service Commission had a little picture made called *Won Through Merit*, which described the way the merit system worked in modern government in 1912—a reassurance for citizens and job-hunters alike. This is probably the earliest example in the Federal Government of a specific film planned for public relations purposes, but it stood alone and was not followed by any departmental program.

Except for the Agriculture Department, the only large Government film-producers before 1936 were the Interior Department and the Army Signal Corps. Interior Department activity on such topics as conservation, national parks and the CCC was partly contemporary with the work of Pare Lorentz, but it had very limited goals, quality and influence. Signal Corps men, who had asked the help of Agriculture men in making the Wright flight test films, made no significant use of motion picture photography even for training purposes till World War I—a development actually pushed by private educational film producers. Not till 1941 did training include "orientation" and orientation include documentary.

This is not to say that America was altogether laggard, before the arrival of Pare Lorentz, in using the film as a carrier for governmental information. Over the years, some remarkable results were achieved in the public interest, without high costs and without elaborate ballyhoo. But compared with what might have been done by way of communicating the problems of government to the people, the performance can only be described as perfunctory. Quantitatively the record is surprising. Qualitatively, it is disappointing.

---

[1] Raymond Evans, "USDA Motion Picture Service 1908–1943," *Business Screen*, Vol. 5, No. 1, 1943, p. 20.
[2] Arch Mercey, "Films by American Governments," *Films*, Summer, 1940.

The Record of the Early 1930's

In 1937 John Devine made a study of government films for the Committee on Public Administration of the Social Science Research Council. His emphasis was on the use of training films in government as a means of increasing the efficiency and morale of administrative services, and he dealt in large part with local areas. But there was plenty of evidence that national departments used this kind of help in explaining both techniques and programs to their employees.[3]

In 1936 a Boston University student made a summary study of Federal agencies having motion pictures for distribution. He found 20 of them. Several of these had two or more bureaus offering films. They varied in scope: the Post Office Department had a single-reeler available, the Department of Agriculture nearly 200 of varying lengths.[4]

In 1940, the U.S. Film Service, then in the Office of Education, put out a directory which showed 17 agencies as offering films to interested borrowers or purchasers. A list of agencies gives little idea of the quality or quantity of their activity, but here is the list: [5]

Agriculture Department
Commerce Department
Interior Department
Justice Department
Labor Department—Children's Bureau, Division of Labor Standards,
   Women's Bureau
Navy Department
Treasury Department: Coast Guard
Federal Loan Agency: Federal Housing Administration

[3] In fact the same lesson became clear here, though less widely noticed, as in the case of the British General Post Office. When films about the Social Security Board, the Rural Electrification Administration, or the Coast Guard, made for public relations purposes, were shown also to the employees of those agencies, morale was perceptibly improved. Workers at all levels saw more clearly the usefulness and inter-relations of their jobs. The U.S. Post Office used a film made privately by the St. Paul Joint Council of Postal Employees, *Here Comes the Mail*, showing it all over the country to post office workers. The FBI borrowed and used locally made police training films. The WPA, enmeshed in the daily grind of appraising and approving projects, showed staff members films made as project records; without these they would have been "unable to gain any sort of reliable image of what the project is like." (John Devine, *Films as an Aid in Training Public Employees*, p. 5.)

[4] Hyman H. Platt, Sources and Content of United States Government Motion Picture Films, thesis for Master of Education, Boston University, 1938.

[5] Directory of United States Government Films, March, 1940.

Federal Security Agency: National Youth Administration, Social
    Security Board, U.S. Film Service, U.S. Public Health Service
U.S. Housing Authority
Works Progress Administration
Pan American Union
Post Office Department
Tennessee Valley Authority
Marine Corps
Veterans Administration
War Department

In 1940, William Hartley selected some nontheatrical films which
he thought might be especially worthwhile for school courses in history
and social problems.[6] A good many of them were Government films.
There were four by the Women's Bureau of the Labor Department, six
by the WPA, seven by TVA, four by the Commerce Department, and
many others. *The River* and *The Plow that Broke the Plains* stood out
above all of these, in his estimation, in quality, usefulness, and popularity.
But they were not the first or the only Government films which attempted
to deal with the subject matter of social science or to influence some
segment of public opinion in some degree.

The films for the armed services were mostly recruiting posters in
motion and travelogs at best. During World War I, however, two steps
forward were taken toward film-making for other, internal purposes. At
the urgent insistence of a private producer, the Bray Studios, and after
sample offerings of animated slow-motion teaching films had been made,
the War Department ordered a series of training films—62 of them in
all. At the same time a real attempt was made to collect a motion picture
history from combat photography. Some of this footage went into films
for the public, through the Committee on Public Information; some
went into newsreels; some went into Army training films. The 62 were in
circulation till 1928. The historical scenes were used again in 1924 in
Flashes of Action, a four-reel picture for troops, which Hartley describes
as "episodic, with little continuity," but which apparently had realism:

Reel one: General Pershing embarking with troops. At sea, soldiers
seen boxing and dancing. Periscope is sighted. Convoy throws down
a smoke screen and depth bombs are dropped. Arriving in France, the
soldiers seen boxing and dancing. Periscope is sighted. Convoy
throwns down a smoke screen and depth bombs are dropped. Arriving
in France, the soldiers get into boxcars and travel to front. 38th and
59th Infantry are seen at the front advancing into action under fire.
Other troops seen going into action along the Meuse.

6 William Hartley, *Selected Films for American History and Problems.*

Reel two: Exermont first aid station, prisoners carrying the wounded, front line trenches, attacks and counterattacks with gas, destruction of German observation balloon, attack on Sultzeren.[7]

In 1937 Devine reported that the Signal Corps Laboratory at the Army War College in Washington maintained a complete motion picture production unit which made about six subjects a year—since 1933 all in sound, and increasingly on 16mm as well as 35mm stock.[8]

The Interior Department film program, at first pretty largely an advertising program, became something more for only a brief period. Devine pointed out that its work, which had been "going on for about twenty years" was "mostly for the purpose of telling the public about the activities of the Department. The majority of the films deal with the national and state parks and the recreational opportunities which they offer." There were also pictures about Indian reservations, the Bureau of Reclamation (*Boulder Dam, Grand Coulee Dam*), cattle ranges, the General Land Office, the territories and the Office of Education. In an article published in 1937, Fanning Hearon, then director of the division, described these as "written, photographed, edited, and mechanically produced by the Division of Motion Pictures." The output amounted to about 25 reels per year during the 1930's. In 1940, the division had 69 films available in 16mm and 35mm, some with sound, some silent, one or two reels in length.[9]

Most of these were fairly humdrum products, which, however much they might brighten a grade school classroom, were not planned as contributions either to controversy or to art. *Seeing Yosemite from a Saddle* and *A Visit to Mesa Verde* (both 1930), *Forests and Men* (1933), which was probably the first CCC film, and *In the Wake of the Buccaneers* (1936), a travelog about the Virgin Islands, are representative titles. There were large numbers of CCC films—separate reports from a wide variety of states, as well as such more general coverage as *Reclamation and the CCC*.

Yet sometime after the reorganization of all department film activities (with the exception of the Bureau of Mines)—a shift which took place on November 25, 1938—there were evidences of striving toward something more comprehensive in informational scope.[10] A one-reel pro-

[7] Hartley, p. 172. The American Legion also sponsored a film from some of this footage and edited by army officers called *The World War*. (See Filmotopics, March, 1948.) See also Frank P. Liberman, "A History of Army Photography," *Business Screen*, Vol. 7, No. 1, December 30, 1945, and James Gibson, "Producer: Signal Corps," *Signals*, March–April 1947.

[8] Devine, pp. 3, 60. See also Chapter 7.

[9] "Interior's Division of Motion Pictures," *School Life*, September 1937.

[10] See Fanning Hearon, "The Motion Picture Program and Policy of the U.S. Government," *Journal of Educational Sociology*, November 1938.

duction called *Home Rule on the Range* made an attempt to show how the Taylor Grazing Act of 1934, by setting aside special lands, prevented exhaustion of grazing areas. *The Price of Progress* (1937) contrasted in its first reel the world of nature and the world as man has misused it by farming and lumbering. In Reel Two, the need for conservation is shown as partly met by the various activities of the Department, which are pictured bureau by bureau.[11]

The beginnings of a kind of service agency for other Government departments can be seen in *Service to Those Who Served*, a description of the Veterans Administration, and *Help by the Carload*, a tour of the Government Printing Office. There was an attempt at historical significance in a film showing the 75th anniversary celebration of the Battle of Gettysburg, and an interesting study of archaeological work done at Moundville, Alabama, with a certain amount of assistance from the CCC.[12]

The Division of Motion Pictures, however, was abolished in 1938. Its films, which had been offered free to school and college libraries, were still to be had, but the only production program left in the department was the Bureau of Mines' scheme of industrially sponsored films. The particular company dealt with in the film provided the money and actually controlled the content. Devine estimated that in the 1930's about $75,000 a year was contributed by various firms to this relatively low-cost program of silent educational films, and in 20 years a million dollars had been spent. In 1936 alone they were supposed to have been shown to nearly seven million persons, largely school children. There was no advertising in them, beyond a statement of sponsorship at the beginning. These sponsors have included Westinghouse Electric Company, Sinclair Refining Company, U.S. Steel, the Copper and Brass Research Association, Johns Manville, Stone and Webster Engineering Corporation, General Motors, Standard Oil, and Ford.

Industry was meanwhile being dealt with in a quite different fashion by the Women's Bureau of the Labor Department. Over a period of ten years, four silent pictures were produced which were noteworthy for their social consciousness but not for their art.

It is difficult to imagine that such primitive appeals as these, technically speaking, were being ground out at a time when Hollywood was reaching its peak of creative activity with sound on film. It was in 1936, the year of *Mary of Scotland*, *Dodsworth* and *The Story of Louis Pasteur*, that the Women's Bureau produced *Behind the Scenes in the Machine Age*. This picture—hardly a motion picture, since it depended heavily on still photographs, still diagrams and studies of machine operations—began with the solemn contention that "willful waste brings woeful want" and ended with a bright little drawing of an industrial train running on

[11] Hartley, pp. 144, 175.
[12] *They Met at Gettysburg; Temples and Peace.*

a well-laid track marked "economic planning." Strung out between these highlights was a series of rhymes referred to as a "daily dozen," based on the standards of employment set up by the Bureau. One of these, for example, pointed out that

> It will in health and efficiency pay
> To have for the job an eight-hour day,
> With place for employees to rest and play.

One is forced to the conclusion that the author of such lines as these had indeed been harnessed to an assembly line too long.

The Story of the Women's Bureau (1929) explained the demands for a separate bureau in the time of Theodore Roosevelt and its final appearance in 1920 after a temporary wartime existence; various people are shown preparing reports, holding conferences, tabulating records and visiting workers' homes. *Within the Gates* (1930) traced (a) the industrial revolution in textile production, (b) the increase in the number of women in factories, (c) the manufacture of a man's shirt from cotton field to shipment, and (d) the fields women have entered.[13]

The Children's Bureau also went in for movies just before the second World War, and besides a two-reeler on posture, and a couple of specialized reports on nursing problems during births, gave considerable attention to *Judy's Diary*. She was six months old in the first one, and progressively grappled with new problems as she grew older.

The Social Security Board needed explanatory films for the successful operation of its program as much as for public relations, and *Social Security for the Nation* was one of the results. *Social Security Benefits* (1939) showed the interviewing of typical clients, traced a case of an application for old-age benefits, and revealed how records are kept and claims are paid.[14]

Various housing films have seen the darkness of projection rooms, and these range from the practical *Design and Construction of Three Small Houses* (Federal Housing Administration) to *World War Against Slums* (U.S. Housing Authority). Probably the most ambitious attempt at a problem film was *Today We Build* (1938), a 30-minute sound production showing the work of the Federal Housing Administration in promoting both individual and multiple unit housing. Various housing projects in foreign countries and in Pittsburgh, Silver Spring (Maryland) and Arlington (Virginia) were reported on, and a conference between the Administrator and the Federal Loan Administrator provided a touch of bureaucratic realism.[15]

[13] Hartley, pp. 157, 117.
[14] American Council on Education, Selected Educational Motion Pictures.
[15] See National Housing Agency, *Films on Housing and Related Subjects*, June 1945 (and later editions) for lists of films and filmstrips produced by local housing authorities in many cities, and by a variety of private groups and educational movie producers over the years.

The Commerce Department, besides the production activities of the Bureau of Air Commerce (*Federal Skyways*) and the Bureau of Fisheries (*Activities of the Bureau of Fisheries, Alaskan Activities of the Bureau of Fisheries, Speckled Beauties*), had a try at a foreign trade film in 1932. *Commerce Around the Coffee Cup* (one reel) was the sort of thing Kipling had arranged on a larger scale for the Empire Marketing Board's first film in England. Little more need be said, except that the Commerce Department never did try again.

In 1936, the Justice Department brought out a movie about the Bureau of Prisons, Alcatraz, Leavenworth and Atlanta, called *Protecting the Public* (one reel). In 1935 the Post Office Department provided young philatelists and others with a straightforward one-reeler called *Following a Postage Stamp*. The Coast Guard, the Inland Waterways Corporation, and the Pan American Union have been responsible for films about their own activities. The U.S. Public Health Service early experimented with venereal disease films (*Three Counties Against Syphilis,* 1938).

It is one of the anomalies of the whole chronicle of Government films that the Tennessee Valley Authority has not been the subject of a major motion picture. *The River*, of course, approached the subject, and included a dam-building sequence at the end. The Authority's own information division has been responsible for such specialized pictures as *Norris Dam, Scenic Resources of the Tennessee Valley*, and *Timber Growing Today*. The short subjects made by the Office of War Information and by RKO are a far cry from the glamour and size of this distinctive American achievement.

Of all these non-agricultural agencies which tried motion pictures in pre-war days, the only one which gave any serious signs of moving boldly into the business of influencing public opinion was the Works Progress Administration. The WPA was a new agency and an action agency, very much on the firing line of public criticism. As Harry Hopkins told Representative John Taber (R., N.Y.), "We felt that the people were not getting any adequate or proper information as to the way our funds were being expended." [16] By 1937, the Division of Information felt this so keenly that a series of films was planned.

Hands was only a half-reel long but was perhaps the most memorable of the lot, with its many brief shots of

> hands hanging empty, whittling uselessly, fingers tapping nervously, thumb-twiddling hands, all doing nothing worthwhile. The commentator says, "Not so long ago hands were idle, losing the skill that train-

[16] House, 75th Congress, 2nd Session, First Deficiency Appropriation Bill for 1937, pp. 114–15. Taber maintained that the WPA was getting out propaganda. Hopkins maintained that "these are published reports of our work to show what we are doing."

ing had given them." As hands pull ropes, saw wood, turn valves, sew garments, guide draftsmen's tools, use acetylene torches, and typewrite, the commentator continues, "Today these hands are no longer idle."

The next sequence depicts the flow of money and the results of this increased flow. Hands receive government checks, pass money across counters in exchange for packages of food, turn the ignition keys of new cars, point out the rooms on the blueprint for a new house, pass money through a grill for a ticket, hold a newly purchased fishing rod, pull on a new pair of gloves, and feed flocks of chickens.[17]

It is not surprising that the educators who reported to the American Council on Education about this film indicated that the showing "was often followed by spirited discussions." It is an effective piece of cinema and a clear-cut propaganda argument. That the average audience of movie-habituated adults or youngsters would find fault with that message and wish to make qualifications to its claims simply shows that a straight-forward propaganda plea, even by the government, does not necessarily bowl over American citizens.

Man Against the River reported on WPA assistance given during the Ohio River flood of 1937. *Rain for the Earth* described activities of WPA personnel in the dust bowl. *We Work Again* showed how black Americans were put to work in clerical jobs, public improvement projects, household training, musical performances, and the Federal Theater.[18]

Work Pays America, beginning with an ostentatious flashing of the title's initials, claimed to summarize in five reels the work of WPA from 1935 to 1937. It was not a very imaginative motion picture, but it did use sprightly music and an announcer with an energetic voice. Given enough patience to sit through five reels, the observer could not help being impressed by the steady enumeration of work accomplished—roads, reservoirs, stadiums, bridges, public buildings.[19] It is difficult now to reconstruct the old days of recrimination and bickering when leaf-raking and "boondoggling" were supposed by many people to be the very symbols of politics, when it was difficult to separate out from this the sympathy men felt for the dispossessed and the depression-stricken. However

[17] American Council on Education, *op. cit. Hands* was directed and photographed by Ralph Steiner and Willard Van Dyke and released by Pathé Pictures in 1934. (See Association of Documentary Film Producers, *Living Films*, p. 38.)

James McCamy reports in *Government Publicity* (p. 124) that the WPA had "its state directors solicit showings for WPA short subjects in the commercial theaters of their states." Raymond Fielding, in *The American Newsreel 1911–1967*, p. 269, documents the contract between WPA and Pathé for monthly newsreels in theaters. See also *Newsweek* August 15, 1936; *Literary Digest*, August 8, 1936.

[18] Hartley, pp. 180, 190, 158.

[19] Reels 2 through 5 dealt with skilled and professional workers, the arts, assistance given in time of disaster, and recreational activities. It must be confessed that this observer did not sit through them all.

much the fact may puzzle a foreigner, it is true that a film like this—
even if it had been a good one—could not at that time have been shown
on the screens of the main commercial circuits. For the film itself was an
open attempt to argue. It was therefore in that ticklish penumbra of
public information between a report on agreed-upon public achievements
and special pleading for public support in the future.

The Department of Agriculture

The Department of Agriculture Motion Picture Service went through
various phases of expansion after the time of Secretary James Wilson—
after the time of secret operations in an eight-by-twelve attic room. When
pictures were first taken of the first airplane owned by the U.S. Army in
1908, there was "one Jenkins camera and two or three pin racks for tray
development." Not long after Wilson provided an enthusiastic green
light for this new kind of informational activity, there was a time of
re-thinking under Secretary David Houston. A committee finally reported
to him that "while the direct educational value of the motion picture
could not be definitely predicted, the employment of films offered other
advantages which warranted the Department in using them in its extension work." [20]

In terms of organization, the Office of Motion Pictures was not
actually in the Extension Service till 1928. For a year during World War
I, the Office did work for George Creel's Committee on Public Information.[21] Under the long and prosperous chieftainship of Raymond Evans,
growing demands for motion picture services finally called for the building of a sound stage (1935) in the South Building of the department in
Washington. Fully-equipped, with room for several small sets, it has since
been flanked by editing rooms, laboratories, viewing rooms, and storage
vaults. The studios were taken over by the Office of Strategic Services
during World War II for the preparation of visual reports for the President and the Chiefs of Staff.

The primary purpose of the Department of Agriculture from the
beginning has been the collection and distribution of information. This
extraordinary fact is often forgotten when the role of the information

[20] Evans, "USDA Motion Picture Service." Some of the most remarkable scientific
film-making of all time has come out of the collaboration of film laboratory and agricultural laboratory in the Department, including pioneering work in microphotography
and time-lapse photography, the latter particularly valuable in the study of plant growth.
[21] *Meeting the Farm Labor Problem, Home Drying of Fruits and Vegetables,*
and *Control of Cooties,* among others, this last for the Surgeon General of the Army.

process in American bureaucracy is talked about.[22] This, the first of the service agencies in the Cabinet to represent a specific economic interest in the country, was set up because information was needed by farmers about farming. Regulation and planning came later, in conjunction with the pressures of economic change. Originally, Section 1 of the Act of 1862 (which set up the Department under a Commissioner 27 years before it became part of the cabinet) read:

> That there is hereby established at the seat of government of the United States a Department of Agriculture, the general designs and duties of which shall be to acquire and diffuse among the people of the United States useful information on subjects connected with agriculture in the most general and comprehensive sense of that word, and to procure, propagate, and distribute among the people new and valuable seeds and plants.[23]

It is not surprising, then, that the Department went ahead in succeeding, years to build up one of the most active information staffs in Washington.[24] Its problems were the problems of any Federal information office, with the additional responsibilities that come with being part of a very large department. Bureau publicity had to be understood in the light of over-all policies, and departmental statements often had to be cleared with the state agricultural people.[25]

By and large, the departmental policy has not been a promotional one. Even during the Henry Wallace period, drum-beating publicity projects usually originated in the New Deal agencies which had their own public relations staffs—the Agricultural Adjustment Administration, the Farm Security Administration, the Rural Electrification Administration. Such energetic appeals for public favor on the part of new and controversial programs met coolness even within departmental walls.

In the first place departmental information has been devoted to specialist causes, when it has been hortatory at all. The basic clientele has been the farming community, and informational materials are usually conceived in terms of some special segment of that community.

22 "In fact, the Department might be thought of quite properly as having been established as an agricultural information center for the nation as a whole and for farmers in particular. Consequently the program of information was one of the most important aspects of its work." John Gaus, *Public Administration and the Department of Agriculture*, p. 361. See also his comments on p. 13.

23 Section I, 12 Statutes at Large, p. 387.

24 The earliest years of the Department actually emphasized laboratory work, but under Secretary Norman Colman (appointed Commissioner in 1885, Secretary in 1889) a Division of Records and Editing made its appearance. This evolved under James Wilson into a Division of Publications, and under David Houston, in 1914, into an Office of Information. As of March 1, 1947, there were 160 people in the Office of Information itself, and 420 more doing part- or full-time work in information for other bureaus of the department. (Gaus, pp. 15, 34. House, Department of Agriculture Appropriation Bill for 1947, pp. 301–315.)

25 Gaus, p. 363.

Movies, therefore, have usually been made with the same specialized publics in view—the women, the cattlemen, the corn farmers, the western farmers, the farmers afflicted with specific pests. Others may describe certain specialized techniques of road-making, forest management, irrigation or soil terracing. Occasionally a self-congratulatory story about departmental activity is told—the history of the Federal Seed Act, the advantages of the meat inspection service, the effectiveness of hog cholera control, a one-reel summary of the U.S. Department of Agriculture itself —or the world in general is told of the importance of the farming community.

In the second place, departmental information, when it has been hortatory at all, has been devoted to causes that can be scientifically supported. Thus departmental films have stressed better ways of farming both for the public good and for the private pocketbook. When the Department made a little melodrama called *Molly of Pine Grove Vat* shortly after the first World War, there was wide agreement among experts that compulsory dipping of livestock would get rid of the cattle fever tick. The film sponsored by the Bureau of Animal Industry therefore openly called for action, and the Bureau actively pushed the showing of the picture in many communities where opposition was strongest—even in communities where motion pictures had never been seen before. A later production of a similar type about bovine tuberculosis (*Out of the Shadows*) was shown 6,500 times to three million persons over a period of ten years.[26]

It is plain enough that however "scientific" these proposals were, they conflicted with common farming practices and meant a change in ways of doing things. The motion picture medium, more forceful than gray pamphlets, thus played a radical role in educating farm people, in changing their minds.

If, then, the search went on for "better ways" of farming, there were bound to be other, less scientific recommendations made. Occasional exceptions in the Agriculture Department film program illustrate this. It is one thing to exhort farmers to use contour plowing or to prefer certain types of seeds, because science shows this procedure to be profitable. It is another thing to exhort farmers to take social or economic action, even if experience shows that cooperatives pay. It is not easy, in practice and in life, to draw sharp lines between "science" and "experience."

Was *The Tree of Life* a propaganda film because it showed unplanned lumbering operations resulting in abandoned communities, and "sustained yield" experiments resulting in controlled natural resources and stable communities? Was the Forest Service being preferential in its public relations by urging planning? And what about publicity for cooperatives? In *Wool, From Fleece to Fabric—Cooperative Marketing*, the Farm

[26] Evans, "USDA Motion Picture Service," p. 32.

Credit Administration showed contented sheep being sheared, and the wool being sent through a cooperative association to eastern markets, with the cooperative advantages much stressed. Was this outside the functions of the FCA, which was authorized in a whole series of Congressional Acts to give preference to cooperative associations, and whose subordinate units are in more than one case authorized to deal only with cooperative associations? *The Negro Farmer* showed the activities of the Extension Service among the nine million Negroes in the South who worked on farms— the fight for crop rotation, improved housing, better 4-H clubs.

What is to be the judgment of films like these—all produced in 1938? Made of realistic materials, based on experience, they extended the edge of change in human affairs by limited appeals to the emotions. What educational effect they achieved was of benefit to the agricultural community, even though they crossed the border between science and experience, even though nobody with an A.B. in animal husbandry could say definitely that their message, added up, made "better farming." They were certainly within the range of authority granted by the Congress for the Department of Agriculture.

It so happens that the big events in documentary film production in the Government have largely by-passed the Department of Agriculture. Pare Lorentz and the Resettlement Administration were certainly *in* the Department by the time *The River* was in production, but they were not of it. Wartime activity, too, centered in outside agencies.

Still, the agency which first entered the field is also the one which has survived more or less intact, which is more than can be said about the Resettlement Administration and the U.S. Film Service. Its continuing responsibility for films on scientific and technical subjects, forestry and fire prevention, agricultural education and soil conservation has been a responsibility which has served the people well.[27]

---

[27] In recent years departmental film production, always more or less dependent on substantive program budgets in various USDA agencies, has been cut back. In fiscal year 1970, only 10 films were made that lasted longer than 15 minutes. The new concern with TV stations has brought forth, instead, more short newsfilms and ten-second "spots."

4

Pare Lorentz:
A Bold Beginning

Like the British story, the early story of government documentary films in America is also the story of one man. It is not a success story, but it is a remarkable odyssey and is perhaps as nearly a record of success as could have been achieved in the atmosphere and under the handicaps of the middle New Deal period.

Pare Lorentz did not turn out to be an organizer of men, nor a propagandist by choice, as Grierson was. He was an artist, with a variable temperament and a keen desire to watch over every detail of production himself. As such he was personally responsible for the beauty and impressiveness of *The River* in a way that could not be said of Grierson and *Night Mail.* As such, he also had troubles with administrators and Congressmen that might have been sidestepped by a more politically astute personality.

Lorentz' sponsor was Rexford Tugwell, who was no Stephen Tallents as far as public reputation was concerned, and who disappeared from the scene when the story was half finished. The timing was out of joint: the New Deal was heading into squalls in 1937. And not only was the general public attitude toward informational activities in government unreceptive, as it was in England, but there were powerful legislative voices which were positively hostile.

Like Grierson, Lorentz wrote movie criticism before he produced movies, but his approach to public opinion, on the other hand, was hardly in the category of research. His column, "Washington Sideshow," and his picture book, *The Roosevelt Year,* were not influenced by Lippmann or any other theorist of politics. He inherited from his father his strong feelings about the conservation of resources, but his aesthetic views were his own—trenchant, careless of opposition, full of a kind of spasmodic courage.

As motion picture critic for *McCall's* Magazine in August 1939, he wrote:

> There is more talk, analysis, and discussion of technique in a so-called documentary group than there is in four Hollywood studios; for every cameraman or director who knows the first principles of moviemaking, your documentary group always includes 25 critics, 15 philosophers, two poets, one man who knows a banker, and 45 corresponding secretaries. Mostly the group meets; occasionally they actually do manage to turn out a motion picture. . . .

> The movie industry itself is the most backward of all our corporate industries. No money for experimental productions is spent, and it puts aside little or nothing for research. . . .

Thus he loftily proclaimed a plague on both their houses. This statement, though written after the event, can stand as largely characteristic of his temperamental viewpoint during the time he was a public servant in Washington.

The Sponsor: Rexford G. Tugwell

The Resettlement Administration was created by executive order on April 30, 1935, and Undersecretary of Agriculture Rexford Tugwell was appointed administrator. It was a farm relief agency, and got its money from the WPA.

The Emergency Relief Appropriation Act had been passed on April 8, and this four-billion-dollar fund reflected two political facts, among others: the success of federal work projects as a form of relief, and the success of the New Deal at the 1934 polls. According to Robert Sherwood, Harry Hopkins was sorry to have to hand over rural rehabilitation to Tugwell.[1] His report on the use of his funds to the House Appropriations Committee was brief:

> Allocations of $334,000,000 have been made to the Resettlement Administration, $227,000,000 from funds made available by the Emergency Relief Appropriation Act of 1935, and $107,000,000 from the ERA Act of 1936 funds. A major part of this total has been used to

[1] See Robert Sherwood, *Roosevelt and Hopkins*, pp. 64–67, 70.

assist destitute farm families in various sections of the country. Rehabilitation loans have been made to farm families in need of assistance,
but in cases of emergency outright grants have been made. In addition, the Resettlement Administration is using a portion of its funds
to carry forward a program of subsistence homestead development in
rural areas and low-cost housing in suburban areas. The remaining
funds of the Administration are being used to purchase and develop
several millions of acres of submarginal farmlands.[2]

The RA was in operation in a period of pre-election enthusiasm and
post-election expansion, but the lifetime of the RA as an independent
agency was only a little shorter than the lifetime of this second phase of
New Deal expansion. A year and eight months later it had become part
of the Department of Agriculture, Tugwell having resigned from the
federal Government altogether, and its name was changed in September
of 1937 to the Farm Security Administration.[3]

Less than a month after the Resettlement Administration was set up,
the National Industrial Recovery Act was declared unconstitutional. A
little more than a month after the RA was consolidated into the Agriculture Department, the President's bill to reorganize the Supreme Court
began its tortuous route down a blind alley. These 20 months saw the
rewriting of the Agricultural Adjustment Act into the Soil Conservation
Act to meet the objections of the Supreme Court, the passage of the
Wagner Labor Relations Act to salvage the collective-bargaining elements
of the NIRA, the consolidation of social welfare and relief objectives in
the Social Security Act, and the battle to pass the Public Utility Holding
Company Act.

The Resettlement Administration, too, represented a kind of consolidation of ideas.

Although it was a relief agency, and took over emergency functions
from other programs—rural rehabilitation from FERA, subsistence home-
steads from the Interior Department—the RA was based on long-range
thinking about agriculture. If the AAA controls-for scarcity meant a quick
trip to high prices for all farmers, the plans of the men around Tugwell
meant a concerted attack on the problems of the little farmer. The man
who was deeply in debt, the man who was farming submarginal land, the
man who was destitute, ignorant, luckless—he was the farmer who needed
money most and would take the longest time to fit back into the framework of a functioning agricultural economy.

[2] House, 75th Congress, First Session, First Deficiency Appropriation Bill for 1937.
[3] John Gaus says that by 1939 the FSA had 2,000 county offices under 12 regional
offices, with state offices coordinated with state agencies. *Public Administration and the
Department of Agriculture*, p. 243.
   Executive Order 7530, dated December 31, 1936 transferred RA to the Department of Agriculture as of January 1, 1937. Some functions of the Bankhead-Jones
Farm Tenant Act (Public Law 210, 75th Congress, July 22, 1937) were also transferred to the new FSA.

This was an extremely radical business. It meant planning, and it meant moving people around. It meant advising people where to live, how to live, when to move, and how much money they would need. Resettlement was attacked as socialism and upheld as reclamation of human resources. Garet Garrett, a *Saturday Evening Post* writer, titled his article, "Plowing Up Freedom." Putting emphasis on the hardy small farmers who didn't want to give up their log cabins, he exclaimed: "The assumption that a poor farmer translated to good land will become a good farmer is bound to provide many disillusionments." An editorial in the *New Republic*, on the other hand, declared that Tugwell's work "constitutes one of the few remaining fragments of whatever was once hopeful in the New Deal." [4]

"The tragedy lies," Tugwell wrote in *Current History* in September 1936, "not with our pioneer ancestors who cleared and settled the land in the only method they knew, but rather with us, their descendants, who have taken so long to recognize that conditions have changed." Our profligate use of western grazing lands for row crops, our greedy expansion of cotton planting in the South, our destruction of timber areas in the north—these should be replaced by comprehensive, nation-wide measures of conservation. These were the causes of the small-farm decay which put such a burden on WPA funds.

"So long as hundreds of thousands of farm families live in ignorance and destitution they will continue to act as a drag upon the rural communities in which they live, just as city slums exert a downward pull upon the culture and moral standards of metropolitan centers." The Irish Free State, he pointed out, was partly converted from a nation of tenants to a nation of landowners. There was "no reason under the sun why the American people, with their wealth of good land resources, cannot succeed if proper intelligence is applied to the task."

"Proper intelligence," of course, is susceptible of various interpretations. It was precisely his undue emphasis on intelligence which alienated a good many outsiders from the beginning of Tugwell's association with the Government. He had been a professor of economics at Columbia University before he was appointed Assistant Secretary of Agriculture in

[4] "Tugwell to the Wolves?" December 25, 1935. This editorial claimed that 15,000 families had already been "rescued" and put on new land, and that ten million acres had been bought in 44 states.

Much of the attack on the RA centered on four suburban projects known as "Greenbelt towns" from the experiment by that name in Maryland. They were to be planned for leisure living, with numerous open spaces and no through roads. See "Trouble for Tugwell," *Literary Digest*, December 21, 1935, and "Tugwelltown Tussle," *Business Week*, January 25, 1936.

All this had its effect on Pare Lorentz. In 1938–39, when he was head of the U.S. Film Service, he wrote an outline for a film for the American Institute of Planners which eventually became the celebrated documentary, *The City*—a full-bodied argument for the building of Greenbelt towns.

1933. His father was a prosperous farmer but, like his chief, Henry Wallace, Tugwell was suspect because he had theories. The theories involved change. After his doctoral thesis in 1922 on *The Economic Basis of the Public Interest,* he had written (with two colleagues) a book on *American Economic Life.*[5] He had made a trip to Russia after that. Besides all this, he was a good-looking man, confident, quick-thinking and impatient with people who didn't agree. He made enemies fast, and became a kind of prototype of the planners who sketched out big, intelligent ideas and then met opposition from real people who thought in more traditional terms. Both the substance of his plans and the angle of his temperament were radical.[6]

From the beginning, Rex Tugwell must have realized he had a "bad press." At any rate, one of his first decisions after he had been made the head of an independent agency was to allot funds for the most comprehensive information staff ever seen up to that time in Washington, D.C.

The Resettlement Administration had an action program, designed to change people's lives. "Resettlement" had to be explained to them— and also, no doubt, to the rest of the people, not participating and not changed, who nevertheless paid the taxes to support the program. Thus there was plenty of rationale for a publicity set-up going far beyond the WPA experience. In addition, there was the intangible factor of a much-attacked man at the head of the agency who must have felt the need for justification—who certainly felt, like Harry Hopkins, that the people weren't getting the right information.[7]

This did not mean, however, a chain of speech-writers for Tugwell or a personal glory-story, though some looked at it that way, nor did it mean even a good-will catalog for RA projects. If there was any publicity "line," it was telling the story of the problems the RA faced, the reasons why the RA was set up. Roy Stryker got no further instructions about his photographic section than this: "We've got to tell people about the lower third—how ill-fed, ill-clothed and ill-housed they are." And so the director of still photography, originally hired as a "historian," brought in people like Walker Evans, John Vachon, Arthur Rothstein, Carl Mydans and Dorothea Lange, who became famous names through their work in picturing dust storms, Southern tenant farms and migrants. Dramatizing

[5] *Current Biography,* 1941. One of his collaborators on the book was Roy Stryker.
[6] "The comely and cocksure Rexford Tugwell is rated as the New Dealer most devoutly hated by conservatives." "Tugwelltown Tussle," *Business Week,* January 25, 1936.
[7] Shortly after the first RA projects were set up, the *New Republic* complained that "hardly a line about them has appeared in the press," but also remarked that "they have hardly been mentioned by administration leaders." Some members of the RA, according to Jonathan Mitchell, thought that "publicity might mobilize opposition." "Low Cost Paradise," September 18, 1935.

the problems, the reasons for relief, rehabilitation, resettlement and land-use planning—this was the main thing.[8]

Tugwell's first information chief, and the man who largely set the free-wheeling tone of the big new operation as Tugwell himself planned it, was John Franklin Carter, who later became a columnist under the name of Jay Franklin. He had been a novelist and a contributor to *Vanity Fair*, and was the Washington representative for *Liberty* Magazine at the time. Carter had succeeded in getting Tugwell to write articles for *Liberty* in the earliest days of the New Deal, and had frankly told him he would like to help out some day if the right kind of thing came along.[9]

They planned for press releases, of course, and writers who could help magazine staffs—all the usual assistance-to-the-press personnel of a Washington information office. But there were also to be exhibits for public display. There were to be recordings and scripts for the use of radio stations. There was to be a big photographic service with emphasis on quality. No stone was to be left unturned to keep the general public informed about the problems of a part of the public.

And there were to be movies. Whether they would hire a permanent staff and buy equipment—or, on the contrary, make contract arrangements with a private company—all such details were unclear. But movies were on the docket, and they were to show something of the bankruptcy of the land and the bankruptcy of the people on the land when that land had been ignorantly, carelessly, tragically misused.

The Plow That Broke the Plains

Pare Lorentz didn't go to Washington because he passed a Civil Service examination. He went there, as usually happens in the case of a big new job, because he knew somebody who recommended him. His wife's sister had married one of the Cowles brothers, and James LeCron, an assistant to Secretary of Agriculture Henry Wallace, had married one of

[8] See also Beaumont Newhall, *The History of Photography*. This extraordinary achievement in photography-as-communication introduced new models of realism in the world of photography-as-art and stirred up considerable excitement. When Darryl Zanuck decided to make *The Grapes of Wrath*, Stryker provided him with 45 still pictures, many of which he says he "recognized" in the fiction film 20th Century Fox produced. Stryker was later associated with Standard Oil of New York in their photographic department, and with a photo-historical project at the University of Pittsburgh.

[9] Interview, J. F. Carter, December 13, 1949.

the Cowles sisters.[10] It was only natural for LeCron to think of Lorentz when people began talking about doing a movie. Besides, there was plenty of evidence that this young movie critic was sympathetic with the aims of the New Deal.[11]

Born December 11, 1905, Lorentz had spent some time at the University of West Virginia, where one of his accomplishments was his job as editor of the humorous magazine, *Moonshine*. During his junior year he took off for the big city, and became an editor of the General Electric Company's house organ. For ten years after that he was motion picture editor for *Judge* Magazine. With Morris Ernst, in 1930, he wrote a book called *Censorship: The Private Lives of the Movies*, and in 1933 he put together a book of pictures called *The Roosevelt Year*. He worked for a while on *Newsweek*'s National Affairs desk. While there, he wrote a long piece on the dust storms. In 1934–36 he did a movie column for King Features, and during a brief tenure as political columnist from Washington he had the stimulating experience of being fired by William Randolph Hearst because he spoke well of Henry Wallace.[12]

Pare Lorentz had never in his life, so far, been responsible for making any part of a motion picture.

It is not altogether clear who first thought of the idea for *The Plow That Broke the Plains*, but apparently Lorentz was in Des Moines on at least one occasion talking about films to LeCron. Lorentz says he talked to various people for nearly a year specifically about a film on the tragedy of the Great Plains. He had taken a trip himself through the Midwest.[13]

[10] These liberal Republicans have long presided over a journalistic complex which has included, in that order, the *Minneapolis Star and Tribune*, the *Des Moines Register and Tribune*, *Look*, *Quick*, and *Flair* (the last two having only a brief existence), and various TV stations. Gardner Cowles, editor of *Look*, became director of the Domestic Branch of the OWI, 1942–43.

[11] Interviews: Roy Stryker, April 9, 1949; J. F. Carter, December 13, 1949; Pare Lorentz, December 27, 1949. LeCron also had known about Lorentz' book *The Roosevelt Year*, which Lorentz had originally conceived as a newsreel. Lorentz wrote the following, November 14, 1950, in a letter to this author: "One of the errors of people dealing with the Roosevelt administrations is that one gets the impression that they all arrived in March 1933 in Washington and all suddenly started reflecting Roosevelt's point of view.

"My people settled northwestern Virginia before the Revolution. There used to be an old man named Roach who was superintendent of a lumber company and he used to come down on the B & O spur line on Saturdays and go in the barber shop and sit around and talk and I remember vividly his saying, "They are going to dig it and cut it and gut it and the whole goddamn thing will fall down some day." He added the fact that nobody cared enough to save some timber on the ridges or to stop polluting the river with chemicals. My father was that kind of man—fought endless battles trying to keep the bass from being killed off. I grew up among such people."

[12] See *Current Biography*, 1940. It was not until August, 1935, after joining RA, that he became movie critic for *McCall's*.

[13] He went to Hollywood in a vain attempt to get the Great Drought filmed, then came back through the midwest, stopping at Des Moines, where, according to J. P. McEvoy, "influential citizens" sped him on to Washington. "Young Man with a Camera," *Scribner's Commentator*, July 1940, *Readers Digest*, August 1940.

This was about the same time Archibald MacLeish was out there seeing the dust bowl, too, doing an article on it for *Fortune* Magazine.

Tugwell hired the embattled young critic in June of 1935. Lorentz and MacLeish met soon after. He did not choose to make the story the story of one man, as MacLeish did, in part, in his story of Tom Campbell, the 200,000-acre farmer. But he did choose to emphasize the three-fold history of Great Plains exploitation—overgrazing by cattle, overplowing by early settlers, and finally the frantic, widespread overplowing of the plains under pressure of World War needs and postwar speculation. He wrote his script in the spirit of MacLeish's opening words:

> For more than three centuries men have moved across this continent from east to west. For some years now, increasingly in the last two or three, dust has blown back across the land from west to east. The movement of men, long understood, is taken for granted. The blowing of dust, little understood, has filled the newspapers and rolled across the newsreel screens. And yet the two are linked together like the throwing and rebound of a ball. The two are chapters from the same book. . . .
>
> The meaning of the dust storms was that grass was dead. . . .[14]

Lorentz owed one of his most effective narrative lines to the last line of the *Fortune* article: "The grasslands are the grasslands. Men plow them at their peril."

This does not mean that by September 3, when he hired cameramen Ralph Steiner, Paul Strand and Leo Hurwitz, he had a complete script all ready for visual accompaniment. Lorentz did not work that way. He had an outline, approved by Carter and Tugwell. He had a couple of dramatic dust-storm scenes in mind (one of them to be done in the Texas panhandle near Dalhart), and for the rest, he would pick up what looked like exciting material to fit his theme.

The excitement in his film, however, was not going to lie in any simple story of individual human tragedy. *The Plow* was to document great geographic and economic forces, as far as film could do so. "We had a special lens made to get the largest possible spread. The motion in our motion picture was going to be *architectural*, the ominous changes in the land itself." [15]

He started in Montana and Wyoming, working down through the Dakotas and south to Texas in a seven-week tour. In Texas, he faced a

[14] *Fortune*, November, 1935. One of the best descriptions, at once concise and dramatic, of the tragedy of the Western lands, is the chapter "When the Farms Blew Away," in Frederick Lewis Allen's *Since Yesterday*. "The 'great black blizzard' of November 11, 1933—which darkened the sky in Chicago the following day and as far east as Albany, N.Y., the day after that—was only a prelude to disaster. During 1934 and 1935 thousands of square miles were to be laid waste and their inhabitants set adrift upon desperate migrations across the land." (p. 197)

[15] Interview, December 27, 1949.

Frame enlargement from *The Plow That Broke the Plains* (Dir. Pare Lorentz) for Resettlement Administration, 1936

brief confrontation with his photographers.[16] They wanted to change the script (or what there was of it). Lorentz, who was a vague, enthusiastic, New Deal Democrat if he was anything politically, must have scented trouble. Paul Strand, who was second only to Robert Flaherty in reputation among American documentary photographers, was later to be a center of controversy in the difficulties of the Association of Documentary Film Producers, with accusations of Communism freely bandied about. Besides this, he and Steiner were periodically at odds.[17]

[16] See also W. L. White, "Pare Lorentz," *Scribner's*, January 1939, and Robert Snyder, *Pare Lorentz and the Documentary Film*, pp. 30–31.

[17] "One week you could mention Steiner to Strand and the next week you couldn't." (Interview, Roy Stryker, December 6, 1949). Steiner and Van Dyke later became convinced that there was too much undemocratic bitterness in Strand's world-view, and refused to join in his plans for Frontier Films. They set up an organization of their own called American Documentary Films, Inc. (Interview, Willard Van Dyke, Apr. 9, 1949. See also *Living Films*, catalog published by American Documentary Film Producers, 1940.)

One needs only to read his comments around and about a film called *The Red Salute*, in *McCall's* for December, 1936, to see how uninterested Lorentz himself was in Communism or in Russia.

Frame enlargement from *The Plow That Broke the Plains* (Dir. Pare Lorentz) for Resettlement Administration, 1936

Lorentz intended *The Plow* to be a problem film, but he wanted no sweeping solutions at the end, and no sweeping recriminations about capitalist society, either. He was interested in human problems, in the bitter results of human mistakes, in the vast drama of the impact of the elements on human beings.

> We had two prime objectives in making the picture: one, to show audiences a specific and exciting section of the country; the other, to portray the events which led up to one of the major catastrophes in American history—to show, in other words, the Great Drought which is now going into its sixth year.[18]

These were dramatic objectives, not propaganda objectives. There was actually some murmuring about this on the part of Agriculture and Resettlement people when they saw the Lorentz films. They felt both films should have been more definitely "instructional"—should have shown exactly what the RA was doing about all this and what further political changes were going to be needed.

[18] *McCall's*, July, 1936.

Lorentz felt keenly the pains and injustices of our increasingly or-ganized, interdependent world and this was to issue in his twice-begun film project on unemployment which he called *Ecce Homo*. But he never had more than the faintest idea what he wanted done about it. He visualized the pains and stresses, chose blunt and forceful words to describe them, and above all was a consummate artist in the use of sound. The scenes themselves, and the sound, were propaganda, certainly. They force-fully spread the news of desolation and poverty. But he himself was not a political propagandist.

The Plow does end with a long string of Okies turning into a govern-ment camp somewhere in California, but this is obviously not offered as an answer to anything and could as easily have been Republican in its mockery: Is this all we can do about the dust bowl? The picture leaves the audience with two main reactions—a sense of hopelessness at the size of the problem, and a sense of guilt which the history of the western plains lays upon us all.

Lorentz said further, in a quite modest estimate:

> Thus, with some outstanding photography and music, *The Plow That Broke the Plains* is an unusual motion picture which might have been a really great one had the story and the construction been up to the rest of the workmanship. As it is, it tells the story of the Plains and it tells it with some emotional value—an emotion that springs out of the soil itself. Our heroine is the grass, our villain the sun and the wind, our players the actual farmers living in the Plains country. It is a melodrama of nature—the tragedy of turning grass into dust, a melo-drama that only Carl Sandburg or Willa Cather perhaps could tell as it should be told.[19]

Two Battles and a Premiere

Lorentz had various financial and administrative difficulties—and some difficulties with Hollywood—as he blazed his new trails in govern-men film production.

Before he started shooting, one thing had been taken care of—a remarkably foresighted move. Arch Mercey, assistant director of informa-tion, had asked the Comptroller-General for an opinion on the legality of using Resettlement Administration funds for making a movie. In the letter to the General Accounting Office (which is in intent an arm of the Congress), it was stated that "the primary object of the motion picture is to help the Resettlement Administration and its employees to visualize

19 *Ibid.*

and understand better the problems confronting them." The Comptroller General's response had been favorable.[20]

On Lorentz' return to Washington, however, the Treasury Department had to be appeased. He had incurred a few expenses. He was only indistinctly aware that this created a problem. He knew there might be some trouble, though he had only the slightest acquaintance with budget justifications, Civil Service requirements, travel vouchers and disbursing agents. It seemed that the bundle of receipts he brought back from his midwestern expedition—some of them scratched on wrapping paper—were not instantly exchangeable for cash.

He had a long talk with the chief disbursing officer of the Treasury —a talk which must have had its own independent value as an entertaining dialogue—and Lorentz evidently won him over to the cause of government film-making at the same time he was being enlightened about the financial operations of the Federal Government. The frequently warm and persuasive Lorentz personality worked well that day, though he himself emerged at the end in the somewhat cold and colorless role of a disbursing agent of the U.S. Treasury. This minor coup seemed to solve the problem for the time being.

There had been other such problems. The decision to hire Lorentz had been in itself a rejection of the two opposite alternatives: (1) complete laboratory equipment and staff in Washington, or (2) a straight contract arrangement with an established producer. This had meant that Lorentz and Mercey could not in the beginning offer photographers and film editors the security of Civil Service, but after a special battle, they were permitted to hire two or three cameramen for short periods at a $25 per diem rate, which was higher than Civil Service jobs could offer.[21] Lorentz himself was for a time on a daily fee as technical consultant to John Carter, an arrangement which later expanded into a $10,000 salary as head of the U.S. Film Service.[22]

[20] "The Administration's own employees consist not only of its employees in Washington but of a large staff in the field. The employees of the cooperating agencies (among which are the National Emergency Council, the Agricultural Adjustment Administration, the Department of Agriculture, the Agricultural Extension Service, the Indian Service, the Civilian Conservation Corps, the Federal Emergency Relief Administration and the Public Works Administration) are likewise located in the field as well as in Washington. A moving picture of the character described above will be one of the most effective, quick and inexpensive means of explaining some of the problems of the Administration to its employees and to the employees of these agencies."
The Comptroller replied: "In view of your explanation as to the objects proposed to be accomplished by the motion picture, this office is not required to object to the use of funds under the allocation for administrative expenses of your Administration for such purposes." (15 Comptroller General 148, August 19, 1935)
[21] Arch Mercey commented that September 3, 1935 is some kind of a landmark since this was the first time such artists were hired at such a fee. Letter, October 12, 1950.
[22] Interview, Pare Lorentz, December 27, 1949. See also Hearings, House, 76th Congress, 3rd Section, Department of Labor-Federal Security Agency Appropriation Bill for 1941. There was a sliding scale of per diem payments for technicians and consultants ranging from $25 to $8 a day.

His free position as government-sponsored independent producer also had its shortcomings when he faced certain technical needs. If he had been head of a contracting film organization or even an experienced director, with both know-how and friends, his path would have been considerably easier. One of his biggest headaches was the difficulty in getting stock shots of harvest time. He had gone on location too late for any good tractor-and-combine pictures. He also wanted to intercut some scenes of World War I. He naturally hoped to buy some of this footage in Hollywood.

But on arrival in Hollywood to ask for these favors he was greeted instead with the news that Will Hays was circularizing the producers, urging all major studios to deny Lorentz the use of their film libraries. Ordinarily, of course, stock shots were available at a reasonable price to anyone who wanted to buy them. But from the point of view of the producers, this was a practical opportunity to discourage the U.S. Government from making films. Pare Lorentz found the studio libraries politely unable to meet his needs.

The whole episode obviously has its petty aspects, and leaves a very real stain on the record of the film industry of the mid-thirties, then at the very height of its cinematic triumphs. The studios which were producing such extraordinary motion pictures as Mutiny on the Bounty, Mr. Deeds Goes to Town, The Story of Louis Pasteur, A Tale of Two Cities and The Informer could have afforded some trifling dealings with an amateur director working for a relatively small agency in Washington. The fact that Lorentz managed to outmaneuver them hardly softens the judgment we must make of their strangely fevered reaction.

The RA film director viewed the situation as a battle. With the help and hospitality of King Vidor, he got in touch with directors who were in sympathy with his plans and was admitted quietly into certain projection rooms to view various stock shots he might want. He carried off some of these to New York with the blessing of the directors and without the knowledge of the producers. Later, when the situation had thawed out a little, he paid for it all in the accepted manner.[23]

When he finally had the footage he wanted, he was faced with the crucial task of editing it, plus the addition of narration and music. Shuttling back and forth between his own office at *Judge* Magazine and the

[23] A letter in the RA files is revealing—addressed to King Vidor and dated May 11, 1936: "A great part of the credit for The Plow That Broke the Plains should be yours. We all appreciate your sympathy and interest." Through the Washington office, the subject was taken up with Mabel Walker Willebrandt, a former assistant to the Attorney General, who was now a representative of the movie industry at the capital. She made some phone calls to Hollywood, pointing out (with some passing references, perhaps, to the anti-trust laws) that cooperation with the Government was the best policy in the long run. (See also Variety, May 12, 1936.)

Lorentz maintains that this Washington intervention "had no good effect." (Letter, November 14, 1950)

H.E.R. Laboratories on West 40th Street, he wrote narration and matched it to the shots he had. "The girls at the lab showed me for the first time how to wind film and cut it." [24]

He interviewed various composers and finally persuaded Virgil Thomson, who had written the music for Gertrude Stein's *Four Saints in Three Acts*, to sit with him in the projection room and work out suitable lengths of American folk music. Alexander Smallens, who had conducted the Stein-Thomson opera, was interested enough both in conservation and in films to persuade, in turn, about 40 musicians from the New York Philharmonic and the Metropolitan Opera to play the new score Thomson worked out. Thomas Chalmers from the *March of Time* read the narration.

The Plow That Broke the Plains had its premiere May 10, 1936, at the Mayflower Hotel in Washington with the help of the New York Museum of Modern Art.[25] The large audience of invited guests was first shown some foreign documentaries for comparison. Only one of the offerings was critical of existing conditions in a way comparable to *The Plow*—Rotha's *Face of Britain* (1934)—and it was produced privately by Gaumont-British Instructional. Others were government films—an ecstatic picture called *Harvest Festival* by Ukrainfilm of Kiev (1935); *Nidi*, made in the same year by the French State Railways; and an excerpt from the Nuremberg Nazi party display by Leni Riefenstahl, *The Triumph of the Will*. There was also an experimental bit by Len Lye of the British GPO called *Color Box*.

Thus the premiere was not unlike the first showing of *Drifters* in England, though *Potemkin* was noticeably absent. It reflected the anxiety of all concerned about the problem of distribution. Here was the first U.S. Government film ever produced which offered any real promise of either critical or public popularity. Yet the prospect was, as the Baltimore *Sun* remarked, that *The Plow* would play "the old Federal circuit of army posts, naval vessels, CCC camps, clubs, Sunday Schools and colleges." [26]

As far as the critics were concerned, this fate was not deserved. Washington movie reviewers (even on the Hearst *Herald*) were much impressed. The National Board of Review magazine listed it as one of its few "exceptional photoplays." Mark Van Doren, writing a month later in *The Nation*, called it "thirty minutes of unforgettable film"—"a work of art" which nevertheless declared "its practical purpose at every moment of its flight across the screen." *Time* Magazine did not vouchsafe a clear-cut opinion, but did offer a clear-cut summary of the contents, with five pic-

---

[24] Interview, Pare Lorentz, December 27, 1949. He also had the help of Leo Zochling on the editing. (Arch Mercey, "Films by American Governments," *Films*, Summer 1940.)

[25] Sometime in March there was a preview at the White House. On Friday, May 1, there were two showings for RA personnel only.

[26] "New Deal Movie Wins Critics But Theaters Bar Doors to It." May 13, 1936.

tures and a picture of Lorentz, remarking that the photography was done by "a trio of cameramen, all able, all Left-wing in politics."

Senator Alva Adams of Colorado declared, "This film is a vivid dramatic persentation of the unplanned cooperation of land-hungry men, war, drought and wind in the destruction of the grasslands of the West. It is a remarkable film production." Senator Pat Harrison of Mississippi was even more fulsome, if somewhat less clear: "This film in my opinion is an agricultural *Cavalcade*." [27]

But Hollywood wouldn't distribute it. There were various levels of reasons given for this. One level was that the thing was too long for a short subject and too short for a feature. Another level of reasoning was that most moviegoers would object to propaganda. Parallel with this was the fear that "the Republican party and other groups opposed to the New Deal might insist on similar treatment for their output of cinematic propaganda." This was not at all unlikely—much more likely, for instance, than the full-scale competition of Government with Hollywood.[28]

Again Lorentz and Mercey viewed this as a battle. Lorentz arranged private showings for local critics. Mercey got in touch with RA regional information officers and told them that they had now become movie salesmen. They were not only to arrange showings for government agency people and for farmers' groups. They were also to try to get theater bookings.[29]

The Broadway debut was at Arthur Mayer's Rialto Theater and it played soon after at three other houses in the metropolitan area. The Europa in Philadelphia, the Fine Arts in Boston, the Little Theater in Washington, all took the film, and other independent bookings followed. The biggest boost for *The Plow* came in the Middle West, where large chains of independent exhibitors signed up—600 theaters in Illinois, 500 in Ohio, 200 in Wisconsin, smaller circuits in Texas, Arkansas, Tennessee, Indiana, etc.[30] In the final accounting, this beating of the bushes in the

[27] See Remarks of Maury Maverick, *Congressional Record*, House, May 7, 1936, for these quotations. Later, in an exchange with Lowell Mellett in an Appropriations Committee meeting, Senator Adams was not so favorable, accusing the film of "deviating from the facts." (Senate, 76th Congress 1st Session, Work Relief Appropriation Act of 1939, June 22, 1939.)

[28] "Federal Movie Furor," *Business Week*, July 11, 1936. Baltimore *Sun*, May 13, 1936. Among others, a special effort had been made to get a release through United Artists, and Lorentz and Mercey saw to it that Tugwell sent a personal invitation to Mary Pickford to see *The Plow* in Hollywood. This leading United Artists board member averred in polite response that while she was much impressed by the photography and the drama of the film, it certainly seemed to her to be very close to propaganda! (Telegram, FSA files, March 25, 1936.)

[29] Chief among these salesmen were George Gercke (New York), Dean S. Jennings (Chicago), and Paul Jordan (Lincoln, Nebr.). Mercey handled the southeast area himself, and California came later.

[30] Resettlement Administration memorandum, July 16, 1936, Arch Mercey to Grace E. Falke, Executive Assistant, subject: " 'The Plow' Distribution as of July 15th."

hinterland netted some 3,000 independent theater showings. This was a substantial outcome, even in comparison with the 14,161 operating motion picture theaters in the United States in that year.

The film-makers of the Resettlement Administration had come a long way from the "primary intention" of their letter to the Comptroller General to help "the Resettlement Administration and its employees to visualize and understand better the problems confronting them." Clearly, they had not only grown proud enough of their film to want people to see it for its own sake. They also felt that the whole American public—or as large a part of it as they could reach—ought to know what problems were confronting the Resettlement Administration and its employees.

If the American people could be made to understand the seriousness of the Great Plains tragedy, they would see to it that the Resettlement Administration program was continued and strengthened. Drama would build conviction and conviction would support policy.

The River

According to Lorentz, after *The Plow* he was through making films for the Government. He was tired, and the critics' reviews weren't enough reward. He didn't like having to be a disbursing agent. He didn't like quarreling with cameramen or dickering with musicians. His salary wasn't in the least comparable to a Hollywood producer's salary. And anyway, why produce films if you can't distribute them?

And yet it had been quite an experience, after all. He had broken precedents and was on the way to becoming famous. He was well aware that some thought of him as the American Grierson.

The best of his film-making, and after that, the worst of his troubles, were yet to come.

His story has it that he was going out of Tugwell's office one day after a farewell visit. As he reached the door, Lorentz caught sight of a big map of North America on the wall nearby. He stared at it a moment, then swung around and said to Tugwell in a voice charged with emotion:

"Rex, here is the great picture that ought to be made—and sometime you ought to make it. You ought to take a drop of water and follow it from here"—he was pointing to the northern beginnings of the Missouri River —"all the way down to the Gulf."

He said good-bye and was out in the hall before Tugwell moved. "Pare!" he exclaimed. "We'll do it! Come back here. We'll do it somehow!" And despite the gathering wrath of various Senators, an impending election and the jealousy of Hollywood, they did it.

The story of *The River* (which began under the working title, *Highway to the Sea,* but fortunately yielded to simplification) is much the same as the story of *The Plow That Broke the Plains*. The photographers were different, the negative cost was much larger and the result was a film of greater unity, drama and poetry. But the production process, with one exception, was basically the same. The Comptroller General did insist, this time, that greater care be taken in incurring expenditures, and a man named John Bridgeman was sent along with Lorentz to be agent cashier. These two actually got along almost too well together, and apparently Lorentz, whose enthusiasm was infectious, did not feel burdened with penury.[31]

Lorentz had read the Mississippi Valley Committee report of the Public Works Administration. It impressed on him some of the larger dangers of water erosion, and some of its causes. Besides this, a man from West Virginia already had some knowledge of floods.

"The problem of checking erosion," the committee had said, "is chiefly one of control of the surface run-off of water on sloping ground."

> In undisturbed natural conditions, the erosive forces act very slowly on account of the forest cover, grass and other vegetation. When this protective cover is disturbed by forest destruction, tillage or overgrazing of livestock, erosion is accelerated. . . . About 25 per cent of tilled land in the Mississippi Basin alone has already lost a large part or all of the top soil. . . .

Lorentz was willing to start with surface run-off, but in his own way. His opening words have become as well known as many a more formal poem:

> From as far West as Idaho,
> Down from the glacier peaks of the Rockies—
> From as far East as New York,
> Down from the turkey ridges of the Alleghenies—
> Down from Minnesota, twenty-five hundred miles,
> The Mississippi River runs to the Gulf.
> Carrying every drop of water that flows down two-thirds the continent,
> Carrying every brook and rill, rivulet and creek,
> Carrying all the rivers that run down two-thirds the continent,
> The Mississippi runs to the Gulf of Mexico.

And later on, he used a sharp visual image which summarized for the public imagination everything the committee said about "run-off":

> Year in, year out, the water comes down,
> Down from a thousand hillsides,
> Washing the top off the Valley.

[31] Interview, John Fischer, December 1, 1949.

"Levees were begun along the river in front of New Orleans in 1717," the report explained.

> The levees were gradually extended until by the end of the last century, they were practically continuous to the upper end of the alluvial valley. . . . As the levees were extended and raised, it became evident that the grade was not high enough to confine the higher floods, so in 1898 the (Mississippi River) Commission established a new grade line averaging about five feet higher than the 1883 line. . . . A third one was established in 1914. . . . The greatest reliably recorded Mississippi flood occurred in 1927. The levees were again broken in many places. . . .

The bald report carries its own sober horror, but Lorentz saw it in more sweeping terms, adapting it, at the same time, to the effective shots he got of levee-building with mules:

> New Orleans to Baton Rouge,
> Baton Rouge to Natchez,
> Natchez to Vicksburg,
> Vicksburg to Memphis,
> Memphis to Cairo—
> We built a dyke a thousand miles long.
> Men and mules; mules and mud;
> Mules and mud a thousand miles up the Mississippi.

From the brief prefatory note of the Mississippi Valley Committee he took his key statements:

> But you cannot plan for water unless you plan for land. . . .
> But you cannot plan for water and land unless you plan for people.[32]

And this led him into his only plug for the RA (which, by the time the film was completed, became the FSA), describing briefly its financial help for "farmers who were caught by years of depression and in need of only a stake to be self-sufficient." He hoped to get some flood scenes, but didn't know yet whether they were available as stock shots. The final sequence, he knew, would be about the TVA—the plans and the work going ahead for flood control and erosion control.

This much he certainly had in mind before the shooting started, but not much more. The narrative words and their poetic form would not be determined till after the footage was shot and partly cut to the music.

[32] The Committee phrasing (see frontispiece): "We cannot plan for water unless we also consider the relevant problems of the land. We cannot plan for water and land unless we plan for the whole people." U.S. Government Printing Office, Oct. 1, 1934.
 The free verse form of the narration was used for the film because of the popular success of an article in *McCall's* about the floods of 1937. Lorentz wrote the magazine version in a weekend and with some changes it became the film narration. He told Robert Snyder there were 150,000 requests for copies of the *McCall's* piece. *Pare Lorentz and the Documentary Film*, p. 61.

He took Horace and Stacy Woodard out to West Virginia with him and sent Willard Van Dyke south for cotton close-ups. Floyd Crosby was hired somewhat later, and joined the crew in Louisiana.[33]

The camera job was pretty nearly finished by January 1937, when it suddenly became clear that flood waters were pouring down from upper tributaries of the great river. Van Dyke and Crosby got a phone call from Lorentz while they were in New Orleans; following his instructions, they took themselves to Memphis as fast as they could. But there were "a thousand miles of disaster to cover," Van Dyke recalls with a shudder. They didn't have enough of a script to know where to start. Lorentz yielded, flew to Memphis, and wrote them a script for the flood scenes. These turned out to be some of the most extraordinary documentary sequences ever filmed.[34]

Much of the flood footage has since been used for other purposes, but only a small part of it, of course, got into The River. This extra shooting gave the second Lorentz production an extremely high proportion of film exposed to film used,[35] and contributed to Lorentz' reputation for profligate use of film negative. It should be remembered, however, that this was the second film he had ever made.

He spent about six months editing it, with the help of Lloyd Nosler, an experienced Hollywood editor who had worked for King Vidor. Again he had Thomson, Smallens and Chalmers helping him. He was worrying all along about distribution. By the end of August he had it ready and showed it to some Department of Agriculture people, including Henry Wallace.

Then one evening, on a hunch, George Gercke, of the New York FSA Office, an old friend of Roosevelt's from Albany days, took Lorentz on a flying trip up to Hyde Park with a copy of the film.[36] They weren't exactly invited, as Gercke admitted, but he had a feeling the President wouldn't mind a postscript on his evening's quota of movies. He didn't. In fact the President had just been asking at dinnertime what had hap-

[33] Van Dyke, who has since become one of the best-known of the documentary producers, remembers how he took off by himself in a station wagon to take a tour of Tennessee, Mississippi, Louisiana, Arkansas and Ohio. Lorentz hired him "on a gamble," and gave him "a guy to hold the slate and pay the bills." Lorentz joined him for a few days at Greenville, Mississippi, but spent most of the time with Stacy Woodard and Crosby. Van Dyke went ahead taking pictures he thought would be interesting (he was responsible for the levee-building scene) and hoping his camera would be in the mood and tempo the director had in mind. (Interview, Van Dyke, April 9, 1949.)

[34] There had been floods in 1936, too. In 1937, from January 21 to the end of the emergency, the Coast Guard had 1,800 men and 350 boats on duty evacuating more than 67,000 refugees. WPA workers in great numbers helped in the flood areas, and 150,000 worked on the levees alone. (See Study Guide, The River, U.S. Film Service, 1936.)

[35] Van Dyke estimates about 30 to 1. According to Time, November 8, 1937, they took 80,000 feet in the flood area.

[36] Gercke had been Albany correspondent for the New York World when Roosevelt was Governor.

pened to the new Lorentz film. The movies were late that night because he was getting ready for a trip west to dedicate Bonneville Dam, but *The River* came on the screen about midnight—after Sonia Henie in *Thin Ice.*

So far as Lorentz can remember, Roosevelt's comment was something like this: "Magnificent! What can I do to help?"

The two of them grasped at the opportunity to worry openly about whether anyone would actually see the film. Lorentz also specifically raised the question of his own role, and the role of movies, in the Government. Tom Corcoran was called in at once, and Corcoran it was who helped out on both counts.[37] Shortly afterward, a plan was begun for a "permanent" and separate Film Service under the National Emergency Council. Action was not taken until several months later, and this—the beginning of the end of the Lorentz era—makes a separate story which deserves a chapter of its own. Meanwhile Corcoran also had some conferences with Barney Balaban, new chairman of Paramount Pictures, and head of the Balaban and Katz chain of theaters in Chicago. The result was a theatrical distribution contract with Paramount, a matter of considerable importance in the history of *The River.*

The critics were generous. *Time* remarked upon its "powerful locomotive quality" and described it as "a motion picture of startling photographic beauty, sweeping scope and social importance." Bernard DeVoto, ostensibly reviewing the book which contained the narrative and some still pictures, objected to the TVA sequence, but said that "all the superlatives you have been hearing about it are justified." Frank Nugent, in the *New York Times,* held it to be "a poetic, stirring, and majestic picture," and went on to say in his Sunday column:

> Not the Mississippi of "Showboat," all prettified, with Negro baritones caroling on the levees, but the story of a mighty brute which served men faithfully until man mistreated it. . . .
>
> It could have been filmed as baldly as a subcommittee's report, with charts and graphs and the concomitant speeches of Congressmen. Mr. Lorentz has seen something more in his story of the river, a great deal more. And he has let us see it, too. It has an epic equality, this tale of revenging nature and of man—resolutely, repentantly—striving to placate it and conquer it again. So the narrative runs like an epic poem, cadenced and rhythmic and mournful. . . . *The River* runs for about half an hour, which is not half long enough. To call it a great documentary does it an injustice. It is a great motion picture.

Howard Barnes, in the *Herald-Tribune,* was no less fulsome:

[37] He was upstairs at Hyde Park at the time. Corcoran was what might be called a second-generation brain truster. Part author with Ben Cohen of several New Deal measures, including the public utility holding company bill, he is described by Frederick Lewis Allen as "a natural leader of the young liberal lawyers." (*Since Yesterday,* p. 242.)

There have been few documentary films to match it for the striking presentation of facts or for sheer screen artistry. . . . He has used the screen as an instrument to make social history vital, understandable, and dramatic. . . . Photographers have taken shot after shot of brooding beauty and impact. . . . With tremendous economy, Mr. Lorentz has fitted them into a swift-moving and engrossing unity and has leavened them with his poetic commentary. . . . The motion picture is of course propaganda, in the largest sense of that word, but it is the most persuasive propaganda ever brought to the screen. It is impossible to sit through it without being deeply stirred, mentally as well as emotionally—a film that demands attention with a serene authority. . . .

Gilbert Seldes was even more eloquent in *Scribner's:*

Mr. Lorentz starts you near the headwaters of the great river . . . and then the atmospheric pressure of the picture is changed, and the brooks and rivulets are no longer flowing together to make a river, but are destroying the land through which they course. And so, without your knowing it, you arrive at the Tennessee Valley—and if this is propaganda, make the most of it, because it is masterly.

This unanimity of critical opinion [38] was further upheld in the announcement in September of 1938 that *The River* had received the top prize among 71 subjects in the documentary classification at the International Cinema Exposition in Venice.

The formal premiere was held on October 29, 1937 for an invited audience in New Orleans. New Orleans was Lorentz' own idea. He wanted to take the story first to the people who were most concerned. If he could win over some of the Valley people in the very beginning, he would have less misunderstanding in the end. This was the rationale for similar screenings in Memphis, St. Louis, Des Moines, Minneapolis and Chicago, before showing it in Washington.

It was all pretty well worked out from a public relations point of view. The manager of the Strand Theater in New Orleans, for instance, provided the New York office with a useful telegram before the Minneapolis opening: [39]

HELD WORLD PREMIERE OF THE RIVER OCT 29 FOR THREE HUNDRED AND FIFTY LEADING PEOPLE AT NEW ORLEANS. REACTION WAS WONDERFUL. I PERSONALLY CONTACTED SEVERAL OF THOSE PEOPLE AFTER PREMIERE: THEY CONGRATULATED ME FOR BEING ABLE

---

[38] *Time*, November 8, 1937. See also Otis Ferguson, "Old Man River," *New Republic*, November 10, 1937. *Saturday Review of Literature*, April 9, 1938. New York *Times*, February 5 and 6, 1938. New York *Herald-Tribune*, February 5, 1938. *Scribners*, January 1938. Later Seldes had broader second thoughts about government films.

[39] A collect telegram, reproduced in the Paramount broadsheet advertising the film to theaters.

TO BRING FILM OF THAT NATURE TO MY SCREEN.
NINETEEN SCHOOLS OF THE CITY HAD REPRESENTA-
TIVES FROM THEIR HISTORY CLASSES TO SEE THE
RIVER. ALSO SHOWED THE RIVER TO SOME TWENTY
THOUSAND PATRONS AUDIENCE REACTION GREAT.
THE PUBLIC NEEDS MORE HISTORY SHORTS LIKE THE
RIVER. HOPING MINNEAPOLIS ENJOYS IT AS NEW OR-
LEANS DID

W. C. LOOMIS MANAGER STRAND THEATER

But there was also an unmistakable public response. A letter dated
December 15, 1937 from the Balaban and Katz Corporation carries its
own stamp of authenticity:

The following is a copy of a memo received from the manager of the
Apollo Theater regarding the audience reaction on the picture entitled
The River:

"We are very pleased with the comments we are receiving on the government short, *The River.* Our audiences applaud it after every
showing.

"During the last day or two we have received numerous calls on the
telephone inquiring how long we are going to run it. Many of the inquiries are in the nature of people asking if we intend to show it at
our out-lying houses.

"In short, it is our belief that this subject has received more favorable
comments than any short of this nature that we have ever shown."

The real popularity of this extraordinary "short subject" could not be
denied then or since. *The River* has stood up well. For many years it was
the most used film in many of the commercial and educational 16mm
libraries. The English film historian and critic, Roger Manvell, called it in
1944 "the most important single documentary America has so far produced." [40]
The Little Theater in Washington also reported "applause at every
showing," and an increase in business instead of the usual slump at
Christmas-shopping time. It was billed above the feature, and was on
December 30 going into its fourth week—neither point surprising in
Washington, of course. *The River* ran five weeks in Boston, with *The
Life and Loves of Beethoven.* It was held over at the Criterion in New
York, according to the *New York Times,* while "the little Class B feature
(*Scandal Street*) which shared the bill during the first week has moved
on." [41]

[40] *Film*, p. 120.
[41] Frank Nugent, "One Down, Two Doubled," *New York Times,* February 13,
1938.

Politics, Truth and Drama

Despite the fact that *The Plow* and *The River* were primarily propaganda about problems and not about politics, these two extraordinary films were nonetheless linked inextricably with partisan politics. They made an impression on eye and ear which was memorable, and if they did not call for specific action—did not say, "Vote for Democrats!" or even "Support the Farm Security Administration!"—these films were certainly on the side of action.

A paragraph or two in the *Study Guide* for *The Plow That Broke the Plains* helps to reveal what kind of local action the FSA wanted to induce through its publicity and through its county representatives:

> The Federal Government alone cannot accomplish the gigantic task of making the Great Plains more livable. Local people, directly and through their State and local governments, must take a major part.

> One of the extremely important problems to be dealt with, for example, is how certain landowners may be made to follow soil conserving practices when their land is blowing dust and they refuse to do anything about it. Frequently such wind erosion, by blowing soil onto neighboring lands, injures the property of other landowners. States have enacted laws that permit local landowners to form Soil Conservation Districts. These Districts, similar in many ways to school districts or other local public institutions, have the power to require landowners to protect their soil, even if the landowners may not live on the land and have no direct interest in preserving it for their own account. Such measures can only be carried out if a large majority of the local people are in favor of protecting the land and will express their opinion in an election held for that purpose.

The party which was taking this kind of action was the Democratic party. The Democrats were in power and the Democratic administration had made the film.

It hardly seemed an accident that *The Plow That Broke the Plains* was being circulated with persistence, pride and vigor during the summer months of 1936. It was an election year which found regional offices of the RA energetically promoting the movie among midwestern theater chains. And however justified Hollywood distributors were in fearing government production competition, they were certainly justified in fearing political demands for "equal time" to counter "New Deal propaganda." Had it not been widely reported that Roosevelt had actually considered sending *The Plow* to Congress as a Presidential message? [42]

Whether or not Tugwell meant it from the first to be a campaign document—and there is no direct evidence that he did—the Republicans made it into one by attacking it and Democratic Congressmen by using it. On May 15th, for instance, Maury Maverick requested "government films for distribution in my district in order to educate my people regarding the work the Resettlement Administration is doing." [43] Fred H. Hildebrandt, of the first Congressional district in South Dakota, was enthusiastic, and in a letter to Tugwell on June 15 he enclosed a copy of an article he wrote praising the new film. It was to be published in various district papers as his weekly newsletter, and he took pains to point out that he had been "a consistent supporter of the efforts of Dr. Tugwell and his co-workers to transfer farmers from exhausted land to territory that has fertile soil."

There was an even more serious objection to *The Plow* than the straight political one. This deserves extended treatment since it reveals the heart of the problem of truth in film-making, and also shows how close is the relationship of documentary method to the publicity purpose, especially when the publicity is for a government agency's program in a democratic state.

An examination of the script alone is enough to bring out important discrepancies between statement and fact. The grasslands, in the beginning, are pictured on a map and described as "a half million square miles of natural range"; the rest of the picture is supposed to be a statement of what happened to those areas "from the Texas panhandle to Canada." But of course the dunes of dust and the bankruptcy of farmers were not uniformly characteristic of the entire half-million square miles. It was not necessary for the quick comprehension of a terrible problem to leave with Easterners such a far-reaching generalization.

Four times the narrative describes this area north of the Texas panhandle as a country "without rivers, without streams, with little rain." On the face of it, the presence of any rain at all means the presence of streams of some kind. Lorentz seemed to be ignoring the Missouri, the Yellowstone, the Platte and the Arkansas for the sake of a sonorous phrase. Even a poet should not subject geography to his imagination to such an extent as that.

Another and even more disturbing misstatement is the pictorial assumption that farm incomes were constantly increasing from wartime to 1929. Soaring stocks, jazz and mountains of wheat are lumped together in

[42] *Time* Magazine, May 25, 1936. It was presumed by some that this liberal extension of the ghost-writing privilege was only withheld because there weren't any projection facilities in the House of Representatives. Film historians and political scientists must surely regret that this precedental opportunity was missed.

[43] Letter to R. G. Tugwell. Maverick was from the 20th District in Texas.

montage, and suddenly the crash produces not only falling prices but drought. The speedy crescendo of visual impressions in the film itself almost forces that very conclusion on the passive mind. Only by thoughtful and informed analysis in the light of history and economics can it be made clear that depression struck the farmer much earlier than 1929 (and for reasons, certainly, closely related to the film's message of wartime and postwar overproduction), and that the drought itself struck much later. Certainly there was no connection between drought and depression except that both injured the individual dust bowl farmer. Obviously the drought raised the prices which depression lowered.

It is easy to say these things years after the difficulties of making a film are past. But these are the very hazards which face a producer of those factual films which are also designed to be dramatic. Only the toughest kind of research integrity on social science subjects will survive the criticism of men and women who know the facts. This is the double load of criticism which lies on the documentary producer—to be interesting and to be truthful.

Bitter comments about the balance and the truth of *The Plow That Broke the Plains* were offered immediately after the picture came out, and they were not offered only by Republicans. Democrats in the Great Plains area were not unanimous in their praise. In fact, the Texas delegation at the National Democratic Convention passed a resolution criticizing the film and requesting that it be withdrawn from circulation. At the same time, the *Amarillo Globe-News* and the *Dallas News*, among others, were bitterly attacking the movie as a libel on the Southwest. There could be no doubt of the hostility of real estate men.[44]

A thorough and balanced statement of the things some midwestern people objected to is contained in a July 2 letter to Tugwell from the Resettlement regional director in Dallas, D. P. Trent. It was written as a summary of the views of twenty or more RA staff members immediately after a special showing of *The Plow*.

> We recognize the possible value of the film particularly in other parts of the United States and we do not feel that there is justification for serious criticism of the film. However, the showing of the film in Texas at the present time would arouse controversy and rather bitter criticism of the Resettlement Administration. It is the judgment of our group that the showing of the film would serve no particularly good purpose at this time and it is our judgment that any good purpose which it might serve would be more than offset by the controversy and criticism which would be aroused. . . .
>
> (1) The film greatly overdraws and unduly magnifies the true situation in the western plains. The statement that there is no water

44 Letter, D. P. Trent, Regional Director, RA, Dallas, Texas, to R. G. Tugwell, July 2, 1936. Interview, John Fischer, December 1, 1949.

within 200 miles is not true in any location in that area and is obviously a serious exaggeration. All of the grass which is shown in the film is dead dry grass which is being whipped about by the wind. The land which is shown is in every case dry, hard and dusty. The "one-way" which is shown in the picture, in process of attempting to prepare land for wheat, is operating under exaggerated conditions because farmers do not undertake to prepare land in such dry conditions, but usually await the time when there is moisture in the soil. There are seasons every year when an abundance of green succulent grass grows on the western plains and when there is moisture in the soil and the land may be easily prepared with the "one-way" and other farm implements.

There are places in this western country where the sand from eroded fields is piled up against the buildings and over the highways, but these are only isolated conditions. The dry, dusty and barren condition portrayed in this film is an exaggeration and the extreme wind erosion is not characteristic of any considerable portion of that area.

(2) The film only presents the distressing side of the situation without offering any solution. The conclusion which a great many people would naturally draw from seeing the film would be that it was a mistake in the beginning for people to settle in that area and that the only solution lies in the complete evacuation of the entire area. Those who are familiar with conditions are convinced that there are measures which can be adopted by way of conserving the limited rainfall, preventing erosion and increasing vegetation and that the widespread adoption of these measures will make much of that area a permanently prosperous country for a progressive citizenship.

If the film had set forth some of the simple and practicable measures which might be adopted and which are being applied in a widespread way at the present time, it would be somewhat less objectionable to the citizens of that area.

(3) The film includes in the dry and windswept area a great deal of country, in Texas at least, where no such conditions exist anywhere as those portrayed in the film. The map includes a large portion of western Texas extending almost as far east as Ft. Worth. It includes the winter garden area in southern Texas.

(4) The film fails to point out some of the natural advantages which exist in that country and which for many years have made it possible for farmers to endure the hazards and still prosper. The nature of the land is such that the average farmer with a tractor, a combine and other power machinery can easily operate 400 acres or more. . . .

Conditions which exist among the dense tenant farm population in eastern Texas and eastern Oklahoma are just as deplorable as conditions in the high plains and a portrayal of those conditions where normal rainfall prevails would indicate more clearly and more truly the situation with which the Resettlement Administration is attempting to deal. We should be delighted to cooperate in the preparation of a film of that nature and I offer the suggestion for your consideration. . . .

These points are not easily answerable. They were made by working staff members of the RA itself and they show the toughness of the public relations problem when a film cuts only one way. These men were asking, actually, for a film which would be still more of a propaganda film.[45]

They wanted, first, a more favorable, more optimistic picture made, which would not only show that there were other, better places in the plains but that there were other places outside where social and economic problems were just as bad if not worse. Then, beyond that, they wanted to encourage optimism in the beholder by pointing out solutions "already being applied." The result would have been better publicity for the RA staff and the Texas area. It would not, however, have induced a feeling of guilt or a desire for action on the part of the audience. The intensity of the picture's message would have been nicely diluted with a variety of facts tending to show that the message, while strictly true, was not so terribly important.

Here is the dilemma between the documentary producer and the operating bureaucrat. The latter is likely to vote for balance and dilution, the former for intensity and distillation. No general rule applies, of course, because professional status does not prescribe attitudes—politicians, bureaucrats, publicity men and documentary producers all break down into differing varieties of conservatism and radicalism, of "balance" and excitement. But it is useful to note that the distinction is not between Congressmen and administrators, or between outsiders and members of the Government. It is between those who want balance and dilution, and those who want intensity and distillation. In this case there were members of the agency and members of Congress on both sides of the fence, and the instance given above shows that for once there was caution in the field and daring in Washington.

Granted that the objections raised earlier about some of the geographical and economic facts in *The Plow* could be met, it seems unlikely that the objections the Dallas men offered could be met without radically changing the nature and purpose of the film itself. If strong feeling and some kind of action are the purposes, a documentary must surely be written and photographed very much as Pare Lorentz did it. If a clear, reassuring report, with much factual content interestingly offered, is the purpose, a documentary must surely be written and photographed much differently.

At any rate, there were so many people who agreed with the Dallas point of view—including Representative Karl Mundt of South Dakota—

---

[45] Snyder reports (p. 37) that there was originally an epilogue showing "how the RA was relocating 4,500 stranded families in new houses on small farms in ten states," but it was cut from the film.

and things got so much better in the dust bowl, what with tree-planting, soil conservation measures and generous rains, that the film was withdrawn from circulation.[46] The return of devastating storms to the dust bowl in 1950 did not occasion its re-release.

Actions and Films

The River did not call forth the kind of acrimonious dissent which greeted *The Plow*. It was still "New Deal propaganda," certainly, and the last part of it even more openly so. But while it was used for political purposes in 1938,[47] *The River* didn't actually appear in an election year. It represented, too, far more than did *The Plow*, a feeling on the part of many articulate people that conservation of resources was unquestionably a good thing, and to a large degree a government responsibility. This was a matter of water, and the government had been in that business for a long time. Resettling people and telling them what to do about their soil was a pretty unfamiliar business, however closely it might resemble the conservation of forest and mineral lands. But the government had been building dams and dredging channels for years, under the commerce clause of the Constitution, and in connection with recurrent rivers and harbors bills.

Besides, the audience response to *The River* was extraordinary. It is difficult to attack a film as either dangerous or partisan when both the critics and the public have given it such deafening applause for its poetry and photography and message.

There are factual criticisms to be made of *The River*, but mostly for small confusions, irrelevancies and oversimplifications. There was no need

[46] First by the National Emergency Council, when Karl Mundt went to see Lowell Mellett, and again by the Department of Agriculture after World War II. There were a good many prints in private hands and in film libraries, however, and it is still possible to get *The Plow* from such sources as the Museum of Modern Art in New York. Educational institutions may buy prints and replacement footage from the National Archives.

This is the official statement of Addison Foster, then executive officer of the Office of Government Reports, to the Appropriations subcommittee: *The Plow* was "withdrawn on April 18, 1939, and has not been subsequently reissued. *The Plow* was produced at a time when agricultural conditions in certain sections of the country were particularly bad. Substantial improvements in these conditions made it desirable to add new footage to the film before distribution was continued. We are advised by the U.S. Film Service that *The Plow* has not been reissued pending this revision, which has not as yet been undertaken because of lack of funds."

[47] Theodore Amlie, for example, wrote the FSA from Elkhorn, Wisconsin, on July 27, 1938, requesting both *The Plow* and *The River* "for use in the coming primary campaign" and said he would "want the film for the next two months at least."

for comment on the Civil War (even if the sound of drums, trumpets, and guns added liveliness to the sound track) because the over-cultivation of cotton was the villain Lorentz chose to attack. Nor was it necessary to give the impression that most of the land in middle and eastern America was now lying fallow and desolate:

> For 50 years we dug for cotton and moved west when the land gave out. . . .
> For 50 years we plowed for corn and moved on when the land gave out. . . .

Then, too, there was no relationship shown between the process of cutting the top off Wisconsin and sending it down the river and the tragedy of the floods below. The mud of Idaho and Pennsylvania lying along the bottom of the Mississippi is part of the problem of floods, but part of it is control of water flow at critical times. The sequences on mud and flood were joined together without so much as a comma between them, and without explanation. Finally, the description, at the end, of soil conservation, dam-building, power-houses and farm loans was hurried, disjointed and vague.

The River has been criticized, in a more general way, as having been too poetic. It appealed to discriminating movie-goers but not to ordinary people nor even to all the people of the Tennessee Valley. George Stoney, when he worked for the FSA, found that it was over the heads of rural audiences in the South. It was not, of course, meant for them. But a little more attention to points of clarity would not have ruined the poetry, and would probably have made its audience almost universal.[48]

These are all comparatively small matters. The fact of *The River*'s pre-eminence remains. As a teaching film or an informational film, it is somewhat confusing and really needs a study guide. As a documentary based on factual research, it could do with a little more factualness. As a drama in photography and sound, it is superb. More than any other combination of words and images, these three reels of motion pictures have achieved exciting visualization of the problem of a great river-valley system.

It is doubtful whether such a fact can be effectively related to the question: Should the Federal Government occupy itself at all with this kind of film-making? It is not easy to say, "This was not worthwhile." In the shadow of an achievement like *The River*, it is not easy to say, "This was not a proper thing to do, nor does it fit in the accepted patterns of government public relations." An idea clothed with greatness finally looms larger than proprieties or accepted patterns. Rather turn the question

[48] Interview, Philip Brown, then information director for Farmers Home Administration, December 15, 1949.

around: How can Government be censured for producing films when it can produce one like this?

And ask the further question: Who would have made *The River* if the Government had not made it? Only the Government had the facilities and the interest in 1937.

There is no need to sweeten the pill and pretend that it was harmless, neutral and merely educational. Both *The Plow* and *The River* were propagandist in effect. They were propaganda for the New Deal, for specific government agencies, for a certain view of history and for a certain way of looking at public affairs—an attitude which stressed action. They portrayed problems which many people agreed were public problems, and in this alone they were serving in the public interest. But they portrayed them with drama, with a sense of urgency. They were different from any peacetime films the Government had ever made before.

Beyond the truths they contained about conservation and about history—admittedly not the whole truth, admittedly in some details unnecessarily distorted—they offered a special kind of truth which is not often recognized in appraising the rights and wrongs of Government publicity. They represented with a high degree of accuracy the mood and temper of the action agency which sponsored them.

These movies were a report on something going on in the United States—not only the continuing crisis of land and water, but also the attitude of mind which was eager to take action. The public interest is also served when the plea for action as well as the plea for peace is given publicity. Action is part of life. Change, as well as conservatism, was part of the New Deal. The viewpoint expressed in *The Plow* and *The River* was widely held in the administration, in Congress and in the country. Its representation in film form was not shocking, but salutary.

Neither of these pictures was a plea for administrative power. These were historical films, emotionally charged with tragic overtones. They told of widespread neglect and national need, and made no specific demands. They did call, in a general way, for public responsibility.

The story of an action program—of its background and the need for it—however favorable, however enthusiastic, is a story whose telling is in the public interest. To say that it is dangerous for such viewpoints to be expressed (1) by government and (2) in films, is simply to say that proposals for change should not be heard in a time when government is actually taking up new policies and when communication is actually reaching out into new channels.

Those who oppose an action program and those who have their doubts about it need not fear that the country will be bowled over by poetry, montage and melodrama. There are other sources of propaganda out in the open, and other media of communication. Furthermore, the average man is thoroughly accustomed to the bombardment of competing propagandas. The inherent conservatism of democracy in the absence of crisis or war is a strong guarantee that dangers will be small and of short duration. And there are further limitations, built into our political way of life and our governmental framework, which, as Lorentz was soon to find out, hedge about the ambitious public relations program and plant the documentary producer's path with thorns.

5

The U.S. Film Service

The decline of the documentary movement within the U.S. Government began with the beginning of the U. S. Film Service. As soon as the Lorentz group came out in the open, it was marked for attack, and the political strength of Lorentz and his associates was not such as to offer a successful counter-attack. On the face of it, honesty seems not to have been the best policy.[1] Perhaps it would have been better to hide under some other name in some other agency for a while longer. And yet, however or wherever concealed, this small band of enthusiasts would have been brought under committee scrutiny sooner or later. It is difficult to hide a nationally distributed motion picture.

The emergence of the Film Service as a separate entity marked the beginning of the end, but it was not itself the reason for the end. The reasons for the demise of documentary were more complex than that. Indeed, so far as outsiders could see, it seemed that the Film Service marked the beginning of a great new development in government responsibility for public information.[2] Critical response to *The River* had been remarkable

[1] Although Senator Alben Barkley (D., Ky.) offered the agency's honesty—whether self-imposed or otherwise, he did not say—as a defense of the Film Service: "It is a little difficult for me to make up my mind to hit at this one agency, which, so far, is the only one that has come out into the open by asking for an appropriation." *Congressional Record*, April 26, 1940, 76th Congress 3d Session, p. 5100.

[2] In a book published by the American Association for Adult Education, the following appeared: "The most helpful development in the educational use of films of Government origin lies in the recent creation of the U.S. Film Service. . . . Educational and cultural groups throughout the country are now able to obtain information concerning the availability of Government films directly from this single body. . . .

by any standard. Important political figures had praised it. Most people seemed to agree that regardless of the credit it gave to the New Deal, it was an extraordinary film on a significant subject of national importance.[3]

Encouraged and emboldened by these heady draughts of praise, Lorentz and Mercey laid plans for expansion. The film-makers were given new status under a White House agency. Within the next two years they had begun an ambitious motion picture on unemployment, completed a full-length feature on childbirth, and gotten well under way on major films for two agencies in the Department of Agriculture. They had set up a center of information and distribution for U.S. Government films. They had under consideration a broad program of factual films for exhibition in South America. There was even an answering echo outside of government in the form of the American Film Center, which began to act as liaison between sponsors and film-makers in early 1939.

But every one of these developments was heading into storms. Not that there was a major national crisis over the use of documentary films by the Federal Government. The U.S. Film Service was silenced by a House subcommittee and a single Senate debate.

The decision against the Lorentz group was not a clear-cut decision against motion pictures in government, nor even against a central production agency of some sort. It was mostly a decision against the people who had sponsored Lorentz and the methods they had used. The broader reasons were there, certainly. Some opposed the Film Service because it was started by the New Deal, some because it was using relief funds, some simply because it was an information agency, some because motion picture production was not yet accepted as a proper activity for government at all, some because war clouds in Europe were turning their attention more and more to foreign affairs. But the leading reason for the final disappearance of the Film Service was its multiple heritage of antipathies. It did not make the right kind of friends fast enough to counterbalance its enemies.

Lorentz himself, aware of such antipathies, but unaware of their cumulative effects, unacquainted with the finer points of inter-bureaucratic courtesy and legislative-executive relationships, went far afield in his filmic subject matter. He made few of the kind of friends needed by producing *The Fight for Life*, though it may have been he was looking for friends outside of Washington by then. He need not have produced films about 12 leading corporations, as Commissioner of Education John Studebaker once proposed; nor did he need to do family biographies of the McKellars and the Tafts. But he might, by way of self-protection, have found some

---

Ample proof exists crowned by the work of Pare Lorentz that the dramatic appeal of informational films can be assured by good production and intellectual integrity in the treatment of subject matter." T. R. Adams, *Motion Pictures in Adult Education*, 1940, pp. 49, 80.

[3] Walt Disney wanted to bill it along with *Snow White*. (Philip Sterling, "Following 'The River,' " *New York Times*, October 15, 1939.)

way to demonstrate to Congress the usefulness of film by making understandable to the American people the aches and pains of lawmaking.

The Changing Atmosphere

Coercion, as well as preference, was involved in the move to set up an independent film service. In a letter to Undersecretary of State Sumner Welles,[4] dated June 13, 1938, Henry Wallace explained plans for the new arrangement and indicated a leading reason for taking action:

> I regret that it is impossible for the Department of Agriculture through the Farm Security Administration to continue to produce pictures of the type similar to *The River* and *The Plow That Broke the Plains* but it appears that there is no legal basis for this agency to continue this activity. The General Accounting Office has recently taken exception to the use of funds appropriated for relief purposes in the distribution of films of this character. . . .

There were other, more subtle coercive factors which can only be guessed at, here and there. They had to do with a changing environment of personalities and information policies. Relationships with the Department of Agriculture, especially the Division of Information, had never been too cordial, even after the Resettlement Administration was brought into the Department and became the Farm Security Administration.[5] With Tugwell long since gone, the man close to Wallace who seemed most interested personally in the Farm Security Administration's publicity problems was Assistant Secretary Paul Appleby, and probably more problems were taken to him informally than were taken to the USDA information director, Milton Eisenhower.[6]

Will Alexander, the new Farm Security Administrator, was a former Methodist minister and executive vice-president of the Rosenwald Founda-

[4] Exchange of films with Latin-American countries was already under discussion with the State Department at this time. Nothing ever came of it in the lifetime of the Film Service, but some of the ideas were used by Nelson Rockefeller as Coordinator of Inter-American Affairs.

[5] There had been two changes in the director of information under Tugwell since the time of John F. Carter—Kenneth Clark and M. E. Gilfond—but things had gone along pretty much as before, with increasing attention given to the public relations process by Grace Falke, an assistant to Tugwell who later became his wife.

[6] Eisenhower, who possessed notable general administrative gifts, was doing a great deal of general departmental housekeeping and early in 1958 was given the extra job of Land-Use Coordinator. This meant that Morse Salisbury, of the radio division, was taking over much responsibility, and his concept of information was more moderate than the dynamic Tugwell-Carter view.

tion. More responsible than any other man for the report to the President on farm tenancy which led to the Bankhead-Jones Act, he certainly had at heart the social and economic objectives of the FSA. But he did not rush into print at every opportunity and he seemed to feel that the FSA should justify itself mainly by action.[7]

Thus by 1938 there was still sympathy, but dispersed and restrained sympathy, for the program begun by Tugwell and Carter in 1935, when Tugwell was both Resettlement Administrator and Under-secretary of Agriculture. Agency consolidation had set in. All of the department's information officials met weekly to coordinate programs. The carefree days of easy delegation of responsibility were drawing to a close.

Alexander and his new information chief, John Fischer, were also painfully aware of the poor public relations resulting from excessive attention to public relations. The furor over the RA's first annual report was still remembered by members of Congress, and this cast a shadow over everything the agency did.

Something of that earlier fiasco is worth retelling here, as an explanation of the changing attitude toward publicity and also as a prelude to the more direct Senatorial contest over the Film Service in 1940. In February, 1937, the FSA appropriation for 1938 was under attack on the Senate floor. There was a movement to cut it by $14,000,000, largely because of what Senator Arthur Vandenberg (R., Mich.) called the "unconscionable amount of overhead in relation to relief" in that agency. Nobody knew just how much of the relief money the Resettlement Administration spent had gone for administrative overhead, but $5,000,000 was one estimate of the cost of the Washington office alone.

The final action, after support of the rural rehabilitation record by leading Democrats and an eloquent defense by Senator George W. Norris (R., Nebr.) was a cut of only $1,000,000, directed at the Washington office.[8] Even Norris didn't object to that, because Exhibit A in the debate was the RA's annual report. The report had a few pictures in it, and that was unusual. But that wasn't the main thing. The main thing was the cover—a so-called "dust cover" which folded in around the edges. Spread out, it was a large four-color U.S. map, with drawings of grain and farm animals on it—a map which did little, if anything, to enlighten the reader about the activities of the RA. During the appropriation debate, Senator James F. Byrnes (D., S. Car.) remarked at length about it:

---

[7] "Roots for the Farmer," *Christian Science Monitor Magazine Section*, May 5, 1937, appears to be his only important magazine article during the first year of his regime. He had been second in command under Tugwell.
[8] Senator Byrnes pointed out during the debate: "The committee has in mind only the thought that because no specific amount is carried in this bill for administrative expenses, it could not remedy the situation . . . in any other way than by making a reduction of a million dollars, and then placing in the report the reason for that action." (*Congressional Record*, February 2, 1937, 75th Congress 1st Session, p. 679.)

I have in my office, and other Senators have in their offices, the best illustration of the situation, being a report to the President and to the Congress wherein there is contained a map so expensive, so unusual, that the Government Printing Office could not print it and according to the information I have, it cost $1.05 to print each one of those maps outside of the Government Printing Office.[9] I understand that now the Joint Committee on Printing is going to take some steps to limit the expenditure for the printing of maps by any department. . . . The most elaborate and most expensive report ever printed by any department of the Government . . . the report in question, containing the map, is of no personal service to the members of the Appropriations Committee.

Next day Senator Josiah Bailey (D., N. Car.) took up the cry in more flamboyant fashion with Exhibit A in hand: "I suppose there never was a nobler man in the world than Professor Rex Tugwell. . . . We gave him $100,000,000. (Exhibiting document) He left us a memorial. (Laughter)." Senator Vandenberg interposed after a while that "the Joint Committee on Printing this morning unanimously made it impossible for any more 'bonanza catalogs' . . . to be printed hereafter at public expense."

Lorentz certainly had no responsibility for the annual report and felt no involvement in the quarrels about it. But it involved him all the same, just as the earlier attacks on Tugwell's policies and personality involved him. Motion pictures were probably the most prominent form of publicity an agency could use, and should it come to the point of justifying an information budget separate from and outside of the capacious provision of relief monies, a hard time would be had by all.

Hence the quieter tone of things under Will Alexander and John Fischer.[10] *The River* was well under way by the time Fischer arrived in early 1937, and he was of no mind to interrupt such an undertaking in any case. He had been a Washington correspondent for the Associated Press, covering the Senate, among other things, and was later to observe the Washington scene with impartial humor for *Harper's* Magazine. His familiarity with the publicity process and his real enthusiasm for the agency's social and economic program did not blind him, however, to the darkening political situation in Congress. Therefore he made a very considerable effort to keep track of Pare Lorentz. There can be no doubt that Lorentz often chafed under his gentle remonstrances.

Lorentz and Mercey both wanted a new central film agency. It meant prestige in the eyes of the public, and it also might mean greater influence

[9] He corrected this next day—the whole report cost $1.05.

[10] They had known each other only casually. Meeting again one day on a train going to New York, they talked of the South's economic problems. A month later, Alexander called Fischer and offered him the information job. (Interview, John Fischer, December 1, 1949.)

over film production in other government agencies. It might well result in greater economies through sharing skills and information. It certainly should, they felt, result in a central catalog of all government films and perhaps even a central distributing office.

Not long after Lorentz and Gercke made their visit to Hyde Park with the print of *The River,* Tom Corcoran instructed them to make up a plan for an independent film service. The organizational outline was written by Arch Mercey and John Bridgeman. It was to be placed under the general direction of the National Emergency Council, another organization supported wholly by relief funds. Lowell Mellett, head of the NEC, was also administrative assistant to the President. He had been editor of the *Washington Daily News,* a Scripps-Howard paper, where he had managed to write a good many crusading editorials in favor of New Deal projects. He sounded a little like J. F. Carter and Rex Tugwell combined.

A New Sponsor: The National Emergency Council

The National Emergency Council had been set up on November 17, 1933.[11] It looked like a super-coordinating agency, since it contained the entire Cabinet and the leading alphabetical agency heads, with an executive director who was to carry out their instructions "to coordinate inter-agency problems of organization and activity of Federal agencies." It was actually a relatively powerless affair, since the obvious relationships within this top-heavy representative group were conducive to steady logrolling. Interference in the affairs of one agency would naturally be restrained for fear of further interference elsewhere.

But if it had little power at the center, the NEC could very easily meddle at the edges. Mellett's own understanding of his functions put emphasis on the field representatives, who were not only to operate local "clearing houses for information concerning Federal agencies," but were to "serve as chairmen of committees composed of the chief state representatives of the various Federal agencies," and as "liaison officers between Federal agencies and the State administrations." To top it all off, they were to prepare reports to the Director, including "critical appraisal of the effectiveness" of the people down there in the state offices.[12]

Here, unfortunately, was another agency with a heritage of ill-will.

[11] Executive Order 6433-A. See also executive order 6889-A, October 29, 1934, and 7073, June 13, 1935.
[12] *U.S. Government Manual,* 1938–39, p. 388, published by the N.E.C.'s U.S. Information Service.

Wherever local offices of Federal departments had been "reported on" and wherever state officials had been "liaisoned" against their will, Senators and Congressmen were likely to hear about it. Department heads in Washington heard even more. It was no wonder that the NEC was almost abolished as of December 31, 1937. It was only rescued at the last moment (December 27) by another Executive Order which extended its life to June 30, 1938. A later extension carried it another year.

In 1937–38 the Council had made some enemies of the most durable sort. In certain states there was evidence of active political participation by its employees, and especially in the attempt by President Roosevelt to "purge" certain Congressional opponents of his own party. This came to the surface on the Senate floor in a bitter attack by Burton Wheeler (D., Mont.) and Bennett Champ Clark (D., Mo.), occasioned by an Associated Press report that an NEC staff member in Iowa had been campaigning against Senator Guy Gillette.

A defense of the NEC as an effective coordinating agency and as thoroughly nonpolitical was immediately taken up by a whole battery of Democratic Senators (including Bankhead, Hayden, Russell, Minton, Pepper, Pope, Byrnes and Barkley) in a spirited interchange which involved a hurried telephone call to Mellett himself—the man in Iowa, it seems, was actually no longer an NEC employee and had not been for a year.[13]

Nevertheless the implications remained. It was further brought out that the main "coordinating" energies of the Council in the states were occupied with state relief agencies, and the accusations about relief rolls and politics were still very much alive in 1938.

The U.S. Film Service was created by the National Emergency Council in September, 1938, with Pare Lorentz as Director. Arch Mercey was appointed Assistant Director, Floyd Crosby became Director of Photography, and others of the old Farm Security crew were in evidence, including George Gercke and John Bridgeman. According to Mellett's own interpretation, the Service was "to acquaint Federal and State agencies, educational institutions, and interested civic organizations and groups with the availability of silent and sound motion pictures produced by various Government bureaus. A consultation service is maintained, and visual educational study aids for classroom and adult education may be obtained upon request." [14]

Thus the new trend was toward a central distribution service. Not a word about Film Service production. But production plans were certainly afoot. They depended on the kind of funds available on transfer from other agencies. The WPA was ready to help again, and probably Farm Security.

Nine months later the Film Service was transferred to a brand-new

[13] *Congressional Record*, May 31, 1938, 75th Congress 3d Session, pp. 7742–51.
[14] *U.S. Government Manual*, 1938–39, p. 389.

permanent sponsor—the Federal Security Agency—as a part of the Office
of Education, which had hitherto been in the Interior Department. Reorganization Plan II finally abolished the National Emergency Council and
placed its Film Service and Radio Service in the Office of Education to be
administered "under the direction and supervision of the Federal Security
Administrator." [15]

The reorganization plan took effect on July 1, 1939, and the Film
Service was destined to last one more year from that date.

Congressional Scrutiny—First Round

The issue was already settled in 1939, as far as the House Appropriations Committee was concerned. They had given no permission for the
Film Service to last another year.

In the Emergency Relief Appropriation Act of 1939 (for the fiscal
year 1940), the general statement was made in Section 13 (c): "Except as
authorized in this joint resolution no allocation of funds shall be made to
any other Federal agency from the appropriations in this joint resolution
for any Federal agency." [16]

Provision was made for transferring funds to the Radio Division
($20,000), but as the House committee report pointedly said: "No pro-
vision is made for the U.S. Film Service, which has been set up during the
current year from funds appropriated to other agencies and allocated to the
National Emergency Council." [17]

This report followed an unusually unpleasant encounter on May 25
between Lowell Mellett and certain Republican members of the subcommittee.[18] On this occasion there was also a meticulous inquiry by Democratic members into the present and proposed salaries of the Film Service
staff. Much interest was expressed in the possibility of economizing by cut-

[15] Sections 201 (a) and 301. See Statutes at Large, 76th Congress 1st Session.
[16] Public Resolution 24, approved June 30, 1939, 76th Congress 1st Session.
[17] House Report No. 833, 76th Congress 1st Session, June 14, 1939, p. 18.
[18] See pp. 303–305, Hearings, Subcommittee, Committee on Appropriations,
House of Representatives (76th Congress 1st Session), Work Relief and Relief for
Fiscal Year 1940. Mellett and Rep. John Taber (R., N.Y.) contradicted each other
three times in the space of two minutes while discussing films. The judgment is ines-
capable, even from internal evidence, that Mellett felt he was beaten before he started.
Reorganization Plan II had already been sent to the Congress on May 9, and Mellett
was asking for funds for an agency about to be abolished, on the assumption that it
would be reconstituted in the Executive Office of the President. See also remarks by
Rep. J. William Ditter (R., Penna.), member of the Appropriations Committee, on
the NEC and the Film Service, Congressional Record, June 16, 1939, 76th Congress
1st Session, p. 7349.

ting down on films made by other agencies. Yet it was perfectly apparent that expansion of production was the agency's main objective.

The actual list of subjects under discussion with various departments was tame enough: a full-length feature on American maritime history for the U.S. Maritime Commission, a series on public agencies and their health programs, a training film for census takers, another fire prevention movie for the Forest Service.[19] There was a plan for films about the United States to be sent to Latin American countries, and films about Latin America to be distributed here, and this plan had backing from Secretary of State Cordell Hull. But this very evidence of far-flung activity must have alienated to some extent the doubtful Democratic members of the subcommittee.

Funds from other agencies would still be required for the production costs. In the Senate hearings, questioning on the part of Senator James F. Byrnes (D., S.Car.) tended to show that even without a direct appropriation, the Film Service could continue to operate on the basis of allocations for film-making from other agencies. The point, as he saw it, was to achieve the promised over-all economy immediately. An additional appropriation to the Service itself might mean that less money would *need* to be spent by the other agencies, but it certainly would not prevent them from spending it, since it was already allotted by Congress.

> Why cannot you carry on the Film Service just as you have done this year without looking elsewhere for money for the next year? You say these various departments have advanced to you $265,000 and if you take that much from them the next year it will not hurt you, except that you will be asking from the WPA, the PWA, and the other people what you have been getting this last year.[20]

This was at least a favorable attitude. It held out some hope for the future of a Film Service if economics could actually be effected. The House report had said, "No provision is made for the U.S. Film Service." In the light of what Byrnes had said, this did not seem to be an absolute prohibition. A House committee report is not law.

But the committee had gone on record, and the general prohibition, if not the specific one, was in the law. Only the most extraordinary political skill, plus something amounting to a miracle, could prevent a final blow. Neither of these items seemed to be available in 1940.

[19] Hearings, *op. cit.*, p. 327. Thirteen other possible subjects were offered.
[20] Hearings, Senate Committee on Appropriations (76th Congress 1st Session), Work Relief and Public Works Appropriation Act of 1939 (for fiscal 1940) June 22, 1939, p. 253.

The Fight for Life

The Fight for Life was, in the first instance, a gift to the U.S. Government. Paul DeKruif had seen *The River* and was so impressed by the apparent gifts of Pare Lorentz that he turned down Hollywood's offers for his most recent book and offered it free to Lorentz instead.[21]

This was not necessarily an unmixed blessing, either for the newly famous documentary director or for the future of the Film Service. Lorentz was already at work on something else which was close to his heart, and it so happened that the ultimate outcome of DeKruif's munificence was a peak of artistic triumph followed immediately by the depth of financial failure—that is, the failure to get further support from Congress. This result stemmed in large part from the fact that certain Senators could not see why a film like *The Fight for Life* should be government-sponsored.

The motion picture from which the Film Service "temporarily" turned aside was to be called *Ecce Homo*. The "man" whom the audience was thus to be exhorted (in Latin) to "behold" was the unemployed man, genus Americanus, A.D. 1930–40. Based on an unfinished short novel by Lorentz himself, the film was to follow the odyssey of a jobless family from deep South to Detroit and on to the far West. A great deal of the basic documentary footage had been taken already, and while it is hard to tell what kind of treatment Lorentz would have given this story of poverty and despair, it is certain that he wanted very much to finish it. Two years later he went to work for RKO studios in Hollywood on exactly the same project, reshooting much of the same footage, but this second try was also doomed to remain unfinished.[22]

Meanwhile the DeKruif proposal caught his fancy. Although rejecting, wisely enough, the suggestion by the famous *Reader's Digest* author that he deal with syphilis, he agreed to "begin where life begins." He would make a feature length film based on the actual work of Dr. Joseph B. DeLee, founder of the Maternity Center in Chicago which bears his name. He would dramatize the need for more and better medical care during preg-

[21] "It was an honor and a pleasure to present the rights of the book *The Fight for Life* to the U.S. Government on the condition that Lorentz would make the film." From a radio address by DeKruif over WMCA, March 6, 1940, quoted in Arch Mercey, "Films by American Governments," *Films*, Summer 1940.

[22] By an odd reversal of circumstances, Lorentz in Hollywood could not get his own background sequences released by the U.S. archives. There was no back door at this time as there had been when he was a government producer begging stock shots from Hollywood. Reorganization at RKO was what finally quashed the repeated attempt to make *Ecce Homo*.

nancy, and he could by implication indict a social and economic way of life which permitted inadequate care and even malnutrition among many child-bearing women at the lowest economic levels.

Arch Mercey described the film's objective, as he saw it, in the House Appropriations Committee hearings:

> It is really a picture on human erosion. . . . Medical experts have found that as soon as a great national health problem becomes apparent to the people, various agencies interested will take some action in alleviating the problem. . . . It dramatizes the efforts which are being made in a certain area by modern science in reducing the infant and maternal mortality rate.[23]

The Fight for Life turned out to be one of the most remarkable examples in motion picture history of sustained excitement and apprehension without the aid of plot or personalities. There was a thread of story, in that young Dr. O'Donnell begins by losing a baby, is encouraged to go on with his work by an older doctor, enters upon a long apprenticeship at the maternity center, and finally gains confidence and success and the determination to "heal the sick wherever and however he found them." But O'Donnell is not so much a person as a symbol. Basically the story was the story of the Center itself, the switchboard humming with its daily drama, doctors hurrying in and out on their perpetually sudden calls, long conferences about ways and means of defeating childbirth diseases.

The final climax comes after O'Donnell's lonely wait at the bedside of an expectant mother—a wait which is not as long as reality, but far longer than the imitation of reality which Hollywood normally offers. The documentary atmosphere of the film was thus both convincing and harrowing. Lorentz, an artist in sound, grimly set the biggest scenes against the background of a loudly ticking metronome.

This melodrama of lives beginning and lives preserved used eight professional actors—including Myron McCormick as O'Donnell and Dudley Digges as the Head Doctor—and among these also were two who had studied at the Chicago Center. Other roles were filled, in the documentary tradition, by members of the staff themselves, although many of the scenes were photographed on Hollywood stages. Louis Gruenberg, who had written *Emperor Jones* for the Metropolitan Opera, did the music; Floyd Crosby was photographer; and Alexander Smallens again led the orchestra, this time made up of members of the Los Angeles Philharmonic. The cost of this feature-length work, as consistently reported in Congressional hearings, was approximately $150,000.

Columbia got the contract for distribution. Lorentz claims that every major studio bid for the rights on this one. Thus he had his triumph over

23 February 20, 1940. 76th Congress 3d Session, Department of Labor Federal Security Agency Appropriation Bill for 1941.

Hollywood. No need for long-drawn-out critics' showings this time. The critics were as kind as ever, and the *New York Post* even went out on a limb to declare, "There will be no better motion picture made in 1940." The *New York Herald-Tribune* (Howard Barnes) called it "a stirring and eloquent drama, as well as a document of profound significance. Here is a memorable tribute to the medical profession, accented by challenging social overtones. . . . It is a film like no other you have ever seen. It is one you are not likely to forget soon." And *Time* Magazine said: "In its realism it sustains the suspense luckily caught a few minutes each year on epic newsreels." [24]

As impersonal, symbolic drama, *The Fight for Life* rang the bell. As truth, and as a responsible public message, it left much to be desired.

The attempts at philosophizing can certainly be forgiven. ("Maybe there's a design. . . . A life for a life. . . . As biologists we know the stuff of life has never died. . . . Perhaps human erosion is normal.") Even the economic commentary is not too alarming, though this is what stood out to members of Congress. Against a photographic background of slums and squalor, the narrator asks: "Why do we bring them into the world?" The doctor recommends green vegetables and sunshine to keep the baby well. "Where do we tell them to go for the green vegetables and sunshine?" A man approaches a garbage can and fishes out something. "We tell them to eat fresh vegetables and mark malnutrition on the record—why don't we just say 'they're hungry'?"

The inchoate nature of these protests was balanced to some degree by the individual dedication of the doctors and the declaration about healing men and women wherever they may happen to be. Attitudes and actions, from telephone girl to head doctor, show the exhilaration of the battle against defeatism.

But the main count against the film, as film, is its insistence on fear. Lorentz was bent upon frightening us in order to induce action—more maternity centers, more research, better doctors. He succeeded in frightening mothers as well. Death at childbirth was dramatized in the first major scene, and the metronome pounded on the nerves of the audience in dramatic rise and fall as heartbeats ebbed away. Twice more, motherhood was shown as a dangerous, fear-filled experience, with the woman walking in dull terror back and forth through the house. The final operation—hot water, instruments, grim faces—was played as a race with death.[25]

It is no wonder that in some audiences women fainted. A New York

[24] Reviews appeared in the newspapers on March 7 and in *Time* March 25.

[25] This was what impressed President Roosevelt. He asked Mellett if he was trying to scare all the expectant mothers in America. (Interview, Mellett, October 13, 1950.)

There was another reason for the hue and cry, quite unforeseen by Lorentz. It happened that the death scene was in a hospital, whereas lives were saved after that only in the at-home environment which the Center doctors visited. Hence hospital staffs protested vigorously.

maternity center protested that it was "a dangerous film" because it depicted "abnormalities of child-bearing in such realistic terms that the
movie-goer is overwhelmed, dazed, frightened." A thoughtful critic must
surely be moved to ask the question: Why was this film made? What was
the really compelling purpose behind it? Was it message or drama? It is
hard to avoid the conclusion that Lorentz got so wrapped up in making
The Fight for Life exciting that he forgot about balance or research or
facts and kept on banging away with his metronome sledge-hammer till he
lost sight altogether of his role as reporter. It is important, of course, to
wake people up, but it is not necessary to inflict on them a permanent fear.
Many women who saw the picture—especially inexperienced and unedu-
cated women—carried away a psychological wound based on an assumption
that a high percentage of child-births end in death for the mother. This
is not true, and it was false and misleading for the film to seem to say so.
It was the more seriously misleading since the film was supposed to be
based on research and presented by the documentary method.

If it is to deserve governmental support, documentary must do more
than achieve melodrama. It must relate to some agreed-upon government
program and achieve broad public understanding of objectives and accomplishments. *The Fight for Life* hit only the outer edge of this target: it was
about public health in a local area, but could hardly be claimed as further-
ing a Federal program.[26]

When Lorentz made this remarkable film, he was no longer intent on
groping for a formula for government film production which would satisfy
Congress. It seems clear that he was trying to impress the film world. It
is doubtful whether anyone could succeed in doing both of these things at
once. It certainly was not possible for Pare Lorentz.

The Land and *Power and the Land*

Meanwhile, Lorentz was trying to expand and delegate. Those who
criticized him for being unwilling to let others run the show should not
have neglected the fact that in 1939 and 1940 he was bringing in two
world-famous documentary directors to work for the U.S. Film Service.
Robert Flaherty, the American inventor of documentary, and Joris Ivens,
the Dutch exponent of realistic photography, both found it an honor to
accept his invitation and the invitation of the U.S. Government.

[26] Even though Surgeon-General Thomas Parran was glad to have the film produced and checked all the medical facts in it. (Letter, Pare Lorentz, November 14,
1950.)

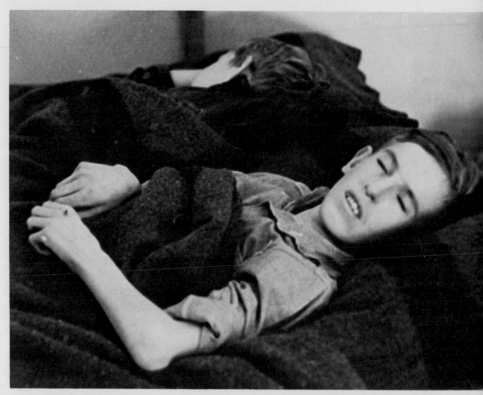

Frame enlargement from *The Land* (Dir. Robert Flaherty) for Department of Agriculture and U.S. Film Service, 1941. "He thinks he's picking peas."

Flaherty set to work on a project for the Agricultural Adjustment Administration to be called *The Land*. This was to be another conservation story, with erosion acting as counterpoint for a new theme—price stabilization for farm prosperity. Iris Barry remarked of *The Land* that it was the "least characteristic" of Flaherty's films. He "had never before made a picture in his own country but did not here (as he had in arctic Canada or Samoa or Ireland) turn away from present problems to the pleasanter vision of a romantic past." [27]

Essentially a silent picture, and a disconnected one at that, *The Land* is a puzzling series of shots punctuated by fade-outs, as if Flaherty expected to link them with printed titles. The theme was too big for him to handle: he was not intellectually up to it, nor was his experience the sort which would have prepared him. The maker of *Nanook of the North*, *Moana* and *Man of Aran* knew the long, strong commitments of simple people to the

[27] "The Documentary Film: 1922–45," Museum of Modern Art, program for documentary showings January–July 1946. See also Arthur Calder-Marshall, *The Innocent Eye: The Life of Robert Flaherty*, pp. 185–201. On pp. 261–279 *The Land* is synopsized and Russell Lord's narration printed in full.

land and to ancient traditions of self-help and survival. He knew nothing
of the industrial revolution. *The Land* was his own re-discovery of America and part of his slow odyssey toward some kind of self-education.

The spectacle of erosion is more fully documented here than in *The
Plow*. The migrant workers he stumbled on and photographed are more
convincing than any in *The Plow* or its fictional film counterpart, *The
Grapes of Wrath*. The child filling a basket two-thirds his own size, the
boy whose fingers still twitch in his sleep ("he thinks he's picking peas")—
these are images of sorrow and collective guilt. Yet they lead to no climax
and find no focus, except a kind of desperation. The "solution" imposed
in the final moments by the sponsoring AAA is a paean of praise for the
idea of contour plowing and the "ever-normal granary—a vast reserve which
now gives us tremendous strength." Yet this concept of planned hoarding
has already been undercut by the most powerful editorial juxtaposition in
the film: a series of shots of grain flooding into elevators and ships is followed suddenly by a ragged group of migrant children, their hollow eyes
staring at the camera.

More often the editing, accomplished under great difficulties by Helen
van Dongen, simply yields to the simplicity and poignancy of the camera
work. There is also a deafening score, played by the National Youth Administration symphony orchestra, obviously intended to keep things going.
The narration, written by Russell Lord but drawn in part from the feelings
Flaherty expressed about his experiences, is spoken by Flaherty himself. It
is surely his own nostalgic anguish that speaks in the lines:

> And now the machine has come in—the corn-picker.
> You don't see many people in these fields any more,
> even at harvest time. . . .
> Out in these wheat-fields farther west
> You don't see many people either.
> Thousands upon thousands only a few years ago
> harvested wheat . . .
> And here they are, some of them,
> crumbs of the machine . . .

The men, women, and children lined up to get their food packages are
prophetic of the millions on welfare in the cities in the years to come.

Flaherty took two years to make the picture, as he usually did, and
World War II caught up with him. Agricultural tragedy seemed to be
reversed again, for a time. Neither conservation nor AAA payments
played the leading role in the war prosperity which overtook farmers in
1941. The film became a historical item before it was available and it was
never released for general public showing.

The Ivens project had better luck. The optimistic story of American
farm life which was finally titled *Power and the Land* had its rationale in

Frame enlargements from *Power and the Land* (Dir. Joris Ivens) for Rural Electrification Administration and U.S. Film Service, 1940

an explanation of the advantages of rural electrification. The Rural Electrification Administration sponsored it and got what it paid for—a substantial report on the objectives and accomplishments of the agency's program. It also got some imaginative and satisfying documentary photography. This picture is an important instance of persuasive reporting on a government program by means of film. It was widely distributed, first by RKO in neighborhood theaters, and later nontheatrically. The commentary was written by Stephen Vincent Bênet, the music by Douglas Moore. Floyd Crosby and Arthur Ornitz were the photographers.

The script—which the usually scriptless Lorentz asked Edwin Locke to help Ivens prepare—called for a typical American farm family of less than average income who get electricity on their farm for the first time as a result of taking part in the REA program.[28] The opening scenes are documentary at its best. Farmer Parkinson, up before sunrise, carries his lantern out to the barn to do his chores. Through the day, he milks, pumps water, works on tools, pitches hay, fills lamps. His wife cooks, washes and irons. "Yes, there are machines to do washing, but they run by electricity." These people know that in the cities a man need only turn on a faucet to get water. They know also that "one man alone can't change" the way they live. The Parkinsons and their neighbors talk it over "in the slow cautious way of country people," and decide to take advantage of the government agency which can help them get power. From there on, the film is slightly magical, as the kilowatt hours—which "don't get tired"—take over, the electric lines go up, and refrigerator, iron, washing machine, stove and radio appear.

Whatever its shortcomings of informational structure and of plot *Power and the Land* nevertheless stands as a leading example of what a government documentary might properly be. It is a straightforward report on social change as it affects one family when it takes advantage of services provided by Congressional and administrative decision.

These two films represented a practical way of financing and producing Film Service documentaries, and might well have set the pattern for a whole series of dramatic reports to the people. But as the next round of Congressional scrutiny was brought to bear, any fundamental grappling with the subject of government public relations as a responsibility to the people seemed to be ruled out.

[28] The production crew of *Power and the Land* had one or two major troubles which are instructive as illustrations of the documentary production process. They wanted a typical farm, without electrical equipment, and a family which would be not only real but interesting. They went through all the REA's suggested places in northern Pennsylvania and in Ohio, but the farms were all too big or too broken down, or else there was a hopelessly disagreeable old couple in charge. Finally they stumbled upon a place with just the right kind of setting and the right kind of barn. But it was already outfitted with electricity. By this time they didn't care any more. They figured closely and decided they could remove one or two items of equipment and "shoot around" the rest for those early scenes, and that is what they did. (Interview, Edwin Locke, August, 1949.) See also Joris Ivens, *The Camera and I*, pp. 187–206.

Verdict by Committee

Since September of 1938, to be sure, the Film Service had been doing more than producing films, especially after its transfer to the Office of Education. In accordance with the statement of its activities in the Government Manual, it was also occupied with cataloging, publicizing and distributing Government films.

Prints of *The Plow* and *The River* were kept in stock for sale and loan—the rental libraries that purchased them, *The River* especially, found that government films can be popular and profitable.[29] Study guides were written for both of these and educators circularized to inform them that such guides were available. A long-needed catalog of all films produced by Federal agencies was made up and issued. Inquiries began to come in to the Film Service as the supposed central government agency, and these inquiries were forwarded to the particular information office which could reply.[30] Advice was given to departmental officials on proposed film activities. The program for South America was still largely in the negotiation stages. But George Gercke, in the New York office, was already making up Spanish and Portuguese sound tracks for existing government films.

These were the activities Arch Mercey wanted to stress when he reported to the House of Representatives subcommittee on appropriations on February 20, 1940. Rep. Malcolm Tarver (D., Ga.) asked him, in view of an estimate amounting to only one-third of the last year's expenditures, whether he expected to get more WPA money for next year for production.

"That remains to be seen," Mercey replied. He pointed out that the new budget request for $100,400 included "no allocation for production ex-

[29] There can be no estimate of the number of people who saw *The River* or *The Plow* in 16mm form since many prints were sold to dealers and libraries and schools. Mellett reported to the House appropriations subcommittee in May, 1939, that *The Plow That Broke the Plains* had educational distribution since August 1938 which included 3,060 play dates for 375,000 people. The first month *The River* was released for nontheatrical showing (March 1939) 193 play dates were booked for an estimated audience of 112,000. (House, 76th Congress 1st Session, Work Relief and Relief for Fiscal Year 1940, p. 295.)

In April 1940, the Film Service reported to the Senate committee that *The Plow* had had 5,694 play dates and *The River* 5,476. (76th Congress 3d Session, Labor Department–Federal Security Agency Appropriation Bill.)

[30] Mercey reported at the House hearing (as noted above) that during 1938–39 the Film Service, in response to inquiries, had "cleared" 2,847 films from the 26 agencies.

penditures," that it was "almost entirely a film distribution program." [31] At one point he even predicted that Pare Lorentz would probably resign, since the estimates provided only $7,500 for the Director's salary instead of the $10,000 he had been getting. At this time, both Lorentz and Mercey apparently saw the Film Service as more and more a consulting agency, with information officials, documentary producers and script writers coming together in the office to plan, on a separate contract basis, motion picture reports to the American people.[32]

The House and Senate committees cannot be blamed for turning instead to the past record. This was a film production record, in large part, and it involved a rather remarkable financial record as well.

No money, of course, had ever been appropriated by Congress itself for such a film service, and yet it had been in operation for five years, mainly by allocations from relief agencies. The Resettlement Administration was wholly a relief agency; the Farm Security Administration in the Department of Agriculture carried on with funds appropriated specifically for it under Emergency Relief Appropriation acts; and under the National Emergency Council (itself appropriated for under ERA acts), and under the Office of Education, the Film Service got the bulk of its support from relief monies.

For the fiscal year 1940, the WPA had allocated $162,500 to support not only the beginnings of *Ecce Homo* but also the distribution work of the Film Service. An important part of the funds for *The Fight for Life* also came from WPA—$75,900—and an equal amount from Public Works Administration, with the Farm Security Administration contributing $16,700. Meanwhile the Ivens and Flaherty undertakings were both financed on a reimbursable basis by agencies in the Department of Agriculture—the REA and the AAA.

The House hearings were not so heated this time. The subcommittee was a different one, since the appropriation was now for a permanent agency—the Office of Education in the Federal Security Agency. But the story of the allocations was fully told. The next subject of discussion was *The Fight for Life*, with some attention given to the "garbage can scene." The final point was the question of legal authority in the organic act establishing the Office of Education, and the chairman asked Commissioner John Studebaker to forward an opinion by the agency counsel.

[31] The Budget Bureau had been asked for $433,350 but cut it to this. (House, 76th Congress 3d Session, Department of Labor–Federal Security Agency Appropriation Bill for 1941, p. 265. For quotation see p. 297.)

At this time, the Film Service had 68 employees, 39 in distribution and 29 in field production work, with 25 of the field men on a per diem basis, when actually employed. Per diem ranged from $5 to $25.

[32] P. 297, *Ibid.* This was because "a complete reallocation of salaries was made, consistent with the salary standards in the Office of Education" (p. 287). During part of this time, Lorentz had also been doing regular articles for *McCall's* Magazine and had done various outside jobs, such as the script outline for the film *The City*.

This opinion, offered by the Federal Security Agency legal department, stressed the last clause of the first paragraph of the law of 1867 as fully adequate to cover the making of motion pictures. Not only were "the purpose and duties" of the Office of Education to "collect statistics and facts showing the condition and progress of education in the several States and Territories" but also "to diffuse such information respecting the organization and management of schools and school systems, and methods of teaching, as shall aid the people of the United States in the establishment and maintenance of efficient school systems, and otherwise promote the cause of education throughout the country." [33]

The House Committee didn't agree that "otherwise promote" was enough. Its final word was published on March 21:

> Two estimates, one in the amount of $40,000 and one in the amount of $106,400, were before the committee, involving the establishment, on a permanent basis, of a radio service and a film service, respectively. The committee, after consultation with parliamentary authorities, has concluded that there is at the present time no existing law that would authorize the carrying on of these services. The sums named have, therefore, been eliminated from the bill. The committee reserves judgment on the merit of the two activities and in the event enabling legislation is passed, will review the estimate of need for funds to carry on any work under these heads in the light of then existing conditions.[34]

The Senate subcommittee did not hear the Film Service case until April. Relations here were considerably less agreeable than in 1939. This time Lorentz himself was there. But there was no efficient questioning from Senator Byrnes. The only Senator present for most of the period was Kenneth McKellar (D., Tenn.) who showed from the beginning no sympathy for the purposes Lorentz and Mercey professed. Economy didn't seem to interest him. He went after the provision in the Emergency Relief Act against allocation of funds. Reading from it, he concluded triumphantly: "No provision is made there for making moving pictures, and whoever gave you that relief money for that purpose undoubtedly violated the law, and you gentlemen in accepting it have undoubtedly violated this law." [35] Pressed further on this, Mercey stated plainly what funds had been allocated by what agencies. Lorentz, evidently alarmed, interrupted to make a disorganized statement apparently intended to distract attention from these well-known facts, whereupon Commissioner Studebaker intervened in an attempt to educate Senator McKellar on the subject of modern mass

[33] See U.S.C.A. Title 20, Sec. 1, or Ch. 158, 39th Congress 2d Session, 14 Stat 434, Act of March 2, 1867.

[34] House Report No. 1822, 76th Congress 3d Session.

[35] Senate Hearings, 76th Congress 3d Session, Labor Department–Federal Security Agency Appropriation Bill.

communications as educational media. But the upshot of it was that Mr. McKellar thought a film service was "unwise," not "justified by the law," and "futile."

The Senate version of the Labor Department-Federal Security Agency Appropriation Bill for 1941 included no provision for a Film Service. Meanwhile the House Committee on Appropriations also wrote into the Emergency Relief Appropriation Act for 1941 a specific denial of funds from that source for the Film Service:

> Except as authorized in this Joint Resolution, no allocation of funds shall be made to any other Federal agency from the appropriation in this Joint Resolution for any Federal agency. No such allocation shall be made for the exercise of the functions of the Radio Division or the U.S. Film Service transferred to the Office of Education of the Federal Security Agency.[36]

The Committee's report further stated:

> The joint resolution (Sec. 12c) as does the present law, prohibits allocations of funds to agencies unless specifically authorized. The committee recommends a specific prohibition on allocation of funds to the Radio Division or the U.S. Film Service or for carrying out the functions of such agencies transferred to the Office of Education. While such provision may be unnecessary because the general language prohibits such an allocation, since the provision in existing law was ignored in such a case a specific prohibition is written in.[37]

Both bills went into conference committee more than once, but when they emerged the specific prohibition was still in the relief bill. In the Federal Security Appropriation the only thing that even resembled celluloid was an old provision in the same paragraph with general office and travel expenses for "purchase, distribution and exchange of educational documents, motion picture films and lantern slides." The amount appropriated for all of this, including travel, was $26,500.[38]

The immediate reasons for the Congressional disapproval of Film Service appropriations were thus of several different kinds, but they were simple compared to the many cumulative reasons which crowded the background. The immediate reasons were more rational than the others, but not necessarily more important. They were: (1) the doubtful legal status of a film production service within an agency established in 1867 and under language which was admittedly pretty general, (2) the general prohibition against allocation of funds from relief to other agencies for other purposes—a prohibition which had been side-stepped by the Film Service, (3) the impossibility of giving convincing evidence that econ-

---

[36] Public Resolution 88, Sec. 12(c), 76th Congress 3d Session.
[37] House Report 2186, 15 May 1940, 76th Congress 3d Session.
[38] Public Law 665, 26 June 1940, 76th Congress 3d Session.

omies were being achieved when it was plain that the agency interest was
rather in making more movies, and (4) the irrelevance for Government
public relations of *The Fight for Life*.

Behind these objections, brought out during the first and third sessions of the 76th Congress, were the other things, the non-rational memories and grudges and prejudices which any agency in the Federal Government normally accumulates—especially if it emphasizes publicity—but
which the Film Service acquired in abnormal quantities. There was the
distant but continuing relationship to the relief program, so that any strong
antipathies toward Harry Hopkins, or "boondoggling" in general, or even
the Federal Theater Project of the WPA specifically, got carried over in
the minds of many to this film-making "project." There was the whole
well-remembered story of Rexford Tugwell—his brains, personality,
methods, program and publicity program—and more particularly his
elaborate first annual report as head of the Resettlement Administration.
There was *The Plow* itself, its poorly balanced truths and its use in the
1936 campaign. There were the more recent questions about Lowell
Mellett's National Emergency Council, its "interference" in the states and
among local Federal offices, its possible tie-up with politics-in-relief, its
rumored activity in the attempted purge of Democrats. Above all, there
was the way these film people kept getting money from new sources without direct Congressional permission—they seemed, unfortunately, to be a
pretty slick bunch. Then there were less directly applicable things, even
less possible to measure—the question of the alleged Communist inclina-
tions of some of the documentary people on the outside who were also enthusiastic Lorentz supporters, the constant underground and above-
ground opposition of Hollywood financial interests.

Above and beyond all this there was the easy opportunity to hit at the
New Deal. The Film Service was strictly vulnerable. It had friends in
general, but no special friends. It was part of the New Deal, but no
particular part. It was simply a publicity outfit. It was possible, then, to
strike at the New Deal through the Film Service without actually striking
down any substantive program of the New Deal or injuring any noticeably
important special interests. There was perhaps a general public interest in
improved, modernized, dramatized Government reporting, but no block of
votes in any constituency was going to be shifted because of that issue.

Finally, it must be emphasized that the clouds of war in Europe were
beginning to overwhelm everyone's attention during 1938 and 1939. As
Lorentz himself wrote, long afterward:

> The Munich pact was signed September 1938. Mr. Roosevelt made
> his famous "quarantine" speech in Chicago in the fall of 1938. On
> September 2, 1939, the day I finished shooting the last scene of *The
> Fight for Life*, Hitler's armies invaded Poland. From the beginning
> President Roosevelt was himself more interested in our work than

any one of his cabinet officers. He himself knew a lot about the actual craft of motion pictures. However, we were a domestic unit concerned with the internal problems of the U.S. The President and his high-ranking associates were increasingly concerned with foreign affairs during the last year of the life of the U.S. Film Service, and with the fall of France in 1940 the President made his decision to run for a third term and was wholly concerned with foreign affairs.

I recall that he asked Senator James Byrnes to appear on our behalf at the Senate Appropriations Committee meeting, but Byrnes also had been told to ram through the increased appropriation for the U.S. Navy, which he barely managed to get over by a majority of two or three votes.

Lorentz added to this a note of hindsight, tinged, perhaps, with a degree of wishful thinking:

It is interesting to note that within two years after the demise of the U.S. Film Service, Nelson Rockefeller's Coordinating Committee was given $13 million for motion picture production. Thus, politically, had I wished to turn the work of the U.S. Film Service towards international affairs, we probably would have remained in existence in some new national defense department.[39]

Debate in the Senate

There was one last attempt to revive the issue on the floor of the Senate itself. Senator Elmer Thomas (D., Okla.) stood forth as advocate for the U.S. Film Service, and asked an amendment to the Labor Department–Federal Security Agency Appropriation Act, re-inserting the Budget-approved sum of $106,400.

Senator Thomas undertook to meet the objection of the House Appropriations Committee that there was no statutory authority for the existence of a separate Film Service. He admitted that this seemed to be true. But he contended, as had the legal department of the Federal Security Agency, that the general clause in the 1867 law covered the situation. Later on in the debate, he pointed out that many other agencies in the Government operated under general clauses about information activity—the U.S. Housing Authority, then under the Federal Loan Agency, and the Bureau of Mines in the Department of the Interior both were distributing films under general authorizations to "disseminate information."

[39] Letter, Pare Lorentz, November 14, 1950.

Senator McKellar's method of attack was to profess his continued amazement that a "film industry" existed in the U.S. Government and to claim that it had been secretly built up by misuse of funds.

> I have been on the Appropriations Committee now for more than 20 years and this is the first time that an appropriation for film service has ever come to light. Governmental agencies have obtained such appropriations in a clandestine kind of way. . . . Money which has been appropriated for work relief has been used for film service and for building up a United States Film Service. Remarkable to tell, we find it in a number of departments. I did not know it was so.[40]

McKellar quoted from the hearings the exchange between himself and Mercey which showed that the REA and AAA had transferred funds to the Film Service. He asserted that it was "monstrous" to do this when "there is a prohibition in the WPA law against using the money except for work relief." What he apparently meant was that it was "monstrous" for the Film Service to have used WPA money and therefore it was "monstrous" for these other agencies, which had the legal right to do so, to follow the example of the WPA.

Senator Thomas pointed out, as was certainly the case, that films were a familiar instrument of information among government agencies and that there was nothing clandestine about it.

> Mr. President, there is no illusion about this matter. It is nothing new. It is at least 25 years old. Each bill carries funds available for the dissemination of information. The Congress does not give the departments specific instructions as to how information may be disseminated. The Congress does not say that information shall be disseminated by postal card or by letter, or by handbills, or by any other particular method. That is left to the discretion of the Department.[41]

He then gave in exhausting detail the titles of some of the films produced by the Department of the Interior, according to the U.S. Film Service catalog. He did this chiefly to show that film-making was familiar, and incidentally to show that many of the subjects were useful scientifically as well as useful to the states concerned (in the case of the geographical and national park films).

Thomas also listed the agencies which had "film services." Obviously none of them was spending the amount of money or making the kind of films made by the U.S. Film Service, though this was not made clear. Nor was it made clear that some of these agencies merely had one or two old movies on hand for loan when requested. This did support his case, however, because it not only showed the familiarity of government film spon-

[40] *Congressional Record*, April 26, 1940, 76th Congress 3d Session, p. 5088.
[41] *Ibid.*, p. 5089.

sorship but also the usefulness of a central agency to distribute the films already made under other agency appropriations.

> The finest film in the world would be of no benefit whatever unless some agency were provided to distribute it, some central agency to which a school or a club or a group or organization could write suggesting a film they want. . . . Unless there is some place from which they can get such a film, all the money we are spending for agencies is entirely wasted.

This was not entirely true, and Senator Robert Taft (R., Ohio) was at pains to say so:

> Mr. Taft: Is it not true that each department distributed its own films up to 1938?
>
> Mr. Thomas of Oklahoma: They can do that.
>
> Mr. Taft: Did they not actually do it?
>
> Mr. Thomas of Oklahoma: They can do that, but they do not stress that work, as I understand.

Senator Thomas went on to read some of the favorable reviews of the latest Lorentz film *The Fight for Life* and seemed to take pride in these. But he kept returning to the point which Taft had already half demolished:

> This agency is a clearing house. As I have said, it has produced two films, both of which have been very popular, but that is not its main function. Its main function is to act as a clearing house for the products of the other 25, 26, or 27 film agencies.

Byrnes and Barkley both supported this view at other points in the debate, with more attention to the possibility that a central agency might save money by coordination of film activities in the Government.

But Senator Taft was interested in the substantive question. His attack on the Film Service was a reasoned and factual analysis of the real situation and it constitutes a concise statement of the case against Government production of documentary films. He began by pointing out that the Film Service, in its earlier phases in the RA and FSA particularly, was primarily a producing organization.[42]

> So far as I can see, the Department [of Education] has been much more interested in the question of production of these large films than it has been in the distribution of films. I think it is perfectly clear that there is no legislative authority for that particular function.

[42] *Ibid.*, p. 5092.

He went on to inspect further Thomas' legal justification for film production in the Office of Education:

> To promote the cause of education is a general term. If it is broad enough to cover the production of a film such as this [The Fight for Life], and the distribution of motion pictures, it is broad enough to authorize the Department to establish schools in every county and every city in the United States. Those words are obviously simply intended as a general catch-all clause to carry out the specific functions of the Office of Education in studying the problems of education and assisting the general educational system of the United States.

After some skeptical remarks about the usefulness of the Interior Department's films on rat extermination, Taft launched into a general statement about documentary.

> I believe the whole business has been greatly expanded beyond any real value in relation to the functions of the Federal Government. There may be cases in which the use of films is the proper method. I think particularly that farm organizations can use films on particular technical subjects. Perhaps a farmer can be taught things about his farm by pictures better than by instruction by books and direct literature, but I somewhat doubt it. Insofar as films are used simply for general education to provide moving pictures for everybody, I think it is far beyond the functions of the Federal Government, and it is particularly dangerous when films are produced which only in a general way illustrate functions of the Federal Government.

> I do not care who is controlling the Government, if it is to produce films and put them out, they are bound to become propaganda for the particular department and the particular work of the department that happens to be covered by the film. . . . If the Republicans were given power, it would be used to advance particular measures in which they might be interested. It is true, certainly, also of the present administration. . . .

> A United States documentary film is a United States propaganda film. I do not care how good the purpose of that kind of a film may be, I do not believe it is an undertaking in which the Federal Government should engage. It may encourage private citizens to do it. There certainly is no objection to some kinds of propaganda by private organizations, but the Federal Government itself ought to stay out of it. For instance, if we offer a service such as the national parks to the people, I do not see why the Federal Government should be engaged in advertising to everybody in the country where all those parks are located. We ought not to have to spend money sending out films to do so. If the parks are not worthy of the attention of the people, and if they do not get attention on their own merits, I do not believe that additional propaganda advertising by the Federal Government is going to make them any more attractive.

The Fight for Life is a picture showing the experiences of a young interne in delivering babies in the slums. It is probably good from an artistic point of view, and probably teaches correctly a great social lesson. However, all it does and all it is intended to do is to convince audiences that slums should be removed, and by a particular program, I might say, or that there should be better medical care for the poor, and by a particular program. *The Fight for Life* cost over $150,000 of relief money, and no relief workers were employed to produce it. One scene in the picture shows a person getting food from a garbage can. It occurs to me that $150,000 spent in seeing that the man got proper food instead of illustrating a picture of a man getting food from a garbage can would be a more effective use of the particular $150,000.

The Children's Bureau in the Department of Labor has a film called *Prenatal Care*. It is a picture that is related directly to the subject of the proper method of taking care of babies and the proper method of delivery. It probably cost about $1,000, instead of $150,000 for the other technical picture, and is probably of at least as much educational value. The other kind of film is a propaganda film. I do not care how good the subject is, or how good the purpose for which that particular film is being used. That is the whole issue here. . . .

This whole business of film service and radio service for the Government not only has been used for purposes of propaganda, but it is bound to be so used. I believe that when we have a chance to vote on it—and this is the first chance we have had to vote on this kind of thing—we ought to say to the bureaus of the Government that the time has come when they should attend to their particular business, and they should not be out spreading propaganda. We should not provide money to stir up our constituents to come and lobby with us to do the things which we ought to do without any lobbying and without any propaganda.

Thus Mr. Taft was (1) not opposed to specialized scientific and health films so long as they were strictly informative and not dramatized. (2) He was opposed to films for "general education" as beyond the functions of the Federal Government. (3) He was also opposed to this more general type of film, as represented by the term "documentary," because it would inevitably become propaganda for a particular program. (*The Fight for Life*, incidentally, did not support any particular program, either for health or for slum clearance.) (4) Again, he was opposed to this kind of film-making because he saw no need of telling the people any more than they already know—about national parks, for instance—which is almost the equivalent of saying that the government information process should not be used to make people happier even when no special interest is hurt thereby. (5) Finally, he was opposed to documentary because it was designed to stir up the people to "lobby" with their representatives. He would not, apparently, have accepted the idea that documentary could be looked at as "lobbying" the other way around: as a dramatized report to the people of the reasons why both the administration and the Congress have seen fit to spend money as they have spent it.

There was no real answer offered to his arguments. Senator McKellar took up his previous refrain, castigating the purposes of the U.S. Film Service, one by one. Majority Leader Barkley did say, at the close of the debate:

> It has always been my understanding that these films have been used to advise the people of the activities of agencies of the Government. . . . I have always derived considerable information and inspiration from such pictures. As a rule, I think no American citizen can observe one of these pictures without feeling somewhat proud of the activities of the Government. It may be more enlightening and more entertaining than merely reading about it in a book, pamphlet or newspaper.

But when the yeas and nays were ordered, there were 24 in favor and 36 against (with 36 not voting) and the U.S. Film Service had had its last appeal.

President, Congress and the Public Relations Man

The details of the long battle over the Film Service help to answer the question which must naturally arise from this history of the democratic documentary: Why was there no "documentary movement" in the United States Government after *The Plow* and *The River?* Why did Grierson's *Drifters* start a historic trend, and Lorentz's *River* mark the beginning of an end?

There were at least two causes of a more general nature, deeper and more stubborn than the rational arguments offered by Senator Taft, more familiar and more difficult than the short-term problems discussed in the hearings or the specific antipathies developed over five years. These were the historic constitutional opposition between the executive and legislative branches of the American Federal Government, and the long-continued opposition of the U.S. Congress to administrative publicity.

First, it needs to be said that England in 1929 was not the same place or time as the United States in 1937. Nor did British administrative experience come to the same thing. British experience since the war had included a gradually increasing role for governmental organizations and corporations. Change through administration was a familiar process all during the 1920's, and social legislation, transit authorities and electric grids were commonplace government activities.

Whereas the climate for experiment in politics—change through administration, action through information—was about as favorable in the U.S. in the year 1933 as it was in England in 1928 (when Grierson joined the EMB), by 1935–37 consolidation was setting in in Washington. Change required more justification, budgetary and otherwise, as the years wore on. The disappearance of Tugwell himself from the scene was only symptomatic of that general shift in atmosphere. The explosive expansion of administrative agencies had been a shock. There was nothing gradual about it, however limited and relatively conservative most of the New Deal goals may now seem to be. Hence the consolidation afterward had its own peculiar problems, centering around the shifting support of senior Southern Democrats in Congress.

Tallents, information head for a quite respectable agency sponsoring expanding trade, in the first instance, and for an old-line domestic agency in the second instance, had only to persuade board members and Treasury representatives in the first instance, and the head of the GPO in the second. Tugwell, head of an emergency agency using relief funds and with a vested interest in social change, and Mellett, head of a nebulous executive office occupied with administrative coordination, faced a host of Southern and Republican Congressmen who cared little for the information process as an administrative responsibility. They saw it rather as a tool for expanding administrative power.

Tallents and Grierson persuading a Treasury representative, and Mellett and Mercey trying to mollify appropriations committeemen—here is a characteristic contrast between budgetary methods in the two countries. In England, the Treasury is responsible for the budget, and Parliament cannot make changes except at the risk of raising a party issue. In the United States, the budget is anybody's target, even after the Budget Bureau has made judicious cuts. Intransigent individuals on appropriations subcommittees can in effect decide broad naval policy or reduce an agency's quota of clerks by one.

The difference between Parliamentary and Congressional responsibility for both policy and budget is a familiar one. The contrast between party discipline in the one case and the complex process of committee persuasion in the other is well known. Combined with intricate partisan and intra-party feelings, this had its effect on the history of the U.S. Film Service. But the more general effect on the process of public relations itself is seldom remarked upon, and this too can be seen at work in this case.

Information is ordinarily an executive function. There is no particular reason why Congress should not have information officers, but this has not yet happened. Congressmen individually talk to the press or send out franked mail. They make tapes for radio and films for television. Congress-men collectively issue reports or permit the press to take pictures. But how-ever salutary it might be for American democracy if there were information offices for both House and Senate—and factual motion pictures showing Congressional policy-making at work—up to now the organized form of public relations has been normally a departmental activity. Programs—whether of bond-selling, crop loans, or Civil Service recruitment—once de-cided upon by Congress are put into action by administrators. Information programs accompany action programs. Banks of mimeographs, stacks of pamphlets, reams of press releases and rolls of film are the paraphernalia of executive business.

Hence it is that information processes, powerful for expanding the scope and success of executive programs, are normally under fire from legislative ranks. Minority Senators who voted against the action program in the first place feel no compunctions in attacking its implementation in-directly by means of direct attacks on its information program. Representa-tives who voted in favor of the action program may nevertheless claim different shades of opinion as to the extent to which it should be pushed, and they may be alarmed by vigorous publicity. Thus the public relations man, however carefully he may have read the Act of Congress authorizing his agency's program, may be frequently taken aback at the ferocity with which his own part in all this is attacked.

The peculiarity of his dilemma is not the fact that opposition develops. The agency head may expect that. The strange thing is that opposition often develops because attention is drawn to the publicity as a thing in itself. It is first decried as far too costly or is said to be inept, and carefully selected examples are paraded. Then it is described as partisan propaganda. Finally it is discovered to be dominated by Communists or by the Communist line—an accusation which discredits the agency program itself without taking the responsibility of debating the program. In due time not only the publicity program, but the agency program, and the President himself, may become discredited in the public eye.

The public relations man may not realize at first that he actually occupies an exposed position in the everlasting battle between two fixed positions—White House and Capitol. It is a battle which shifts historically with conditions of crisis, party organization and personality. But the constitutional basis of the conflict is an enduring one. Since neither branch can actually dislodge the other, since terms are fixed and powers relatively stable, since both sides can both initiate and veto action, since party dis-cipline is vitiated by geographical dispersion of power and by seniority rules in the Congress, the result is a kind of congenital frustration. Any real agreement is a triumph of patient persuasion. Compromise and cooperation are not uncharacteristic of the system. But equally characteristic, whether agreement is achieved or not, is a withering cross-fire of pot-shots.

Woe to him who is in an exposed position. The less attention he at-tracts, the less likely he is to become another leading issue between Presi-dent and Congress. The public relations man may look in vain for an exit from this dilemma: full speed ahead in support of the agency program may mean the stirring up of opposition which will harm the agency pro-gram. If he is mindful of the famous case of the Resettlement Administra-tion annual report, he will be keenly aware of the dangers of too much enthusiasm, too much public relations.

His way out, short of resigning and joining a magazine staff, is usually the soft answer and the soft pedal. He often becomes, therefore, a brake on publicity rather than a promoter of publicity. He prefers, so far as possible, not to be in an exposed position. Thus the information man reflects the conservatizing process the bureaucracy in general undergoes whenever it seeks new appropriations.

Therefore the question, "Should a democratic government make documentary films?" finally becomes, "Is it possible for American govern-ment agencies to make documentary films?" Does not the conservative effect of the American separation of powers—as well as the fear of a normally conservative public opinion which objects to "government propa-ganda"—mean that films like *The River* are seldom, if ever, possible?

Perhaps only brand-new agencies, staffed with men devoted to a new enterprise, willing to accept the hazards of action, will enter into the arena of information with the determination to publicize the program creatively. Perhaps such new agencies can come into existence in America only under the pressure of a crisis. Even then, as soon as the crisis and the newness wear off, enthusiasm will become caution, and the spending of money merely to inform the public will be harder and harder to justify.

Having watched, from within, the growing orthodoxy of the Farm Security Administration, the Film Service itself was later changing into a more conservative organization after one encounter with Congressional committees. Had it continued under the Office of Education, it would probably have lost Lorentz and lost its creative, crusading drive. It would probably have become respectable, informational, noncontroversial, dull. It would have produced some useful films and the public understanding of problems of government would have been increased. But it is fairly cer-tain that it would never again have produced anything like *The River*.

6

World War II: The
Office of War Information

WARTIME is a time for action. It is also a time when there is likely to be wide agreement on the immediate goals of action. For both reasons, World War II brought new government support to documentary workers in this country.

To the film-maker war offers the ultimate in exciting subjectmatter. An alert and courageous cameraman can get action shots which may hold attention more fixedly than the best of acting and directing combined. If movement is the life-blood of film, then the panoramic death and destruction of war bring that life-blood to its highest pulse-rate.

For successful prosecution of a modern war, there are directives and public messages which must reach workers and cooperating groups on the home front. Once decisions are made which call for support from money and manpower, the support must be summoned at once. Nowadays it is clear that a formal Presidential message is not enough. Understanding, agreement, action and continuing action must be achieved on a bewildering variety of fronts. War cannot wait for the slow growth of retrospective agreement on one subject after another, long after history has been made. Persuasion is vital, and from war to war its timetable speeds up in a proportion similar to the increasing speed of projectiles.

During World War II the need for simultaneous repetition in all media called for motion picture treatment of war messages. The movie was not as fast as a newspaper, but it was powerful and had a wide audience. It was supposed to reach 80 million people every week (though an uncertain number of these represented youthful repeaters). There was

118

another audience of uncounted millions, especially adults, in the non-theatrical field—churches, clubs, and other groups with 16mm projectors. Whether the need was to mobilize scrap iron or nurses, to understand manpower rules or price controls, here was a familiar medium which could do more than any other—short of direct personal contact—to persuade.

Yet it was the dramatization of messages for domestic consumption which had least success in the three-fold use of factual film in World War II. Movies for overseas propaganda and movies for the orientation of troops went through steady expansion and improvement. Government films for the American public got off to a poor start under unpopular sponsorship, with the same kind of heritage of antipathy the U.S. Film Service had, plus recurring unpleasant memories of the Creel Committee's activities in World War I. The day of the Domestic Branch of the Office of War Information was brief, and its demise left to Hollywood the main task of producing public messages on film and, to the combined information staffs of the armed services, the public reporting of the drama and terror of war itself.

There were, however, net gains for documentary on four fronts as a result of government activity during World War II. The Motion Picture Bureau of the OWI Domestic Branch did succeed in mobilizing the 16mm projectors of the country and organizing something like a nontheatrical distribution system. The Motion Picture Bureau of the OWI Overseas Branch, under Robert Riskin, and the Coordinator of Inter-American Affairs (chiefly with the help of Julien Bryan), produced a number of notable documentary films which are now part of the slowly growing library of Americana on film. Frank Capra and Anatole Litvak took stock film, edited it with care and added an unmistakably American commentary to create a new kind of propaganda documentary for the Army. In the last years of the war, John Huston, John Ford, William Wyler, Garson Kanin and the lesser-known, unsung combat photographers of all the services recorded some of the most extraordinary action scenes in the history of the camera, and many of these front-line reports were rushed onto the screens of the nation in time to reach the public as news.

No new leader rose to prominence, nor was there any really new discovery in technique. The simplicity of wartime agreement on immediate goals meant that film-makers did not have to grapple with subtle problems of public policy and political relationships.

But the relative sobriety of wartime film reporting offers a startling contrast with the bravado of World War I. It came partly from the disenchanted attitude of the common soldier (up to and including Eisenhower) who had lived through a decade of depression and anti-war muckraking and simply wanted to get a dirty job done. The honest film people, who had ears to the ground, caught this tonal quality and put it into their sound tracks. The sobriety came also, in part, from the influence of the documentary method, itself depression-conscious, but more deeply influenced by the factual fidelity of Flaherty, the social consciousness of Grierson and the impersonal drama-in-sound of Lorentz. Documentary people and Hollywood people mingled and worked together, especially in the OWI Overseas Branch, and postwar films showed the effects of this experience as well as the effects of the war itself.

The Creel Committee—A Precedent

None of the ideas for government films in World War II was basically new. Even the use of "orientation" films by the army was an adaptation to large-scale mobilization of earlier techniques of public information. The pattern of the OWI's campaigns was not very different from the activities of George Creel and his film lieutenant, Charles S. Hart, in World War I —and not much more ambitious. The big difference was in tone, temper, and taste, not in fundamental objectives.

The Committee on Public Information [1] appeared on April 13, 1917 but the Division of Films was not established until September 25 and many of its most notable undertakings were not completed till after World War I was in its last stages. According to Mock and Larson, its functions were five:

1. Cooperation with photographers of the Signal Corps and the Navy in preparing and handling pictures they had taken.

2. Writing of scenarios and issuance of permits for commercial films about government work.

3. Production of the documentary films made entirely by the Committee on Public Information, most of which were finished after the Armistice.

4. Distribution and promotion of war films whether taken by our own government, the allies or private producers.

5. Cooperation with the Foreign Film Division in the export of pictures to CPI agents abroad. [2]

These film functions did not develop all at once. The first thing Creel did was to go to the War Department and convince Secretary Newton Baker that the historical films the Signal Corps were taking ought to be

[1] By Executive Order 2594 the Secretaries of State, War, and Navy were made into such a committee and George Creel appointed chairman.
[2] James R. Mock and Cedric Larson, *Words That Won the War*, p. 137. See also George Creel, *How We Advertised America*.

shown to the American people.[3] This material was released to weekly newsreels. In course of time, this naturally suggested the collection of such films under more logical headings. With the addition of such subjectmatter as training camps and armament production, various documentary short subjects began to appear. Such titles as these are typical and self-explanatory: *The 1917 Recruit, The Second Liberty Loan, Submarines, In a Southern Camp, Labor's Part in Democracy's War, Making of Big Guns, Woman's Part in the War.*[4]

These titles were distributed free to "patriotic societies and state councils of defense." At first it was thought that distribution was largely a matter of nontheatrical showings which would not compete with commercial houses. But it soon became evident that to mobilize a really large audience commercial channels were necessary. This was dealt with in two ways. Three full-length features were paid for by the Government, and scenarios were provided for 18 one-reel subjects to be made by private producers.[5] At the last, the CPI was going into production itself and six short films were completed after the Armistice, of which four were shown.[6]

In all these cases, various types of promotion were used, including local sport advertising, special big-city premieres, and solicitation letters to prominent men. The full-length features had thousands of bookings, and two of them—*Pershing's Crusaders* (7 reels) and *America's Answer* (5 reels)—grossed more than $180,000 each for the Government. In this respect, Creel evidently took a page from the notebooks of England and France, who sold their front-line news footage to the highest bidder. Exhibition for pay was one motion picture policy of 1917–18 which was not followed in World War II.[7]

[3] "Investigation developed the sad news that the Photographic Section of the Signal Corps was a hope rather than a fact. . . . Kendall Banning and Mr. Lawrence E. Rubell . . . made a survey of the photographers of the United States, motion and still, and urged selections upon the Signal Corps until an adequate force had been assembled for duty at home and abroad." Creel, p. 118.

[4] *Men Who Are Doing Things*, not quite so self-explanatory, is nevertheless a revealing title; it showed "upon the screen, as far as possible, every person who is mentioned in public print as being active in war preparations." George Creel, *Complete Report of the Chairman of the Committee on Public Information.*

[5] Typical titles: *Keep 'Em Singing and Nothing Can Lick 'Em, I Run the Biggest Life Insurance Company on Earth, A Girl's a Man for A' That, Feeding the Fighter, Reclaiming the Soldier's Duds, Colored Americans, It's an Engineer's War, Waging War in Washington, College for Camp Cooks.* Producer-distributors were Paramount-Bray Pictograph, Pathé, Universal, and C. L. Chester.

[6] *If Your Soldier's Hit, Our Wings of Victory, Our Horses of War, Making the Nation Fit.* The two not seen: *The Storm of Steel, The Bath of Bullets* (about gun factories and machine guns).

[7] It was not followed by the OWI Domestic Branch but was followed for the theatrical exhibitions in certain foreign countries. The Creel committee took in $852,744.39 from their domestic film showings to apply on total expenses for films of $1,066,730.59.

"The rental charged every house was based on the average income derived from that particular house. By this method the small house as well as the large one could afford to run the government films." (*How We Advertised America*, p. 124.)

Terry Ramsaye, in his history of the movies, published in 1926, expanded on this point with his usual frankness:

> A curious problem existed. There had never been one like it. Distribution of propaganda to the press was relatively easy. The press is a commercial institution which gets its raw material, the news, by picking it up free. Its editors are presumed to know news and what it is worth no matter where it comes from. The motion picture, equally but no more commercial than the press, pays high for its material and judges largely by price.

> The government could hand a good story to the news associations and every newspaper reader would see it. If the government handed out a free motion picture nobody saw it. A free picture was not merchandise and could not go through a merchandising machine. The government through the Division of Films of the Committee on Public Information was thereby forced into the motion picture business, as a business. . . . A picture has to be sold to the distributor, sold to the exhibitor, sold to the public at the boxoffice.[8]

There was no distinction made, as there was in 1942–45, between domestic and foreign audiences. The main thing was to get the films intended for American audiences also shown overseas.[9] The CPI, through its advices to the War Trade Board, saw to it that entertainment films were not licensed for showings abroad unless some government material went along with it, and as a result "Charlie Chaplin and Mary Pickford led *Pershing's Crusaders* and *America's Answer* into the enemy's territory." [10]

Some idea of the quality of *Pershing's Crusaders* can be seen in the *New York Tribune* report of the opening at New York's Lyric Theater, quoted in the *Literary Digest* of 8 June 1918:

> Germany and France are shown as though modeled in clay, and then slowly, out of the center of Germany, rises a volcano, and a huge mailed fist appears scattering mud and sand and lava over France.

> The first part of the picture shows how plots, fires, strikes, etc., were fomented by German agents in America; how America is putting her hand to the plow to feed the Allies; the huge cantonments which have sprung up to house the Army; cutting the khaki clothes by machinery. Other subjects are: What American women are doing; how the army shoes are made; feeding America's Army; mighty ships in the building; supremacy in the air will strike down the German vultures; our Navy; camouflage of the sea; our own submarines; in the aviation camps; baptizing the boys ordered to the front; tenderness and skill at the dressing stations; the sniper's job; the victor of yesterday and the victor

[8] A *Million and One Nights*, vol. II, pp. 782–3.

[9] The man in charge of film work in Scandinavia, for instance, reported "90 per cent of the films shown being American"—a considerable change from the earlier strong German influence. (Mock and Larson, p. 280.)

[10] Creel's words in *How We Advertised America*, p. 142.

of tomorrow; and Pershing's crusaders and their Allies, who will get the Kaiser!

A letter of protest to the *New York Sun* by a clergyman, Dr. W. S. Rainsford, gives further perspective. He thought the pictures of setting-up exercises were outstanding, but decried the descriptive insets, which "introduce scene after scene with some boastful declaration of what America has done or will do, or with some meaningless and vulgar sneer at the courage of our foes. . . . In the audience on Tuesday night were men who had seen war, English, French, Canadian officers. I wonder what they thought as one after another of those vulgar and boastful insets were laid on the screen." [11]

Most of the film work of the CPI was done too late to have much effect—whether negatively or affirmatively—in what Creel called "the world-fight for public opinion." The motion picture only barely began to carry "the call of the country to every community in the land and . . . inform and enthuse the peoples of Allied and neutral nations." Yet the intentions and plans were all there as a pattern for a later war. The discrepancy in film technique and in mood—epitomized in such titles as *Pershing's Crusaders* and *Reclaiming the Soldiers' Duds*—should not hide the fact that all the major film activities of World War II were used in World War I: newsreel distribution, nontheatrical showings, features and shorts for commercial theaters, and films for overseas, accomplished through government advice, then government sponsorship and, finally, government production.

The Birth of the OWI

The years of 1940–42 were lean years for the democratic documentary in the United States, and it is difficult to trace across that no-man's-land the threads of continuity from U.S. Film Service to OWI.

More than any other one person, Arch Mercey was a connecting link. When he left the Federal Civil Service to join the Coast Guard in January 1944, it was a symbol of the final dissolution of the revived hope which the OWI had represented. Documentary films about public policy were no longer made by any central agency for domestic distribution after that time.

11 When *Pershing's Crusaders* arrived in Mexico, incidentally, the local CPI agent, who was at the same time a correspondent of the *New York World*, "had it tactfully renamed *America at War*, but enemy agents saw to it that the earlier title was made known in the country from which other Pershing crusaders had withdrawn scarcely a year before." (Mock and Larson, p. 326.)

Mercey, a graduate of the University of Illinois law school, with some radio work in Hollywood to his credit, had come to Washington as an assistant to Senator Arthur Robinson of Indiana, a Republican. He met John F. Carter there and did some freelance writing for him. When Tugwell brought Lorentz in, Mercey accepted a job as administrative chief in the film section. From this time on he made government films his business, and contributed steady loyalty and considerable political awareness to the Tugwell and Mellett programs.

After the U.S. Film Service ended in June 1940, Mercey rejoined Lowell Mellett as an assistant and consultant on films. Mellett was then in the Executive Office of the President as head of the new Office of Government Reports—the somewhat sterilized remains of the National Emergency Council.

Shortly afterward, with the rise in defense expenditures, the Office of Emergency Management (also in the Executive Office of the President as the result of the reorganization of 1939) began to grow. Its information office was set up in February 1941 and Wayne Coy chose as his information director, at Mellett's suggestion, a hustling young man named Robert Horton. Horton thought he would like to be in on the ground floor as far as movies were concerned, since the war seemed likely to draw the United States in at any time. He therefore called on Mercey for advice, and before Pearl Harbor they had already released three short films and planned others.[12]

Power for Defense was the first of the government films of this period released through commercial distributors. It was sponsored, not by OEM or OGR, but by the National Defense Advisory Commission (the agency which preceded the OPM, which in turn became the War Production Board). Its release date was February 8, 1941, and its credit captions read as follows:

> This film is distributed and exhibited under the auspices of the Motion Picture Committee Cooperating for National Defense.

> The National Defense Advisory Commission presents *Power for Defense*, in cooperation with the Tennessee Valley Authority.

> Producer: Arch A. Mercey
> Technical Supervisor: Philip Martin Jr.
> Photography: Exteriors—Floyd Crosby
>   Interiors—Carl Pryer
> Commentary: Robert Collyer
> Voice: Thomas Chalmers

"More dams are on the way," the narrator said, as various TVA dams and construction scenes were shown. Referring to them as "the mechanized

[12] Interview with Lowell Mellett, October 13, 1950. Horton was another Scripps-Howard man.

divisions of peace," the script went on to show that "one-third of the products needed for defense" were completed with the help of the kilowatts generated in the Tennessee Valley. Pictures were offered of cotton uniforms, nitrate and manganese being shipped out, and of aluminum on its way to the airplane plants of Northrop, Vultee, Boeing and North American.

This was the emphasis of the early films, especially before war was declared—production achievements, the need for workers, the need for salvage and conservation and food production.[13]

Two of the most popular government films of this early period (both of them completed before, but released after, December 7, 1941) ought to be given special mention here. *Safeguarding Military Information* was made by the Signal Corps as an official U.S. Army training film but was released to the general public through the War Activities Committee of the motion picture industry (the successor of the Committee Cooperating for National Defense). It pictured a sinking ship and a wrecked train resulting from careless soldier or civilian talk about military movements. Walter Huston, impersonating a military lecturer, warned of "thousands of unauthorized ears."

The New Spirit was a Treasury Department release aimed at the income tax-paying public. If Donald Duck could be convinced of the value of saving and tax-paying almost anybody could be—or so the Treasury thought. According to the 1942 War Activities Committee report, it played in 11,785 theaters (very close to complete national saturation) in six weeks.[14] The people liked it, too, or the Treasury wouldn't have made a sequel called *The Spirit of 1943*.

After Pearl Harbor, the situation in Washington took on a grimmer aspect, and not alone because of the military factor of "too little and too late." There was also an obvious and increasing battle among various government agencies for the attention and support of the public. This bureaucratic competition, in the absence of any law and order in the information field, was a normal and justifiable response to a critical situation wherein everything seemed terribly important. It did, however, confuse the public, as well as the movie producers, and it tended to use manpower in a way that was both inefficient and embarrassing.

Shortly after December 7th, the Hollywood cooperating committee had requested President Roosevelt to appoint some one person to coordinate agency needs and Hollywood proposals. Lowell Mellett was thereupon designated as Coordinator of Government Films and Arch Mercey became Deputy Coordinator. But Mellett was apparently endowed with no inter-

[13] Films about bonds were directly sponsored by the Treasury Department, and army recruiting trailers (two or three minutes long) were provided for the Motion Picture Committee by the War Department.

[14] *Movies at War*: Reports of War Activities Committee, Motion Picture Industry, 1942–45.

departmental power beyond friendly persuasion, and the resulting coordination was infinitesimal.[15]

During the early months of 1942 the chaos continued and burgeoned. The OPM-WPB continued to have films produced, as did the OEM.[16] The Office of Facts and Figures had been set up on October 24, 1941 to supply the people of the United States with the facts about the "defense effort," and Director Archibald MacLeish had asked Leo Rosten to coordinate relations with Hollywood. The U.S. Office of Education was beginning what turned out to be a monumental program of films for training in industry, an operation which quite properly remained separate throughout the war. The Army and Navy were well under way with brand-new training film programs. And off at the edge of official Washington, at 25th and E Streets, was the headquarters of Colonel William Donovan, who was actually called the Coordinator of Information, but whose duty was that of preparing propaganda for, and collecting political intelligence from, foreign countries. Nelson Rockefeller was already Coordinator of Inter-American Affairs, and as such retained authority for information activities in Latin America.

Franklin Roosevelt seemed to enjoy having people around him competing for the same territory of authority. In this case he may have been watching to see if any of these various coordinators were likely to do an outstanding job. It was well known, on the other hand, that he had absorbed the temper of the 1930's on the subject of wartime propaganda.[17] He didn't like it. Furthermore, he did not have, as Wilson had, a man in mind who was certain to fill the bill.[18]

[15] The Presidential letter (December 18, 1941) described one of his functions as "to consult with all Government departments in connection with film production and distribution programs." This was not very strong language. One tangible result of all this was a new OGR catalog of all those government films which might conceivably have some relationship to the war effort. There appeared to be 64 of them in May 1942. (*Education for Victory*, Vol. 1, No. 8, U.S. Office of Education, May 15, 1942.)

[16] Arch Mercey was producer for the OPM film *Subcontracting for Defense*: Philip Martin Jr. was technical director; and Robert Horton and George Gercke consultants. In March the OEM released *Building a Bomber, Men and Ships* (merchant marine training), *Homes for Defense*, and *Women in Defense*. In May: *Tank* (commentary by Orson Welles), *Ring of Steel* (Spencer Tracy narrating the history of the American soldier), *Lake Carrier* (with the voice of Fredric March) and *Coal for Victory*. The OEM also produced the first government film on the specific subject of the TVA. (See editions of *Education for Victory, passim.*)

[17] The Walter Millis-Charles Beard-Gerald Nye line in its earliest phases implied that bankers and munitions makers had propagandized us into war. The Institute of Propaganda Analysis grew out of this climate of opinion. Roosevelt was keenly aware of the broader public feeling about war propaganda.

[18] According to a letter Josephus Daniels wrote to Mock and Larson, no one but Creel had ever been considered for the post of CPI chairman. (See p. 50.) A wise-cracking article by Walter Davenport in *Collier's* for February 15, 1941, predicted Mellett would get the job in World War II. It was favorable enough toward the former *Collier's* editor, but did him more harm than good. Mellett himself didn't want the job and urged the President to avoid setting up any central information agency. (Interview, October 13, 1950.)

From the earliest days of spring in 1941, it was widely understood in Washington that the Administrative Management Division of the Budget Bureau had an executive order "on the President's desk" for a reorganization of wartime information agencies. He finally signed it on June 13th and appointed Elmer Davis, the well-known writer and radio commentator, as director. With Associate Director Milton Eisenhower (lately of War Relocation Authority, formerly Department of Agriculture information chief), Davis set about the task of combining the functions and temperaments of the people in the Office of Government Reports, the Office for Emergency Management Information Division, the Office of Facts and Figures, and the Coordinator of Information's Foreign Information Service.[19] He didn't get the Coordinator of Inter-American Affairs in the shuffle, nor the political intelligence side of the COI, nor did he get any real power over the public relations officials of the armed services. He was to "formulate and carry out, through the use of press, radio, motion pictures and other facilities, information programs designed to facilitate the development of an informed and intelligent understanding, at home and abroad, of the status and progress of the war effort and of the war policies, activities and aims of the Government." [20]

Elmer Davis, as the President well knew, was no George Creel. However lukewarm Roosevelt was toward Davis personally and toward the whole problem of war information, the appointment did represent well enough what was wanted in the way of propaganda. Davis wasn't an advertising man. By profession he was a newspaperman, and by conviction a skeptical critic of propaganda, by whomever sponsored.

Therefore, the OWI emphasis became an emphasis on news, and the chief problem about the news was how to tell all the facts and yet contribute affirmatively to the "war effort." During the first months of Davis' leadership, the OWI became the spearhead of newspapermen's demands for more military news. He seemed to view his role as primarily that of an advocate for the public in its "right" to have abundant information about the way the war was going. This was, in a way, a propaganda objective as opposed to a purely military objective in the use of news. But it also involved the public's right to hear bad news as well as good news from the fronts, and therefore it was an essentially neutral point of view as far as the content of the news was concerned. Indeed, Davis said in early 1943, in the first OWI budget hearings:

> That news is as accurate as we can make it—including bad news when we have it, because it is important to create confidence in the story

[19] The present writer was an assistant to the administrative officer of the OFF and stayed on three months past June 13 in the OWI before being drafted. The three separate but adjoining mail rooms which were still grimly surviving at that time would have made a good case study in informal administrative relationships.

[20] Executive Order 9182, Federal Register VII, p. 4468 (1942).

we are telling, to make people feel that we give them the facts whether encouraging or not from our side.[21]

This preoccupation with facts and news was not in the least to be deplored, but it did mean that the production of argumentative or dramatic matter was not pushed. Davis was interested in soberly reporting, not advertising, America. Least of all did he feel it necessary to convince Americans of anything much. His interest was chiefly in the Domestic Branch of his Office but, within that Branch, chiefly in its news coordination activities. He did not think primarily in terms of audience building or audience attitudes. Like the sound of his voice over the air, his approach to war information was notably undramatic. If people wanted to know things, the things were there to be heard and to be printed. But he was not going to force anything on anybody.

This was his basic orientation. It did not mean that he objected to pamphlets, radio scripts and motion picture production. He accepted them, as important OWI activities from the beginning. It did mean that when he was faced with the necessity of adjustment to Congressional criticism, he abolished the pamphlet program, and admitted freely that he thought informational film production could just as well be turned over to Hollywood altogether.

Whether he would have accomplished more by more forcefully selling these production programs to the appropriations committees is extremely doubtful. The limits on his range of domestic activity were almost oppressive. They included: (1) the general public suspicion of anything that smacked of coercive government war propaganda, (2) the Presidential agreement with that frame of mind, (3) the traditional Congressional suspicion of the Executive Branch and its specific suspicion of any "New Deal" publicity projects which might still be going on in wartime, and (4) the heritage of antipathy borne by Presidential favorites like Lowell Mellett and Archibald MacLeish,[22] who had identified themselves with the domestic information process before Davis arrived on the scene. Add to this his own predilection for straightforward public reporting and for more or less hard-boiled analysis, and even such a liberal critic of affairs as Elmer Davis saw little point in fighting for the right to make pamphlets and documentary films for the domestic audience.

[21] House, 78th Congress 1st Session, National War Agencies Appropriation Bill for 1944, p. 707.

[22] MacLeish seemed to be no more acceptable to the general run of Congressmen and to the more articulate newspapers and pressure groups than was Wallace, though both had practical experience to add to their theories. While MacLeish had not been a farmer, he had practiced law as well as doing some important writing for *Fortune* Magazine as one of its editors. But he was known, of course, as a poet. Even a successful administration of the Library of Congress, eventually admitted by librarians themselves, did not wipe away this stain.

Lowell Mellett and the Domestic Films

For film operations, Davis didn't keep OEM's Robert Horton or OFF's Leo Rosten. He did keep OGR's Lowell Mellett (who was still a Presidential assistant) and Arch Mercey. They became chief and assistant chief of the Bureau of Motion Pictures of the Domestic Branch of the OWI. Besides using motion pictures to "facilitate the development of an informed and intelligent understanding" of the war effort, they were specifically to exercise the Director's duty, as far as motion pictures were concerned, to:

> Review, clear and approve all proposed radio and motion picture programs sponsored by Federal departments and agencies; and serve as the central point of clearance and contact for the radio broadcasting and motion picture industries, respectively, in their relationships with Federal departments and agencies concerning such Government programs.

The production story of the Bureau can be all too quickly told. Arch Mercey reported to the House Appropriations subcommittee on May 20, 1943, that 98 subjects and 110 reels had been released by the OWI. But many of these were converted from films produced by other agencies or private companies. The OWI itself had 27 films made for nontheatrical showings and 19 for commercial theaters.[23]

The titles of the commercial releases are in general no more unexpected than the Creel Committee titles, and just about as self-explanatory: *Salvage, Manpower, Japanese Relocation, Fuel Conservation, Colleges at War, Food for Fighters, Doctors at War, Message from Malta.* Briefer or more urgent wartime messages were offered to the newsreel companies: *Don't Travel, Lend-Lease Report, Farm Manpower, Point Rationing, Meat Rationing, Nurse Recruiting, Rent Control.* Variations in the pattern of short subjects were "regional specials" when specific areas needed to be reached—*Women Wanted, Send Your Tin Cans to War, Get a War Job.*[24]

Two of the most useful films done by OWI Domestic Branch were *War Town* and *Troop Train.* The first reported on the way in which a typical war-boom town, Mobile, Alabama, dealt with its housing and health

---

[23] National War Agencies Appropriation Bill for 1944, pp. 922–942.
[24] This section of the chapter is much indebted to Cedric Larson's article, "Domestic Movies of the OWI," in the *Hollywood Quarterly*, Vol. III, No. 4, 1947–48.

problems. *Troop Train*,[25] suggested to the OWI by the Office of Defense Transportation, showed the transportation of an armed division by rail and was an object-lesson for civilians who might complain about the difficulties of travel; it also appealed to them to give up unnecessary trips.[26]

A picture like *Salvage* served to show men and women who were trying to conserve iron, tin, rubber and fats exactly what was happening to these materials in the war. The need for civilian action on this front was made clear in a way that no speechwriter or speechmaker or newspaper paragrapher could have done it.

All of these theatrical films were subject to the veto of the producers, distributors and exhibitors represented on the War Activities Committee of the Motion Picture Industry. They had to be accepted by a reviewing group which the WAC set up. Starting in January 1943, it was jointly agreed to have 26 government films alternate with 26 industry-produced films for a regular weekly release. The Government supplied 677 prints of its subjects—often produced under the supervision of some other Washington agency—and in turn 16,486 theater owners pledged themselves to include them on their screen programs.[27]

Samuel Spewack was chief of production for the Bureau of Motion Pictures, and he was closely identified with one major undertaking in the first year—a feature-length film. *The World at War* was a compilation of newsreels and other photographic material as a history of 1931–1942. This pattern had been followed by the *March of Time* in a 1940 issue called *The Ramparts We Watch*, a strongly anti-isolationist feature. Spewack's film was accepted by the WAC and widely distributed.

Meanwhile Frank Capra had been hired by the War Department [28] to do the *Why We Fight* series, based on much the same pattern of piece-work, with a propaganda commentary, intended for troops. There was strong support within the Army for releasing the series to the public, and Mellett was asked to submit the idea to the War Activities Committee. He immediately protested. To him, the sound track seemed an affront to

[25] See *Movie Lot to Beachhead*, prepared by the editors of *Look Magazine*, p. 195.

[26] Because of the scattering of wartime personnel and the informal arrangements of wartime production, it is difficult to get accurate information about any film's producer, director and writer or even whether privately produced on government contract or produced by government personnel. The films themselves were likely to credit only the OWI, as the releasing sponsor. The Museum of Modern Art Film Library program, *The Documentary Film 1922–45*, lists *War Town* only as "produced by OWI."

[27] "Desiring to promote the spirit of patriotism among our citizens and to give every support to our government until final victory is attained, I hereby pledge my fullest cooperation in the work of the War Activities Committee Theaters Division of the Motion Picture Industry." *Movies at War*, Reports of the War Activities Committee, 1942–45.

[28] Mellett recalls that he urged Capra not to work for the Government. Stay in Hollywood, he advised, and make those wonderful pictures that mean so much for the entertainment of the war-weary American public. (Interview, October 13, 1950.)

the American people, and besides, it had all been told, as far as the pictures were concerned, in Spewack's movie.

Before the first one, *Prelude to War*, was finally offered to the theater-going public on May 27, 1943, several things happened. Elmer Davis and his chief of the domestic branch, Gardner Cowles, asked Mellett to submit it to the War Activities Committee. The Committee then refused it. A conference was held in Washington, with delegates from the Army and the film industry. According to Mellett, the Army threatened to tell the world that the industry was trying to suppress *Prelude to War*, whereupon Mellett threatened to tell the world that the Army was trying to impose a propaganda film on a free industry. This exchange of subtleties probably didn't influence Davis as much as the fact of his complicated daily relationship with Army people, involving considerable give and take of one sort or another at higher levels of informational policy. The War Activities Committee finally agreed to distribute it, and actually pushed the film with all the simulated enthusiasm they could muster. It was, relatively speaking, a boxoffice failure, and this result supported Mellett's thesis that the subject had already been covered.

A more popular kind of release was the report-from-the-front news film, based on combat footage and organized and edited by Hollywood skill. The first of these was John Ford's *Battle of Midway*. A sequence in this picture about the home life of sailors departing for the battle before it happened, and a thing or two in the sound track, didn't appeal to Mellett. His Indiana frankness and his concern for grassroots politics came into conflict with the Hollywood way of doing things—or at least the way Ford did this particular film.[29] He also felt that Ford had gone back on his word to the newsreels, since they had been promised early footage from battle zones, and Ford had held his footage back to make the unified film.

However right he was about these matters—and as amateur movie-goer he was probably right in feeling that some of the things in *Battle of Midway* were "silly"—the effect of it all closely resembled censorship. He put it on a perfectly sound basis, of course, saying that this was the Government making films—that when the Government speaks to the people there is a different kind of responsibility, dignity and propriety involved—that Hollywood habits of production were not necessarily suited to the needs of a Government-public relationship. But what he actually did was to sit in a projection room and pick out shots that ought to be cut or changed. No amount of making enemies in the Pentagon by fighting battles for Hollywood could make up for the enemies he made in Hollywood by picking

[29] Released September 14, 1943. (*Movies at War, op. cit.*) He also pointed out to the director that his documentary didn't indicate who won the battle of Midway, whereupon Ford added a kind of scoreboard at the end and made clear that the U.S. had done the job.

flaws in films. It was a small-time kind of operation, and demonstrated his lack of skill at larger administrative tasks. He had never made a film, nor had been responsible for exhibiting films commercially or educationally, and therefore carried little weight in Hollywood. As far as the Government was concerned, he carried little weight with Congress, certainly: his very sensible idea of building a central Information Center for small business-men and others visiting Washington was a project well-known in the capital as "Mellett's Madhouse."

Where he did carry weight, aside from a network of old friends in administrative agencies, was with Franklin Roosevelt. Even this didn't help him with *Midway*, because John Ford had his picture shown at the White House before Mellett was aware of what was going on, and Roose-velt's enthusiasm for the movie swept everything else aside. He wanted to get Secretary Frank Knox to release it at once. Nor did it help in the case of John Huston's *Report from the Aleutians*, which Mellett was quite rightly convinced was too long—at least for a release date so long after the events depicted. He declares he "fought it out for months"—which didn't help the release date any (July 30, 1943)—but was finally defeated.

In these cases, Hollywood was not involved *in toto* since these were simply Hollywood directors at work for the Army and Navy, and there were some producers who supported Mellett's position. But concurrent with all this was a running battle on a broader scale over the content of Hollywood-made pictures. As Coordinator of Films, Mellett had taken seriously his instructions to "consult with and advise motion picture producers of ways and means in which they can most usefully serve in the national effort." [30] His appointment of Nelson Poynter as West Coast representative was a conscious attempt to keep Hollywood at bay—not the industry viewpoint but the government viewpoint was the important thing, and that rationale had much to recommend it.

After a year, however, he found that "considerable confusion seems to exist among motion picture producers regarding Government channels." In a letter to the heads of the studios, dated December 9, 1942, he said "it would be advisable" for copies of synopses and of finished scripts to be turned over to the Hollywood office of OWI.

> We should also like to set up as a routine procedure an arrangement whereby our Hollywood office might view all pictures in the long cut. While this is rather late in the operation to introduce any new matter it would make it possible for us to recommend the deletion of any material which might be harmful to the war effort.

This rather sweeping proposal, however harmless it seemed to him, looked like pretty close supervision to the producers. There were immedi-ate and widespread protests. He wrote another letter in May 1943 protest-

[30] Presidential letter December 18, 1941.

ing in turn that he had been misunderstood, that the producers were "completely free to disregard any of our views or suggestions."

> We have no authority enabling us to force our views upon them and have never desired any such authority. In effect our operation is largely one of keeping producers informed of wartime problems and conscious of possible implications of proposed pictures or details of pictures. There is nothing in any part of our operation that can possibly be construed as censorship.[31]

But the damage was done, and Walter Wanger wrote in the *Public Opinion Quarterly* at the time of the controversy: "The OWI shows a growing desire *to write things into* scripts. Indeed, there is a mounting urge to dominate production. The officials moving in this direction are not equipped by any past relation to the motion picture industry." Wanger went on to say, in effect: We have better film ideas than the bureaucrats have, and better notions, furthermore, of what makes good propaganda. This might be a matter of opinion, but it was a matter of fact that Mellett and Mercey and Poynter were, relatively speaking, amateurs.[32]

Any judgment on Mellett's judgment in these matters must be tempered by the realization that he actually had a job which did not fit him well. He was a newspaperman, even as Elmer Davis was, and shrank from any role that looked like a censor.[33] He thought everybody was aware of his attitude, and when he offered suggestions they were to feel free to act on them or not. Yet he had his enthusiasms and his revulsions, and when he felt a thing was "right" he was capable of fighting over it "for months." Those close to him confirm this strong sense of fairness; his loyalty and integrity and honesty were apparent to those who dealt with him on a personal level. His extraordinary capacity for amassing opposition, however, was even more apparent to those who dealt with him otherwise. He was a serious handicap to the Domestic Branch of the OWI.

Elmer Davis found it hard to defend film production by the government. Beset by attacks on the pamphlet program (which he had just abolished in anticipation of further Congressional objection), harried by inquiries as to the political affiliation of himself and his staff,[34] compelled to point out laboriously that the Hollywood feature film *Mission to Moscow*

---

[31] See House hearings for 1944, pp. 937–38.

[32] "The Office of War Information and Motion Pictures," Vol. VII, No. 1, 1943. Mellett claimed that Wanger originally wanted to be the OWI representative in Hollywood.

[33] See especially "Government Propaganda," his article in the *Atlantic*, September 1941, in which he said that the free American press associations were the best propaganda weapon.

[34] Senator Styles Bridges (R., N.H.) asked the question. Davis at the time was a member of the American Labor Party. Milton Eisenhower, it developed, was a Republican, as was Palmer Hoyt, then Domestic Director, and Robert Sherwood had voted both Democratic and Republican.

was not sponsored by the OWI, Davis had to make choices as to what he would fight for.

In the House hearings, Arch Mercey was asked: "Why do we have to produce these films? Why cannot they all be produced by private industry?" His reply stated the important difference between the Hollywood alternate weekly messages, distributed under the title *America Speaks*, and the factual, documentary approach of most of the other producers chosen to make films for the Bureau of Motion Pictures:

> The *America Speaks* series . . . are photographed in restricted areas, made by actors as story films, and made on sound stages. The war information films made by the Federal Government require camera crews to go out into the field and cover war activities in the actual area of operations.[35]

The difference between glamor-coated entertainment pills with a message hidden inside and a straight message, with pictures and reasons, was an important difference. It was the difference Lowell Mellett meant when he talked about the dignity of the government-public relationship. It was the difference between *Prices Unlimited*, in which a beautiful girl had a bad dream after planning to beat the price-fixing regulations, and *Which Way This Time?*, an Office of Price Administration film which soberly traced the history of inflation and pointed out the special danger after a war is over.

But it was not a distinction which carried much meaning for members of Congress. When Elmer Davis was asked in the Senate hearings, "Now what is the necessity for the Motion Picture Division?" he simply replied, referring to war message films: "The present arrangement of our making half of them works very well. . . . Certainly on this matter of production, the industry could do it." [36] And after June, 1943, the industry did do it, in its own way, making some and distributing others which were made and released by the armed services. The Domestic Branch, cut from $7-million to $2-million, became "what it had been in some degree theretofore—a staff operation, coordinating the information activities not only of Government agencies but of private interests which contribute their effort to the furtherance of the Government's war programs." [37] The Bureau of Motion Pictures was allotted $50,000.

On October 18, 1943, Stanton Griffis, an investment banker and chairman of the executive committee of Paramount Pictures in New York,

[35] Some of the earlier subjects: *Letter from Bataan* (Paramount) on the need for conserving food and materials; *Everybody's War* (Twentieth-Century Fox) on the contribution of a small American city; *Plan for Destruction* (MGM), a reenactment of Haushofer's geopolitical plan for conquest; *Men Working Together* (Columbia), a dramatization of a wartime poster showing workers and soldiers.

[36] Senate, 78th Congress 1st Session, National War Agencies Appropriation Bill for 1944, p. 230, June 26, 1943.

[37] Elmer Davis, House hearings, 78th Congress, 2d Session, National War Agencies Appropriation Bill for 1945, p. 4.

joined OWI's Domestic Branch as chief of the Bureau of Motion Pictures, to serve without compensation.

Nontheatrical Distribution

Films had been released in 16mm form for nontheatrical groups before the OWI was formed; the OEM information office was active in this, as can be seen in the announcements in *Education for Victory*, the wartime title of the Office of Education weekly.[38] For OWI, the first chief of the Nontheatrical Division of the Bureau of Motion Pictures was Paul C. Reed, of the Rochester Board of Education, later editor of *Educational Screen*. In August of 1942 regular monthly newsletters started going out to distributors of OWI films. In the first issue, the following was approvingly quoted from a local educational film dealer:

> It is not only a patriotic duty to show these films to your usual audience, but the Federal Government expects all owners of 16 millimeter sound equipment to contribute to the war effort by exhibiting films to local civic, labor, fraternal and social organizations. . . . Donate your equipment and a few extra hours of time to help disseminate information vital to our war effort.

The states varied in their response during the year the Domestic Branch was in full operation, but a divisional memorandum (May 20, 1943) covering the month of March 1943, showed "33 films plus four song shorts in active use, handled by 168 distributors of 16 millimeter films, who had 9,448 prints in circulation and reported a total of 21,316 bookings, with an estimated total of 46,895 showings and an audience of 7,165,555 American men, women and children."

Among the films made available to dealers and educational libraries were such titles as *Lake Carrier, Anchors Aweigh, Winning Your Wings* (with James Stewart), *The Arm Behind the Army, Campus on the March, The Price of Victory, Japanese Relocation, Henry Browne Farmer, The Spirit of 1943* (with Donald Duck), *Out of the Frying Pan and Into the Firing Line* (another Disney production), *Letter from Bataan, Troop Train, Jap Zero*. There were several U.S. News Reviews and one or two British items like *Target for Tonight* and *Listen to Britain*.

In November of 1942 there was a meeting in Washington of 30 distributors and a number of representatives from various government agencies. The talk was of better community organization, more publicity and

---

[38] See especially March 16, 1942, p. 16; May 15, 1942, p. 32; June 1, 1942, p. 32. See also April 1, 1942, p. 8 for Office of Civilian Defense film called *Fighting the Fire Bomb*, which was available from regional OCD offices in the number of 420 prints.

locating still more usable movie projectors. This conference foreshadowed the time a year later when it was up to the private groups to carry on the work of the Motion Picture Bureau.

It was in August of 1943 that the newsletter announced that the Bureau had actually received $50,000 from Congress instead of $1,250,000. Paul Reed resigned, and only five out of the staff of 23 remained in the Nontheatrical Division. C. R. Reagan, a widely-known film dealer from Austin, Texas, and a former president of the National Association of Visual Education Dealers who had been an OWI field adviser, now became head of the division.

Reagan and Stanton Griffis brought together a Sixteen Millimeter Advisory and Policy Committee representing distributors, librarians, and educators.[39] Cooperation was pledged in distributing whatever films other Government agencies might turn out, but it was clear enough that the problem would be to find enough good pictures to fill the now-developed demand. One of the first responses to the need came from the New York State War Film Advisory Council, which "recommended that all existing resources be canvassed for assistance in producing films specifically needed in New York. Any of such films would be made available to such agencies as OWI and OCD for national distribution." [40] The New York Office of War Training promptly produced three movies: *Fit to Fight on All Fronts* (about physical fitness), *Care for Children of Working Mothers*, and *What of Your Child?* (recruiting assistants for child care centers).

For the most part, however, the coordinators were reduced to pointing out what the Hollywood War Activities Committee was doing—"be sure to see *Tunisian Victory* at your neighborhood theater"—and distributing what few of the short subjects were put on 16mm. Increasingly, motion pictures sponsored by other allied countries now took the spotlight in American club, church and schoolroom gatherings. The National Film Board of Canada provided 200 prints of *Sicily: Key to Victory*, which showed the Canadian First Division in action. *New Soldiers Are Tough* told the story of a British commando raid. *The Dutch Tradition*, directed by John Ferno, was distributed here by the Netherlands Information Bureau.[41]

[39] L. C. Larsen, chairman of the Educational Film Library Association; W. K. Hedwig of the Allied Nontheatrical Film Association; Mary U. Rothrock, chairman of the audio-visual aids committee of the American Library Association; J. M. Stackhouse of the National Audio-Visual Education Dealers; Bertram Willoughby, of the National War Committee for Visual Education in Industry; George B. Zahmer, of the National University Extension Association; Camilla Best of the Department of Visual Instruction of the National Education Association; O. H. Coelln, Jr., editor of *Business Screen*.

[40] Newsletter to Distributors of OWI Films, January, 1944.

[41] Not until April of 1945 was it arranged for OWI Overseas Branch documentary productions to be available for sale in this country; these were not war message films but would have served earlier as pride-of-country background. In April, too, it was

Meanwhile Taylor Mills had succeeded Griffis as head of the Bureau. In the final letter, which he and Reagan sent out to the educators and the librarians and the private dealers, it was stated that 77,387 prints of 177 subjects had been released, in the 37 months of OWI operations, through 324 official OWI film distributors for more than a million showings to audiences aggregating 275,000,000.

OWI Overseas: Telling the Story of America

The Overseas Branch of the Office of War Information, which received $24-million even when the Domestic Branch was getting $7-million,[42] had a much easier time of it with the appropriations committees in Congress. Agreement on the use of information as a weapon abroad was strong and substantial, where agreement on the use of information for understanding at home was scattered and doubtful.

One of the biggest arguments Elmer Davis could offer was the feverish activity of our enemies. Robert Sherwood, Director of the Overseas Branch, pointed out as an example that the Germans had at least several hundred people in Turkey just for propaganda purposes, with only one of their six specialized services spending $11,100 a month. The Germans were flooding Europe with hourly newscasts and good music. They were sending to Sweden 30,000 copies of the magazine *Signal* and 50,000 of *German Voices*, with free pamphlets, advertising, window displays, lecturers, scientific propaganda and fashion shows all contributing to the general air of inspired friendliness. The Japanese, for their part, were operating 46 radio stations, using numerous Chinese and Indian dialects as well as their own and European languages.

It was necessary to compete with that sort of thing, and Congress directed Elmer Davis to do so. There was considerable vague enthusiasm for "psychological warfare" and remarks in the hearings from time to time showed that members of Congress considered this kind of activity a worthwhile investment. They listened with much interest when Edward Barrett, executive director, reported on work he saw while he was in the Mediter-

announced that the War Department's industrial incentive films could be released through the OWI's nontheatrical division.

[42] See House hearings, 78th Congress 2d Session, National War Agencies Appropriation Bill for 1945, p. 40, April 19, 1944; Domestic Branch actual expenditures for 1943, $7,625,203; estimated for 1944, 2,407,109; requested for 1945, $2,464,633. Of the 1944 sum, $295,335 was for liquidation of programs in the Domestic Branch, and $49,861 for motion pictures. Overseas Branch actual expenditures for 1943, $24,716,561; estimated for 1944, $33,366,070; requested for 1945, $59,562,101. Of the 1944 amount, $1,285,873 was for motion pictures; of the 1945, $1,640,328.

ranean area for a visit. The OWI rebuilt radio stations, wrote and edited leaflets under field conditions and packed them into shells, issued instructions to the populace for a complete evacuation of Naples during tests for booby traps, adapted transmitters overnight to enable immediate broadcasting of the surrender message to the Italian fleet. Leaflets distributed by the millions, urging Germans to surrender, were written and printed by the OWI. The base in Britain, built up for this and other psychological warfare operations, grew from 160 persons in July 1943, to about 900 the following year.[43]

Besides impressing the minds of our enemies with our ideas and our might, there was the necessity of keeping the confidence of our allies and of the neutral countries. The OWI sent news abroad via all kinds of cable and wireless to its own offices and to embassies and consulates—100,000 total words daily to 22 leading cities—and produced a varied list of periodicals and booklets, including a magazine digest called U.S.A. The Voice of America, introduced by the jaunty strains of "Yankee Doodle," was a familiar voice to foreign listeners of many languages—in 1944 the New York office put out about 2,000 programs a week, and 850 originated on the West Coast.

Here, as in the Domestic Branch, the emphasis was on news, on facts, on "the strategy of truth." Like the massiveness of the American military attack, the propaganda attack was conceived on the basis of weight and repetition. It was a matter of satisfaction to report that whereas the Turkish press touched on U.S. activities only five per cent of the time in the earlier days, the proportion shifted by 1944, so that 50 per cent of the foreign news in Turkey could be traced to the Office of War Information.

> As the committee knows, our operations outside the United States fall into two classes—those in friendly or neutral countries, where we operate under the general jurisdiction of the State Department, exercised through its embassies and legations; and those in theaters of war, where we are under the control of the military commanders. . . . It is the job of the OWI in these friendly and neutral countries to keep continually before the public eye the power and strength of the United States, to keep the peoples informed of our great and increasing contribution to the United Nations war efforts on all fronts; and to assure them that the war aims of the United States, as laid down in authoritative statements of both the Executive and the Congress, are such as will conduce to the eventual good of the entire world. . . .
>
> This country was not founded and has not been conducted on the theory that ignorance is bliss; and we are confident enough in the

[43] Of this number about 60% were locally hired. *Ibid.*, pp. 66–67. Barrett remarked that the OWI people often worked 79 and 80 hours a week, well-convinced that they were actually shortening the war. If they only shortened the war by four and three-fourths hours, he added, it would cover the OWI appropriation.

quality of American life to believe that on the whole, the more foreign peoples know about us, the more highly they will respect us.[44]

Film was pre-eminently a longer-term propaganda weapon, directed only toward areas under American control or areas which were friendly or neutral. Certainly films were used close to combat areas:

When the first patrols enter any city or town, we must be prepared to move in and take over the local press and radio stations and operate them in the local language. We must have motion pictures ready, and posters and publications of all kinds.

We have now stockpiled in Great Britain 6,178 reels of motion picture films. They include straight entertainment (selected products of the Hollywood industry) and educational and news films of all kinds and in all European languages.[45]

But the dominant and continuing purpose of film production by the Overseas Branch was the indirect support of the armed forces and the foreign policy of the United States by telling the story of America to its friends and acquaintances. The big question here, of course, as in the presentation of news itself, was: What parts of the story should be told? The truth, yes—but should it be the whole truth? Or merely nothing but the truth? The whole truth might conceivably include *The Plow That Broke the Plains*—a film not contrived to inspire confidence in the great bread-basket of the American plains. At the same time it was clear that the available Hollywood product was an entertainment product and as such was not made for the purpose of giving a balanced picture of the American way of life.

Therefore, in addition to the *Magazine of the Screen* (a monthly release of very short subjects) and the distribution of Army and Navy and other government films wherever they seemed appropriate, the OWI made documentaries. Sherwood chose Frank Capra's screenwriter, Robert Riskin,

[44] Ibid., pp. 3–13, statement by Elmer Davis.

Wallace Carroll (*Persuade or Perish*, pp. 236–37) has an interesting comment on the conflict between psychological warfare and informational programs within the OWI itself: "Our desire was to speak frankly and honestly to our allies in the occupied countries and to the people of the neutral nations. But at times we could do this only by going counter to our psychological warfare and propaganda aims. . . . If we told the whole truth to the Continent, we would at times encourage the Germans and discourage our friends. . . . I mention this conflict mainly to demonstrate the fallacy in the widespread belief that the propagandist's choice is between truth and falsehood. . . . Our real difficulties came over a choice between giving the news and withholding it . . . between the urge to inform and the passion to save lives, between common honesty and plain humanity."

[45] Letter from London by Robert Sherwood, quoted in House hearings, *ibid.*, pp. 68–69, and dated April 14, 1944. Samuel Spewack had gone to London after the demise of the Domestic Branch Motion Picture Bureau to head the film section of the OWI office there. Spewack arranged showings of the Capra *Why We Fight* series and also brought Capra to London to collaborate with the British on the feature *Tunisian Victory*.

as head of the Motion Picture Bureau. The budget justifications for the 1944 appropriation described the need this way:

> Commercial pictures distributed in neutral and allied nations have given only a partial and often not very serious idea of Americans and the American scene. . . . The Bureau of Overseas Motion Pictures is attempting to spread the true facts about America through the motion picture without destroying the entertainment value of the media.[46]

Sherwood expanded on this in an exchange with John Taber (R., N.Y.) during the hearings:

> Mr. Sherwood: They are films of American life such as are not being made today. We have tried to find them. . . . There has been too much emphasis on Hollywood luxury and swimming pools—
>
> Mr. Taber: Glamor.
>
> Mr. Sherwood: "Glamor" is the right word. We are trying to do some deglamorizing. . . . I may say that in North Africa I was ashamed of the showing that this country was making on the screen. All of the great documentary pictures were made by the British— *Desert Victory* and *Target for Tonight*, for example, are excellent pictures of the British war effort. And we, the greatest motion picture producing country in the world, were represented by films which indicated that we were taking no serious interest in the war and had no interest in anything but frivolity and luxury.

Wallace Carroll, who directed psychological warfare operations and was chief of the London office, wrote in his book *Persuade or Perish*:

> We could easily have used a hundred straight informational films about the United States and its part in the war. There were none. . . . The American film companies in London had two hundred gangster films in their vaults, but not one film about the Tennessee Valley Authority. The crowds that stormed a London theater to see the stirring Soviet documentary film, *One Day of War*, were also treated to a Hollywood film *Orchestra Wives*, which told the story of a touring jazz band and the petty rivalries among the wives of its members.[47]

Sherwood felt fairly certain that Robert Riskin of Hollywood would not continue the glamorizing that Hollywood had been guilty of. Riskin had joined the staff of the British Ministry of Information in London long before Pearl Harbor and had absorbed a good deal of their approach to the making of wartime films for government purposes. Before that he had been

[46] *Ibid.*, pp. 792–797.
[47] P. 140.

an independent producer in Hollywood for a short while.[48] He chose Philip Dunne, another Hollywood production executive, as chief of production for the bureau. But the people they used for the making of pictures during the next three years were the documentary people. The story of the intricate disputations and difficulties involved in coming to agreement about film purposes and film techniques is a story that need not be told here, even if all the facts were available. But the overseas need for movies which soberly described lesser-known facts about American life, the whole wartime atmosphere of diligent attention to practical needs, and the slender but firm tradition of documentary method itself, all combined to achieve a remarkable series of films.

Dunne later wrote an article for the *Hollywood Quarterly* which not only described the way they worked, but reflected his developed understanding of the documentary method and incidentally revealed the difficulty of achieving its goals in a democratic society. The usual crew in the field was small, he explained, including some eight men with a station wagon and light truck, a few lights and two cameras. At the operational peak, in the summer of 1944, there were five such units. The pictures they took were pictures of real people, doing what they commonly did. The director's job was to "cast" these amateurs, change the script to fit the situations he found, and find the best photographic way of explaining the general idea intended in the film as planned:

> Documentary scripts are usually simple affairs, allowing the director plenty of leeway for substitution or invention in the field. They are notably devoid of "situations," melodrama, or suspense developed from plot devices, or from intricate interrelations between characters.

But at the same time, the narration, which is apt to be "simple, sparse, often poetic," may in turn "suggest changes in the editing of the film. Words and image can thus be dovetailed and emerge . . . as an artistic entity." [49]

The excitement in such a motion picture does not necessarily come, therefore, from character clash or a fast-moving chase. It is more likely to come from some kind of a menace, such as the floods in the Tennessee Valley or the sputtering airplane motor and the fog in *Target for Tonight*. For a documentary to be fully effective, "the audience must be *for* one thing, *against* something else."

This last statement brings the very heart of the problem of the government documentary into the open, and shows why the films which were

---

[48] Interview, Robert Sherwood, October 19, 1950. Fortunately, although Riskin could claim much of the success of *It Happened One Night*, *Mr. Deeds Goes to Town* and other Capra films, he was not around when *Mr. Smith Goes to Washington* was made, and could tell the Congressmen so.

[49] "The Documentary and Hollywood," January, 1946.

about the war itself had more to offer in the way of excitement. On the war itself there was agreement among ourselves and among our allies. We were *for* one thing, *against* something else. Physical and technological obstacles were to be conquered, and after that, the Nazis and the Japanese. But more complicated matters of loyalty, including questions of public policy, expositions of the American way of life, the meaning of economic institutions—these things were not provided with broad public agreement on menace and promise, what to be against and what to be for. There were plenty of facts on different sides, if you were studying them, and plenty of people and interested groups on different sides, if you were acting on them. If you set out to be excited and interested, you were likely to turn up on one of the sides of the question.

This was impossible for the Office of War Information. Congress would not permit it, in the first place, and was in any case already very touchy about all information sent overseas about Roosevelt, as "propaganda for a fourth term" (regardless of the fact that the people overseas were quite powerless to vote on that subject). But it was also true that the OWI was supposed to represent a nation united in purposes, not a nation divided and disputing, turning aside from the main task of fighting shoulder to shoulder with her allies in order to carry on arguments about the wage level or the housing shortage. This meant that the whole truth was not to be told. *The Plow* was not on the program. Disagreement was not to be aired. Insofar as documentary film might deal with the very heart of the freedom which democracy provides, it was not a part of the schedule of the Office of War Information.

It is not surprising to find, then, that there is not much excitement in the OWI documentaries. At the same time there is in them much truth about the American way of life, truth which goes beyond the incidental knowledge gained from Hollywood films, which were up to that time dedicated primarily to excitement. The whole story of America is not in the newspaper headlines or the newsreels of disasters or the gangster movies. The story of America is also the story of *The Town*, directed by Josef von Sternberg, a film which described in "simple, sparse" language and straightforward pictures an average midwestern town, with its mixed population, its differing religions, its many styles of architecture, all carrying on certain cultural traditions from the old world into a free synthesis of live-and-let-live.

Some were more laborious than others. *Library of Congress* was basically a lecture illustrated by still photographs. *Cowboy* attempted to show that not all the fellows who were at home on the range lived exactly as Hollywood depicted them. Even such a widely-heralded picture as *Hymn of the Nations*,[50] enthusiastically received in Italy as a kind of message

50 Produced, as was *Library of Congress*, by Irving Lerner, and directed by Alexander Hackenschmied (1944). *Cowboy* was produced by Willard Van Dyke (1943).

Frame enlargement from *The Town* (Dir. Josef von Sternberg) for OWI, 1941

from Arturo Toscanini to a people oppressed, was exciting only in its brilliantly recorded and pictured orchestral music; the single unimaginative scene in the great conductor's living room as he plods obediently across the path of the camera from chair to phonograph can only be described as painful.

For the most part the pictures sent overseas were earnest, honest efforts to pin down some part of the American scene in terms that could be understood by audiences of varying literacy and background. They ranged from the oversimplification of the electoral system in *Tuesday in November* to a detective picture called *Capital Story*, wherein Public Health Service tracing of a harmful ingredient in a shipbuilding process illustrates the relationship of government to the individual. They included a Hollywood approach in *Swedes in America*—the first film made by the Overseas Branch—and documentary re-enactment in *The Cummington Story*, which taught a lesson about the acceptance of refugees in a rural New England town.[51]

[51] Other titles: *City Harvest, Steel Town, A Journey, Social Security, Northwest U.S.A., Madame Chiang Kai-Shek, Song of Arabia, Yellow Springs, Oswego Story,*

In *Valley of the Tennessee*,[52] there were evidences of conflict, of something to fight against. Both the "destruction from the sky" and the human apathy in the face of rain-gutted lands could be met and changed by the "new pioneers"—the experts—and by "reason, science and education." The theme is brought out that the "individual through cooperation with his fellows becomes a more important individual." But the story is marred by a hypersentimental manipulation of characters, who seem to be moving through molasses. The perseverance of Henry Clark in cooperating with the TVA agricultural representative, and the final winning over of a jeering neighbor, are no more unexpected than the rain, and certainly far from exciting.

There were three smaller OWI pictures which can be said to be un-qualified successes. They were successful because they dealt familiarly and proudly with technology, not humanity.

Pipeline told the story of the bringing of oil from Texas, "thousands of miles away from the United Nations campaigns" to the East Coast. The ditch for the pipeline—"three feet wide, four feet deep, 1,400 miles long; greater than London to Leningrad"—is dug by enormous machines but also by a "team of men working together, each respecting each other's skill." In the Alleghenies, the Big Inch starts uphill: the rock fights back, then the spring floods and the mud, and the icy Susquehanna. When finally "the draglines and throwbuckets put baby to bed," you know something about what it took to add 300,000 barrels of oil every day to the American seaboard stockpile. You have also had a taste of American soil and American muscle.

Autobiography of a Jeep was in a different key.[53] A friendly, whimsical voice remarks, "I come from a country of roads—place called the United States of America." (The camera displays roads, clover-leaf intersections, cars.) "Because of the automobile, Americans who live a hundred miles from each other are as close as next door." With the coming war, however, a new kind of vehicle was needed—and "this is what comes out!" (The new jeep is skeptically inspected by GI's.) " 'Can this be an auto-mobile?' men wondered. 'Looks more like a four-wheeled beetle!' Then they tried to break my back on roller-coaster roads." (The jeep goes on maneuvers, through mud, through fences, onto airplanes. It is seen towing airplanes, too, and cannon.) "Lucky I was only 200 pounds heavy . . .

People to People, A Better Tomorrow, Freedom to Learn, Salute to France, French Journalists Tour U.S., San Francisco (about the UN Conference).

Tuesday in November was directed by John Houseman; *Capital Story* was pro-duced and written by Irving Jacoby and directed by Henwar Rodakiewicz; *The Cum-mington Story* was directed by Helen Grayson and Larry Madison (1945).

Swedes in America starred Ingrid Bergman. Sherwood said that this film was well-received in many parts of the world—but not in Norway.

[52] Produced in 1944 by Alexander Hackenschmied, who later shortened his name to Hammid.

[53] Produced and written by Joseph Krumgold in 1943.

Frame Enlargement from *Autobiography of a Jeep* (Dir. Joseph Krumgold) for OWI, 1943

lucky I was 60 horsepower strong. . . . All of a sudden I found myself in mass production. I was a success!" And despite all kinds of popularity at war bond rallies and with such big shots as General MacArthur, King George VI, and President Roosevelt (at Casablanca), it is "my pal the soldier" who matters most. Whatever demands were made, they were "no worse than what my driver was willing to do himself. . . . The jeep is here to stay!"

At Cherbourg, when the ruins were still smoking and the peninsula was still not secure, the OWI showed a feature, a newsreel and *The Autobiography of a Jeep*. The jubilant, liberated Frenchmen, touched by the warm humanity of this little film about a quarter-ton of metal and motor, burst into shouts of "Vive le jip! Vive le jip!" [54]

Another very short one, brought out in 1945, should also be mentioned. Perceptive, humorous, and altogether memorable, *The Window Cleaner* [55] followed the doings of a man who washes skyscraper windows for a living. We share the dangers of this work, meet a few of the people he

[54] Interview, Robert Sherwood, October 19, 1950.
[55] Directed and photographed by Jules Bucher; written by Joseph March.

Frame enlargement from *The Window Cleaner* (Dir. Jules Bucher) OWI, 1945

meets during the day at the Empire State building, and at the end, back on the ground again, he directs our gaze up some 30 or 40 dizzy stories, remarking, "They look pretty good, don't they?"

It might be that in later years and under more favorable circumstances documentaries about American life would be made in which human beings played a more notable and persuasive role—documentaries surmounting the inherent difficulties of a basically silent film with separate narrative and sound track. For the OWI both the technical and political limitations were too great, and probably the experience of the documentary people still too small, to achieve a first-rate series of non-fiction films.

It is impossible to avoid a kind of self-congratulatory gloss in movies which had the purpose these movies had, no matter how much Sherwood and Riskin desired to avoid bragging salesmanship. The comment about them by Walter Davenport, in an otherwise inadequate article, demands to be quoted, for its malicious fun hits near the truth:

> They are aimed at teaching the Pacific islanders, the Hindus, the Arabs and others, that we are, after all, a homey, industrious and even folksy people and not a nation of mobsters, wolves and penthouse slickers, Hollywood to the contrary.

Anyone sitting through them will behold us fighting boll weevils, diligently planting Victory gardens, pushing buttons in magical transparent kitchens, turning out jeeps at the rate of one a minute, virtuously going to church and throwing picnics under large elm trees.[56]

But there also needs to be quoted the following from Elmer Davis' reply two weeks later:

Mr. Davenport speaks of our "overseas ballyhoo" and says that "much of it is straight evangelism, shy of facts but long on emotion." A Republican member of Congress who inspected an entire day's output of our New York Radio Bureau complained, on the other hand, that there was nothing in it but straight news—no propaganda. Our critics agree that we are wrong, but I wish they might come a little closer to agreement as to which way we are wrong.[57]

The fact remained, as far as motion pictures were concerned, that the OWI managed to distribute overseas in an average of 17 languages some 30 or 40 original documentary films, besides monthly screen magazines, other newsreels and various Hollywood-made feature pictures (where commercial arrangements were not yet set up). Within the limits of their foreign policy purpose, the documentaries represented a steady advance beyond the scattered efforts of the 1930's, and were a credit to their writers, directors and producers—men like Willard Van Dyke, Irving Jacoby, Henwar Rodakiewicz, Alexander Hackenschmied, Irving Lerner and Joseph Krumgold. Before World War II nobody had ever consciously set out to tell the world in a series of films what it was like to live in America.

Inter-American Films

A consistent effort to do a similar job had been made by Julien Bryan —educator, explorer and film-maker—for the Coordinator of Inter-American Affairs in his so-called Ohio series. However, his films about the U.S. are less memorable than his work in telling Americans what it's like to live south of the border. The CIAA also deserves fame in the film world for two other activities—the educational cartoons of Walt Disney, and its vigorous exhibition policy carried through by the use of traveling shows.

Established by an executive order of the Council of National Defense

56 "Free Speech and Mr. Davis," *Collier's*, June 3, 1944.
57 "Reply to 'Free Speech and Mr. Davis,'" June 17, 1944.

on August 16, 1940, with Nelson Rockefeller as its head, the CIAA was for a long time primarily concerned with commercial and financial problems of the Latin American countries.[58] But the stepping up of defense preparations and the arrival on the scene of the Board of Economic Warfare meant that the CIAA was more and more identified with cultural relationships. It was a war information agency and, but for the strenuous efforts of Rockefeller himself to keep South America separate as an area for cultural exchange, the Budget Bureau would have combined the agency with the others under the OWI.

Rockefeller's first visit to South America was in 1935, when he went to Venezuela to see a Museum of Modern Art. Active in the support of the Museum of Modern Art in New York, he became its head in 1939. His interests in foreign relations were early developed in his work in the foreign department of the Chase National Bank, and he was familiar with the health activities of the Rockefeller Foundation in Latin American republics.

The Motion Picture Division, set up in October, was placed under the guidance of John Hay Whitney, Vice-President of the Museum of Modern Art and President of the Film Library, who received for his services a dollar a year. A battery of committees was set up in Hollywood to help the people out there understand the problems of relationships with South America, and much success was achieved over the years in preventing irritating things from cropping up in films about the South American countries and customs. The industry also provided many services without charge, including rights to a large number of short subjects, and produced shorts on "hemisphere subjects" for release both here and abroad.[59]

An important item was the agreement on the part of U.S. distributors to withdraw all U.S. films from theater operators who showed Axis films. This was a major achievement in the informational war, and had immediate effects, especially in the showing of newsreels; except in Argentina, German and Japanese newsreels ceased to be generally shown. As a result it was increasingly necessary for the CIAA to provide other materials, and in cooperation with five major newsreel companies, a great many new kinds of events were covered—matters of larger consequence than fiestas and carnivals, on the one side of the border, and the latest speed boat race on the other.

[58] The *History of the Office of the Coordinator of Inter-American Affairs* provides a fairly detailed story of the origin of the CIAA, as well as considerable background on conflicting information agencies of all kinds in the war period, though it is extremely weak on the titles of films.

The idea of exchanging films about Latin America and about the U.S. was a familiar one in the U.S. Film Service, sponsored especially by George Gercke, and encouraged by Sumner Welles in the State Department.

[59] By 1943 about 60 of them, according to the *History*, p. 77: *Viva Mexico, Highway to Friendship, Gaucho Sports, Madero of Mexico, Der Fuehrer's Face, Cuba—Land of Romance and Adventure, Price of Victory*, etc.

As chief of production, Whitney first appointed Kenneth Macgowan, well-known Hollywood production executive and former editor of *Theater Arts Monthly*.

> In accordance with the general plan of the Motion Picture Division, actual operations were to be carried out under contract by the Film Library, Inc., of the Museum of Modern Art of New York. Under the direction of CIAA the Library was to: (1) maintain a comprehensive catalog of all available nontheatrical films suitable for the purpose desired; (2) gather special films from all sources; (3) review them; (4) cut and edit them as necessary; (5) arrange for sound-tracking in Spanish and Portuguese; (6) distribute these prints for showing in other American republics; and (7) arrange for the production of new films where these seemed necessary because of a lack of existing films which were appropriate. In addition, the Library was to serve as the medium for purchasing of suitable film on nontheatrical subjects in the other American republics and arrange for their distribution in the United States.[60]

Since production was last on the priority list, and the newsreels and Hollywood relationships took up a good deal of time in the first year, it is not surprising that the making of documentary films did not begin for a while. By this time Macgowan had left, and Francis Alstock was head of the Motion Picture Division in place of Whitney.[61] Even by the latter part of 1942 there was no production unit; Philip Dunne, who had succeeded Macgowan, grew impatient and went over to OWI, taking Willard Van Dyke with him. Meanwhile the Division had taken over the film called *The Bridge*, which Van Dyke and Ben Maddow had made in South America under the earlier sponsorship of the Sloan Foundation—a film about trade and transportation relationships among the Americas.

But when Julien Bryan was finally adopted as the mainstay of the CIAA film program, a veritable stream of motion pictures began to issue from South America. This traveler and educational film producer undertook to cover practically every geographical area of any difference or consequence in the southern part of the hemisphere. Not often inspired in his use of the camera or the sound-track, he nevertheless accomplished a film reporting job which had not been equalled up to that time. From *Americans All*, a general plea for an understanding of individuals who were shown moving to and fro at various occupations (in obvious and awkward stock-shot situations) to the specialized intimacy of *Brazil's Fishing School* or *Montevideo Family*, Bryan covered the gamut.[62]

[60] *Ibid.*, p. 71.
[61] Interview, Kenneth Macgowan, July, 1949.
[62] Some more titles: *Argentine Primer, Atacama Desert, Bolivia, Brazil, Brazil Gets the News, Brazilian Quartz, Buenos Aires, Columbia, Cuernavaca, Down Where the North Begins, Fiesta of the Hills, Fundo in Chile, Good Neighbor Family, Guadelajara, Hill Towns of Guatemala, Introduction to Haiti, La Paz, Lima Family, Mexico Builds a*

His *High Plain*, directed by Jules Bucher, was an extremely warm and convincing travel documentary, in the tradition of Robert Flaherty. The Indians of the Bolivian plateau, far from modern ways or conveniences, are shown in their daily round of life in all weathers, and a satisfying balance of the primitive and the scenic is achieved by superior editing. If the paternalism of the land-owner is highly oversentimentalized, the facts of life nevertheless emerge in the camera's own truthfulness.

Uruguay, to take an example of the more routine reports, showed on the other hand the notable modernization of an essentially agricultural economy in "one of the most likeable of all countries." Working into the narrative with skill and affability such matters as automobile charcoal-burners, national health insurance, modern Montevideo buildings and gaucho festivals, the film has as much unity as one could ask, beginning with country scenes—"it meets the eye placidly, comfortably, as if partly made of Ohio"—and ending with the reminder that this progressive, partly socialized, heavily middle-class nation has "strong roots in the soil and pastures of the interior."

His production of films about America was less successful, at least in the eyes of the average American observer. Unquestionably he was trying to key the story, timing and wordage to the attitudes and capacity of foreign peoples of low literacy and little acquaintance with America or even with movies. Bryan and Francis Thompson, who directed these films, were trying to show quite simple things about an Ohio town, about a doctor, a mechanic, a county agent and a school teacher.[63]

Walt Disney's role in all this came earlier, beginning with a trip he took with some staff members in 1941 to gather background material for a picture about South America. The outcome was not only *Saludos Amigos*, which had a rousing success in the entire hemisphere, but a number of short subjects, some of which were straightforward scientific education. Most of these last were nontheatrical productions, like *Winged Scourge, Chicken Little, Water—Friend or Enemy*. They tended to have the opposite vice from the Bryan films, moving a little too fast and expecting a little too much from the audience. This was particularly true of *The Grain that Built a Hemisphere*, a delightful one-reel cartoon that raced through history with an ear of corn, beginning with the sacrifices to the corn god in the Mayan civilization and ending with such modern monuments as chemical laboratories and plastics plants. By and large, however, these contributions to inter-American education, while they could not be put in the category of documentary, were successful in their purpose. And if this experience, together with the work he did for the armed forces,

Democracy, Mexican Moods, Paraguay, Peru Coastal Region, South Chile, This Is Ecuador, Venezuela Moves Ahead, Yucatan.

63 For further background on Bryan, Thompson and Hammid, see Loren Cocking, *Francis Thompson: An Analysis of an American Film Maker*, unpublished M.A. thesis, Ohio State University, 1969.

actually formed in Disney's mind the resolve to produce the nonfictional *True-Life Adventure* series, then the beneficial role of the CIAA went far beyond an influence on hemisphere solidarity.

The CIAA pictures were shown, not only in commercial theaters in the big cities, but to specialized groups and to small island communities. "Coordinating committees" were set up in leading towns, made up usually of local Americans, and including one or more professional motion picture men—who were likely to be representatives of major U.S. distributors. More than 300 projectors were sent to the committees and by the end of the war some 70 sound trucks were in use for trips into the surrounding villages and towns.

The figures sound impressive enough, but convey nothing of the mingled danger and exhilaration of carrying to jungle-side settlements not only their first picture of American life, but sometimes their first movie. The projectionists got used to using local methods of communication. They looked for the *alto-falante* (the "loud speaker") to pass along their news about an evening show, as well as setting up signs and starting music going over their own loud speakers. They even got used to such questions from the dazed audiences as: "How do you make all of those sounds by yourself?"

Sometimes they were surprised. One memorable evening, among the Brazilian men, women and children who came long distances in oxcarts or on horses to see this new thing, there was one stalwart visitor who watched the show in immobile dignity—from his horse. Evidently he was not so immobile inside, for when the story of Nazi aggression had reached the point on the screen where Hitler himself appeared, the man excitedly whipped out his gun and shot him right through the head.[64]

[64] Interview, Alan Fisher, April, 1949. Fisher was a CIAA representative in Brazil and elsewhere during the war, having been a photographer with the *New York World Telegram*. He continued with the State Department and was in Brazil in 1949.

7

World War II: Armed
Forces Documentary

I N WORLD WAR II, the War Department managed to establish a continuing and relatively satisfactory relationship between the government and
Hollywood. Like most rapprochements, this one was attended by suspicion,
hesitancy and mis-steps, but in the end considerable confidence was established and some outstanding movies made. There was a very real fear on
the part of some Hollywood people that a corps of film-makers would be
built up by the Signal Corps and become a threat to Hollywood itself. On
the other hand, many said, and probably rightly, that there would be little
art and no public interest in any war films turned out by Signal Corps
"technicians." The eventual compromise, which involved putting directors,
producers, writers and technicians in uniform, did not threaten Hollywood
commercially but did undermine some familiar movie habits—and this
was all to the good.

By virtue of the tough, continuing requirements of working together
on real problems, another kind of rapprochement took place. The factual
needs of Washington and the dramatic experience of Hollywood met and
mingled and found reason for mutual respect. The generals found that
they could not get by with a forcible injection of knowledge. The directors
found that making up a story was not necessarily the best way of doing
everything on the screen. The people in the Pentagon, seeking the physical response of obedience, became more aware than ever before that they
had to deal with what was going on in the minds of soldiers. The people
in Hollywood, seeking to reach soldiers' minds, became aware that well-
ordered facts were the most persuasive dramatic material they had. When

the films began to be made more and more for public showing, this kind of rugged honesty persisted and resulted in achievements of enduring greatness.

The product which came out was documentary, but it was documentary under pressure. Working with limited goals in mind, though not altogether without a sense of their place in history, men like Capra, Zanuck, Ford, Wyler, Kanin and Huston could do very little planning. They could not direct the shows they photographed. They couldn't even direct what the combat cameramen were going to do. Sometimes cameramen had to throw grenades. Thirty-two of them died on the western front alone.[1] Only toward the last did a new writing technique come to full fruition in *The True Glory*, using the idiom of the soldier himself in combination with the filmed events of epic size. For the most part the makers of government war films were simply film editors.[2]

Orientation: Frank Capra and "Why We Fight"

A priority list of film needs had been set up by arms and services in accordance with a letter from the Adjutant General on April 23, 1940, but after Selective Service began to bring men in in great numbers, the problems became more acute. Subjects of basic usefulness to the army as a whole were sought, and *Articles of War, Military Courtesy, Safeguarding Military Information, Sex Hygiene, Personal Hygiene* were among the earliest of these. Hollywood made them, and Darryl Zanuck, vice-president in charge of production at Twentieth Century Fox, accepted two scenarios before any terms were arranged.

On November 26, 1940, Y. Frank Freeman, then chairman of the Motion Picture Production Defense Committee, wrote a letter to the Secretary of War concerning arrangements about training films. He had talked it over with the Chief Signal Officer (Major General J. O. Mauborgne) and with industry representatives. He proposed production by the industry for the War Department on a nonprofit basis. On December 12, Secretary Stimson accepted this offer and an Advisory Council to the Chief

---

1 Emanuel Cohen, "Film Is a Weapon," *Business Screen*, Vol. VII, No. 1, 1945.

2 See Hermine Rich Isaacs: "War Fronts and Film Fronts," *Theater Arts*, June 1944. "The war permits no retakes. . . . [The director] now becomes the editor extraordinary. . . . Perhaps not since the poetry of ancient wars have great events found a medium so eminently suited to convey their impact sharply and effectively to the people who had no part in the proceedings." See also Douglas Gallez, "Patterns in Wartime Documentaries," *Quarterly of Film, Radio, and Television*, Vol. 10, No. 2, Winter 1955, pp. 125–135.

Signal Officer was set up; Nathan Levinson was commissioned a colonel in the Signal Corps reserve and assigned to the War Department Liaison Office in Hollywood. Shortly afterward Darryl Zanuck was appointed to the Advisory Council and made a lieutenant colonel in the reserve.[3]

The nonprofit arrangement had its advantages and disadvantages but finally broke down under the weight of increasing demands and increasing costs. A year after Pearl Harbor a straight contract plan was worked out.

Things moved fast after the Japanese attack. There already existed a Training Film Production Laboratory at Fort Monmouth, New Jersey, in addition to the Army War College photographic laboratories. The need for a big central source of training films finally became not only apparent but compelling. One of the leading reasons was the increasing quantity of confidential and restricted information which had to be taught to specialized troops. The War Department bought outright the old Paramount studios at Astoria, Long Island,[4] and moved in equipment and personnel from Fort Monmouth. The Signal Corps Photographic Center was activated on March 30, 1942, and by December all training films for ground forces were being made there. People from Hollywood now started coming to New York in greater numbers.

[3] See James V. Clarke manuscript (December 1945, revised 1946), *Signal Corps Army Pictorial Service in World War II* (September 1, 1939 to August 15, 1945). Historical Section Special Activities Branch, Office of Chief Signal Officer. The Signal Corps is dealt with in three volumes of the massive history, *The U.S. Army in World War II*, published by the Office of the Chief of Military History, Department of the Army, Washington, D.C., 1957. See especially Dulany Terrett, *The Signal Corps: The Emergency* (to December 1941), pp. 78–82, 223–230. Also George Raynor Thompson, Dixie R. Harris, Pauline M. Oakes, and Dulany Terrett, *The Signal Corps: The Test* (December 1941–July 1943), pp. 387–426, and especially note 6, page 389.

The Hollywood office eventually became the "western branch" of the Signal Corps Photographic Center, first under Lt. Col. Charles Stodter, later (1943) under Lt. Col. Paul H. Sloane.

See Allen Rivkin and Laura Kerr (Mrs. Rivkin), *Hello Hollywood!*, p. 428: "Frank Capra, with Anatole Litvak next in command, Tony Veiller writing and narrating, Edgar Peterson doing *The Battle of China* and *The Battle of Britain*, Claude Binyon, my brother Norman, John Weaver, Ted Geisel, Bill Hornbeck as chief editor, Dimitri Tiomkin in charge of all music, Davie Miller sweating over a nuts-and-bolts documentary, Walter Huston alternating with Tony on the narration and Paul Stewart doing all the other voices—Nazi, French, Russian, Chinese, Japanese, British, Italian . . ."

[4] Owned at that time by Eastern Sound Studios. First built by Famous Players-Lasky. Gloria Swanson and Rudolph Valentino had played there. See letter, War Department Adjutant General's Office February 18, 1942 AG 601.1 (2-4-42) MR-M-C, Subject: Designation and Establishment of the Signal Corps Photographic Center, Astoria, Long Island, New York. See *Film News*, August 1949.

As in many other parts of the armed forces, the first men in from Hollywood were often the second-rank men in the industry. When their bosses joined up later they had to take subordinate positions—a fact which required a new kind of diplomacy all around. Low-ranking officers and even enlisted men often took charge of a production situation where others were nominally in authority.

Carl Laemmle, Jr., a late draftee, and heir of the Universal millions, drove daily to the Center from his quarters at the Sherry-Netherland, changed to his fatigues in his limousine, and set to work mopping the floors and doing other details around the place. He got to be a private first class after a while and finally became a writer.

By the middle of 1942, training needs already began to yield to more dramatic subject matter. "Highest priorities will be given to those pictures which present instruction directly concerned with combat operations." [5] In September, a new series called *Fighting Men* was announced, which would be "short, highly dramatized, and hard hitting. Presentation will in general be by a soldier speaking typical soldier language." [6] This was immediately inspired by a speech of Lieutenant General Wesley McNair at the Army War College, in which he called for greater toughness in training and a realization that the soldier must either "kill or be killed." [7] The resulting pictures emphasized that treachery was to be expected and the ethics of the playing-field did not apply. In *Kill or Be Killed,* a Nazi soldier gets an American to reach for some water for him and shoots him in the back for his pains. Demonstrations of brutality were predominant and *Life* commented that "the trainee can almost hear the crunch of flesh and bone." [8]

Meanwhile, at another level, the Signal Corps was soliciting the services of a popular Hollywood director whose films had been full of the irrepressible faith and humor of middle-class America. Frank Capra was at the very height of his success when the Signal Corps requested him to apply for a commission on December 8, 1941. The response to *Meet John Doe* had been less than unanimous, but the titles of his previous films, year by year, represented a veritable gallery of popular triumphs: *Lady for a Day, It Happened One Night, Broadway Bill, Mr. Deeds Goes to Town, Lost Horizon, You Can't Take It with You, Mr. Smith Goes to Washington.*

The War Department was already well aware that morale was not exclusively a matter of chow and letters from home. It also had to do with a sense of direction on the part of the individual soldier. Pearl Harbor helped, but there could be no forgetting the pre-Pearl Harbor threats of OHIO ("Over the Hill in October")—the widely publicized manifesto of the drafted boys who thought one year was enough. The chief of staff, General George C. Marshall, had already put in effect in November an orientation program throughout the army on the reasons for military service—a program which was assigned to the Bureau of Public Relations. [9]

Thus "Why We Fight" became the next film need. Capra was brought

[5] Letter, Deputy Director of Training, Services of Supply, to all Chiefs of Services of Supply, July 25, 1942.
[6] Letter, Commanding General Army Ground Forces to Chief Signal Office, attention Army Pictorial Service, September 10, 1942.
[7] Interview, R. C. Barrett, wartime commandant of SCPC, December 20, 1949.
[8] "Films Teach Soldiers Lessons of War," July 26, 1943. *How to Be Killed in One Easy Lesson* was an after-the-battle lecture by a captured Japanese on what the GI's should have done. *On Your Own* was a Hollywood-style story about a corporal and a private in a cave who fight on despite odds.
[9] Francis Keppel, *Study of Information and Education Activities in World War II* (manuscript) April 6, 1946. Lt. Keppel was a special assistant in the I & E Division in the office of Brig. Gen. F. H. Osborn.

in as a major for the specific purpose of producing the orientation films which became the most famous film achievement of the War Department.[10] General Marshall called in Capra and Major General Frederick H. Osborn, head of the Special Services Division, and talked with them for an hour about the problem of maintaining morale and instilling loyalty into a civilian army. He told them he wanted motion pictures to help with this job, gave them a general order to go ahead, and asked them to hurry.[11]

The series of films was based directly on a series of lectures prepared by the Army Bureau of Public Relations which were being delivered to troops. These apparently left something to be desired in the way of motivation. General Marshall had occasion to give a public appraisal of the effectiveness of those lectures when the first film *Prelude to War* was under attack on the floor of the Senate:

> I want to say this: That I personally found the lectures of officers to the men, as to what they were fighting for and what the enemy had done, so unsatisfactory because of the mediocrity of presentation that I directed the preparation of this series of films.[12]

Some day there will be an extended depth analysis of the themes and purposes of these films. It can only be said here that, in general, they attempted: (1) to destroy faith in isolation, (2) to build up a sense of the strength and at the same time the stupidity of the enemy, and (3) to emphasize the bravery and achievements of America's allies. Their style was a combination of a sermon, a between-halves pep talk, and a barroom bull session. Capra and his staff searched for pictures to illustrate certain ideas;[13] then the commentary was tailored to fit the pictures which were

[10] Capra was commissioned February 14, 1942. He spent only a short time in Washington, since he found that the stock shots he needed were mostly in Hollywood. (Interviews, R. C. Barrett and Richard Griffith.)

The Hollywood office was a part of the Special Service Division until transferred to the Signal Corps Army Pictorial Service in 1943, though Capra and others were commissioned in the Signal Corps from the first. He returned to civilian life in June 1945, having become a full colonel in the meantime.

[11] *The Signal Corps: The Test*, pp. 387–426. See also Frank Capra's autobiography, *The Name Above the Title* (1971) for his personal story of certain bureaucratic battles in the early days of the war and for his relationship with General Marshall (pp. 314–367).

[12] The attack was by Senator Rufus C. Holman, who had been convinced, he said, by the film, "that Mr. Roosevelt intended to seek a fourth term in the Presidency," and introduced a resolution calling for investigation of government agencies which produce films. (Congressional Record, 78th Congress, 1st Session, February 8, 1943, pp. 674–676.)

Marshall's reply was that "the President, Mr. Roosevelt, had never heard of their preparation, because this was a matter of Army training responsibility, until after A *Prelude to War* had been shown to probably a million troops." (February 18, 1943, p. 1088.)

[13] Eric Knight, Anatole Litvak, Anthony Veiller, Richard Griffith, at the Museum of Modern Art (in uniform and on detached service from *Yank*) found a good many of the pictures they wanted.

actually found; the words were kept simple, direct, hard-hitting, with plenty of time allowed between statements to permit both statements and pictures to sink in deeply.

However familiar its message was by 1943, there can be no doubt that *Prelude to War*, which was shown to total troop audiences of 9,000,000 by 1945,[14] reinforced and sharpened the lessons of the 1930's. Its purpose was to describe "the causes and events leading up to our entry into the war." The film made plain that the war did not begin at Pearl Harbor. The "other world" of totalitarianism had made a choice between democracy and force: its "tragic mistake of choosing the second course" meant that "demagogues" gained power in Italy and Germany. In Japan it was "not one man but a gang," backed by the secret Black Dragon society. But "no matter how you slice it, it was plain old-fashioned military imperialism."

In the beginning, Capra pictured not only our own early leaders, and the Declaration of Independence, along with people like Lafayette and Lincoln who fought for freedom, but also claimed that the belief that all men are created equal went back to old-world leaders as diverse as Moses, Mahomet, Confucius and Jesus. The nations of the "other world" had now surrendered their liberties. Throwing away their human dignity, they "became part of a mass, a human herd." Their leaders were now public enemies. "Remember these three faces"—Hitler, Mussolini, Tojo. "If you ever meet them, don't hesitate."

Following this came the actual picture story of the giving up of liberty, told in a kind of three-way counterpoint. Crowds yelling "Sieg Heil!" "Duce!" and "Banzai!" approved the giving up of free speech, assembly, press and courts, along with labor unions and bargaining rights. The Matteoti assassination, the killings of Japanese statesmen, the Nazi murders of Roehm and others were seen as a pattern. Sneers at culture, destruction of religion and perversion of truth in the classroom all come to a climax in scenes of children marching. The sinister comment is: "I want to see again in the eyes of youth the gleam of the beast of prey."

"What of our world?" We weren't so smart, ourselves, because we were preoccupied with our own little problems. "Let Europe fight her own battles." We turned our backs on the League of Nations and put up prohibitive tariffs. It was true that John Q. Public ran the country; he read what he pleased and attended any church he pleased. But he didn't pay much attention when the German children drilled; he didn't know about the Japanese Tanaka plan for conquest. When the war actually began on September 18, 1931, it was impossible to convince a city bus driver or a midwestern farm boy that a mud hut burning in Manchuria was a threat to his life. Ethiopia came and went, with "Mussolini beating

14 *Information and Education Division*, privately printed pamphlet for members of I & E, with dedication by Maj. Gen. F. H. Osborn, October 1945.

his chest like Tarzan," and though Roosevelt and other leaders gave warnings, we were still hypnotized by our two oceans. But now the two worlds are lined up, the chips are down, and it's "us or them."

There can be no doubt of the effectiveness of such a film as this for young men and women who had lived through the 1930's—simply as a reminder, for some, but more particularly as a forceful organizing of loose thoughts for those who had never bothered to work things out in their minds. This single film may not have deeply affected fighting motivation. Research Branch reports, using questions of doubtful relevance, tended to discredit the effect of the film. But it strengthened those who were most in agreement with the opinions presented, and provided a framework for the opinions of waverers. A propaganda film could not expect to do much more. The most typical comment on *Prelude to War* was: "It's propaganda, all right, but it's good propaganda."

Soon after, came *The Nazis Strike* and *Divide and Conquer*, which dealt in much the same way with Germany's aggression eastward (including Austria and Czechoslovakia) and westward (up to Dunkirk). *The Battle of Britain* was followed by *The Battle of Russia*, which received considerable critical approval when it was released, as was *Prelude to War*, for public showing. *War Comes to America*,[15] also publicly released, was the last of the series, and did not appear until 1945, some time after *The Battle of China*. Neither of the last were as widely seen as the first five, which were all shown to Army personnel for the first time in 1943. They were required seeing. They were supposed to be viewed, and notation made on the service record, before any soldier went overseas.

Eight million men were supposed to have seen *The Battle of Britain*. Pictorially it was probably the most impressive of the group; it is dramatic and inspiring history even today. It starts with pictures of Hitler in Paris. "Where Napoleon failed, I shall succeed; I shall land on the shores of England." As the audience becomes accustomed to thinking in terms of 1940, and the hopeless prospect which then confronted the world, the Nazi plan is ticked off: Phase One—knock out the Royal Air Force and destroy communication and transportation; Phase Two—dive bombers and paratroops; Phase Three—invasion. After that, the United States.

Then the British preparations are described—the army dragged from the sea at Dunkirk, one tank for every thousand square miles, one machine gun for every 1,500 yards of beach, men working 70 hours a week, defense maneuvers which were permitted to use one shell at each practice. But though they were outnumbered ten to one, the British "also had an air force."

We hear Churchill's magnificent words and feel the force of his spirit, and then we watch what happens. The great gulf between the printed

[15] This one started with Jamestown in 1607 and worked its way up to Pearl Harbor.

page and the film has never been better illustrated than here, for the raging inferno of London in August and September can only be named, not reproduced, in words. The film reproduces it. The film gives meaning and depth to the statistics—the 26 major attacks in the first ten days, the 697 German and 153 British planes lost, the 500 bombers and fighters overhead on September 15 and the 185 shot down, the 50 million pounds of bombs in 28 days. And then in October the night attacks. In November, Coventry. On Christmas night, the fire bombs.

The outnumbered people and the little air force are the steady heroes of this remarkable moving picture. No thoughtful American could watch this dramatic and terrible story without a sense of wonder and gratitude that this thing could have been done on this little island in 1940.

The Rationale of "Information-Education"

The names and dates of the administrative organizations responsible for army film-making are difficult to trace and probably relatively unimportant. Neither General Marshall nor Frank Capra permitted the exact details of bureaucratic history to distract them from the purposes they were pursuing. But it may be noted that the Information-Education Division, which was the final headquarters for Capra's information film-makers, was the outcome of a long process of development.

It was the Morale Branch, provided for at the end of World War I and re-inaugurated in July 1940,[16] which saw the growth of such unrelated activities as decorations, army exchanges, recreation, athletics, the Motion Picture Service (which exhibited Hollywood films to troops) and the U.S. Armed Forces Institute (for correspondence courses). The Branch had a civilian advisory committee which included Frederick N. Osborn, Clarence Dykstra, Robert Sherwood, Charles P. Taft, Wayne Coy, Raymond Fosdick and Arthur W. Page.

Osborn was commissioned a brigadier general in August 1941 and made chief of the Branch, which was renamed Special Services in January 1942. The Orientation program which Marshall had started under Public Relations, was transferred in June of 1942, and radio, films and *Yank Magazine* were also under way within Special Services by that time.

The processes of education and information (as opposed to recreation and post exchanges) got a special boost from Wendell Willkie, the forceful and imaginative Republican ex-candidate for President, who took his air-

16 It was first under the Adjutant General, then reported through a subsection of G-1 to the Chief of Staff, and was later a subsection of G-4 in Services of Supply.

plane trip around the world in 1942.[17] When he got back in October he strongly urged Elmer Davis to do something about news for troops overseas. The camps he had visited showed plainly enough that the boys weren't hearing much about American and international events. This was not in Davis' hands, of course, but there were conferences about it. Not long after, along with a general expansion of the information program, the *Army-Navy Screen Magazine* made its appearance (April 1943) and thereafter was released twice a month. Produced by Colonel Leonard Spigelgass, it contained not only a straightforward presentation of news, but also the famed cartoon character "Snafu" and the soldiers' own asked-for pictures of almost anything under the sun, "By Request." It was increasingly popular both in War Department movie theaters and in "GI Movies" as part of the orientation program, and some 70 issues were turned out before the end of the war.[18]

In the fall of 1943, a new Morale Services Division was separated from Special Services, again under Osborn, and there began to be appointed in all commands full-time Orientation Officers. A 26-day course was begun at Lexington, Virginia, and its graduates began to provide regimental and divisional troops with a more serious approach to the Newsmap, Orientation Kits, *Army Talks*, *GI Roundtables*, and other printed material provided for the required orientation sessions.

The name Information-Education Division was finally adopted in August 1944, and Orientation Officers became I and E Officers. About the same time, a concerted effort was made to work out a philosophy for all this activity. It had been well enough known that the main purpose was to keep the American soldier informed. But why was this important, beyond the fact that he had been rather more used to being informed while he was at home than most other soldiers of the United Nations? First, and perhaps most important, was the fact that he was a better soldier if he did not feel that everything was going wrong—that the war was mismanaged and his part in it inscrutable. Hence these remarks in *The Information-Education Officer*, War Department Technical Manual 28-210 (published July 1945, but the outcome of a year's discussion and work):

> The commander alone is responsible for morale. It is a responsibility which cannot be delegated . . .
>
> But where [there is] . . . misunderstanding of military or national policy, lack of comprehension of the war, its causes, objectives and

[17] Keppel, *op. cit.*, p. 26.

[18] See George Raynor Thompson and Dixie R. Harris, *The Signal Corps: The Outcome* (Mid-1943 through 1945), pp. 540–579, especially p. 558. Also, Memorandum, Headquarters Army Service Forces, May 31, 1943 to Director, Special Services Division, subject: "Film Production." See also Charles F. Hoban Jr., *Movies That Teach*, for a summary of types and a few titles of armed forces films. Iris Barry has some comments on the quality of the *Screen Magazine* in the program for the 1946 showings at the Museum of Modern Art, *Documentary Film 1922–1945*.

progress; confusions and doubts caused by enemy propaganda over a period of years; misconceptions of reasons for inconveniences or hardships; misunderstanding of the personal relation of the soldier or his unit to the war as a whole; or lack of knowledge in the other fields peculiarly the province of information and education, the information-education officer properly brings to bear appropriate informational resources through methods described in this manual.

A second reason for the information process within the Army became more and more important to the men in charge of the program as they wrestled with its rationale. The soldier in the American Army was "democratic man" in uniform, a self-reliant fellow, pretty much accustomed to making up his own mind. This was not only the way it was, but a good thing, too, because he made the best kind of soldier. Hence it was the business of the Army to encourage his independent thinking and to feed it with information, discussion and education. Under the somewhat disturbing heading of "Importance of Mental Training," the I and E manual proposed:

> All armies now recognize the need for training the soldier's mind, in order to maintain his zeal for work and combat. The United States holds the belief that the soldier's mind should be free, informed, judicious, able to protect itself from sophistry and falsehood, alert and understanding of the larger problems of command, and of his Nation.

> Such qualities of mind can grow only in the presence of a free press and freedom of speech, and they can only serve the individual and his democratic society adequately if he has the opportunity to nourish such qualities through information and education.

> Free access to information, uninhibited discussion with his fellows, and a common opportunity to pursue self-education are three major resources which support the American concept of the mental training of the soldier in a democratic country.

> But troops in vast numbers, on duty all over the world and segregated from familiar sources of news, of understanding of events, and of education, could hardly fulfill the natural rights of members of a democracy to know the truth and to grow through it, unless the Army they belong to would undertake to supply the needs of their minds as well as their material wants. This the Army does through its Information and Education program.

That the I and E program actually did so much would have been doubted even by the writers of these paragraphs. Especially would they have realized that the average commander in the field, and even the commanders of posts, camps and stations, had only a slight acquaintance with the fundamental philosophy herein represented. But this was their ideal, and its influence was bound to be increasingly felt as the program grew in acceptance.

There were certain stated limitations when it came to free discussion. The logical division laid out in TM 28-210 may well give students of public communication pause. Efforts have been made in the past to delimit subject matter which ought and ought not to be publicly discussed. When a government publication actually makes such distinctions, however tentatively, it is worthwhile to take a look at them, just to see how they would seem if more generally applied.

> *Ideas which are basic to the American tradition* . . . include belief in the integrity of the individual, and a belief in the democratic process of government in the United States; also ideas which flow inevitably from those beliefs. . . . Examples are: that democracy is practical; the belief of Lincoln and Jefferson in the soundness of the majority opinion of the common man when properly informed; racial and religious tolerance. . . .

> As to these fundamentals, the discussion leader will energetically present to the soldier a concluded opinion.

> *Policies of the Government* . . . are expressed in laws enacted by the Congress, in executive orders, and in regulations and directives issued by the War Department. . . .

> In such matters, the discussion leader has a clear responsibility for explaining to the soldier the reasons for a majority opinion, and the reasons for acceptance by the soldier of the majority decision. The soldier may discuss matters pertaining to governmental and military policies, understanding, however, that these are policies to which he must, perforce, conform. . . .

> *Other Current topics* . . . include all issues which do not fall into either of the categories above. These, the discussion leader does not resolve for the soldier, but carefully gives him the facts, pro and con, as they are available.

Thus the information officer is to be vigorous and hortatory on matters which are "basic," explanatory on matters of law and Army Regulations (which are not, incidentally, passed by majority decision), and neutral on matters not yet settled. He might be pardoned for wondering if everything the Army sent out in the way of information actually fell so neatly into categories. And he might be pardoned, also, for wondering if the categories were impregnable. If *The Battle of Russia* presented one of our allies in a favorable light in certain directions, was this Government policy, or did it fall under "other topics"? And what if the War Department film, *The Negro Soldier*, was presented during the information-education hour? [19]

[19] This film, rather lengthy and none-too-subtle but certainly informative, used an unwieldy framework of (1) a Negro pastor talking to his congregation about his-

Obviously racial and religious tolerance, however inevitably it may flow from the idea of democracy, is not in the United States a settled question. "Basic" ideas unfortunately are often subject to definition, and individual definitions vary. Perhaps tolerance as an idea is an absolute, whereas the meaning of tolerance would fall under "other topics." Would the writers of TM 28-210 have accepted that?

The film-makers did not face the complicated problems of weekly discussion faced by information officers in the field. But they did find that they were pretty much limited to "basic ideas" or else to those subjects which flowed inevitably not from basic ideas but rather from War Department directives. There was misunderstanding of foreign peoples by the traditionally isolationist GI. Therefore the film-makers produced *Know Your Ally, Britain,* and did contrary items called *Know Your Enemy, Japan* and *Know Your Enemy, Germany.* In preparation for occupation, they made *Your Job in Germany.* In preparation for V-E Day, they made *Two Down and One to Go,* which later became a veritable legend of simultaneous distribution and single-problem attack:

> Any lingering doubts about the value of film, not only in routine training courses, but also in spreading information quickly and in attacking specific morale problems, were completely dissipated . . . when the army relied almost exclusively on a single motion picture to tell 8,000,000 men something each was more concerned with than any other single thing—discharges. The picture, *Two Down and One to Go,* had been prepared in the greatest secrecy, explaining the army's point system of discharges to be followed after the defeat of Germany. To insure the quickest possible showing 1,363 technicolor prints were dispatched by plane all over the world, and at the same time the men were seeing it overseas, their families were seeing it at some 800 first-run theaters back home.[20]

By request from a general in the China-Burma-India theater of operations, they made a detailed explanation of the reasons for the Burma campaign, called *Why We're Here.* And by 1944 the Information-Education films began to include straight battle reports. Capra went to London to work in cooperation with the War Office on a feature-length sequel to the British *Desert Victory,* called *Tunisian Victory.*[21] His men were also

---

tory and (2) a member of the congregation reading a letter from a soldier about life in the army. The facts about Negro participation in past wars and the pictures showing the jobs they did in World War II are impressive and moving by themselves. This film had the advantage of special advice by Walter White and special attention by Undersecretary of War Robert Patterson. It was directed by Captain Stuart Heisler.

20 Emanuel Cohen, "Film Is a Weapon," *Business Screen,* Vol. 7, No. 1, 1945. Colonel Cohen was executive producer at the Signal Corps Photographic Center in New York. See also *The Signal Corps: The Outcome,* pp. 557–558.

21 Lt. Col. Hugh Stewart was his opposite number in England for this film, according to Hermine Isaacs (*Theater Arts, op. cit.*).

responsible for *Westward Is Bataan,* the story of the New Guinea campaign, and *Attack!—The Battle for New Britain.*[22]

Attack! was one of the best of the films about single campaigns.[23] It gave both explanations of strategy and comments about life in the jungle. Its GI tone was set by the first comment about the scenery around Rabaul —the beautiful "tropical sunsets bringing in the malarial mosquito." The task forces which built up on the New Guinea coastline—collecting supplies, training, trying to make a temporary home—were to strike in two places on New Britain: the feint at Arawe, the main landing at Cape Gloucester. Both landings are shown, along with a wide variety of the forces that made them possible. "For every finger squeezing a trigger there are a hundred others pulling, hauling, and shoving." More memorable than this statement is the scene which illustrates it—two GI's carrying a top-heavy burden of barbed wire, stumbling with it, falling, recovering and going on.

The Air Force and the Navy

_____

Because war in the air and on the sea is not the constant strain of front line war, and because airplanes and warships are more complex instruments than mortars and machine guns, the Air Force and Navy film programs developed somewhat differently. Combat films were fewer and came somewhat later; the training films were more technical.

The Army Air Force had its own Motion Picture Unit, though the AAF was under the War Department. There was a long intra-bureaucratic struggle with the Signal Corps about this, and an uneasy compromise was recorded in a War Department letter as a result of a conference in New York between representatives of the AAF and the Signal Corps. A special Signal Corps photographic unit was set up under each Air Force under the technical control of the Chief Signal Officer but under the command of the Commanding General of the Army Air Force.[24]

The First Motion Picture Unit at Dayton, Ohio—which had been operating at high speed all the time and never could see the use of sending film projects through channels to Astoria, New York—now moved most of

22 See Letter (SPSAFWD-40210.4551) September 2, 1944, from Col. Frank Capra to Adjutant General, Washington, D.C.

23 Although one of the objections to this picture is its overdramatic and ever-present music. It stops long enough on one occasion to show us by contrast how quiet the jungle really is.

24 Letter, Headquarters, Services of Supply, July 19, 1942, "Memorandum for Chief Signal Officer."

its activities to Hollywood and enlisted the facilities of the Hal Roach studios. From October 1942 to October 1945, the FMPU turned out 228 films, with a total running time of 78 hours, 37 minutes.[25]

Apart from such things as *Psychological Test Films, Identification of the Japanese Zero,* and humorous instructional shorts using a conceited ignoramus called "Trigger Joe" as protagonist, the FMPU made both dramatized idea films for training and documentaries based on combat footage for public and military morale purposes.

Such items as *Ditch and Live* and *Land and Live in the Jungle* spoke from the point of view of the combat crew. The outstanding achievement of the FMPU in this category was *Resisting Enemy Interrogation.* This picture dramatized the capture of an American flying crew, showing how each one—whether by ignorance or by being a little too smart—gave information to their captors. The moral: give only your name, rank and serial number. It was an exciting story (62 minutes long) and unusually well acted.[26]

The high point of AAF production was reached when the First Motion Picture Unit joined forces with Hollywood's William Wyler, director of *Dead End, Wuthering Heights* and *Mrs. Miniver. Thunderbolt* came too late (1945) for wide distribution, but it was a remarkably effective photographic treatment of the northward progress of the air war in Italy.

Wyler's *Memphis Belle* (1944) was widely shown in American theaters as well as to the personnel of the armed forces. This story of a bombing mission over Wilhelmshaven owed much to the English precedent, *Target for Tonight.* It lacked the sense of intricate planning and detail that could be felt in the early scenes of the English picture, and almost all of the sound track was narrative rather than spoken by the principals. But some of the photography was notable, and it was all on a bigger scale than its predecessor, as one might expect of an American film. The bombers were larger and flew in formation; the exclamations over the "intercom" reflect a longer, tougher battle with German flak and fighters:

"There's one of 'em at one o'clock high!"
"They're comin' around—watch 'em!"
"I'm on him! I got him!"
"Don't yell on that intercom!"

Such easy authenticity more than makes up for such strained lines as "These are the faces of combat, faces of Americans who have seen their

25 See Alex Greenberg and Malvin Wald, "Report to the Stockholders," *Hollywood Quarterly,* July 1946, for a list of titles and a brief description of operations.

Ben Maddow was a sergeant with this unit. He later joined Director John Huston, writing the script for *The Asphalt Jungle* and other features.

26 See Charles Hoban, *Movies That Teach,* for a description of this film.

comrades die." By and large, Wyler's *Memphis Belle* was a simple and powerful film.

In the early stages of film operations for the Navy, on the other hand, a running battle was carried on with Hollywood. This may have protected the early Navy training film program from over-florid treatment of simple needs, but it served to postpone to some extent the broader development of documentary for public uses.

The Bureau of Aeronautics, which has had the major responsibility for Navy film-making ever since aerial photographic reconnaissance began, called in Louis de Rochemont in 1941, when it was decided to expand motion picture activities. After World War I, he had stayed in the Navy as an officer for four years to do recruiting movies, and had not lost contact with the Department. Shortly afterward, Thomas Orchard, his associate producer at *The March of Time*, turned up as a lieutenant, junior grade, and started organizing a training film unit under the Flight Division.[27]

This operation grew into a Photographic Division, with a Training Film and Motion Picture Branch employing 200 persons in Washington alone in 1945. By that time it had made 1,100 Navy training films and 2,200 filmstrips, mostly by contract with private educational and scientific motion picture producers.[28]

During the early phases of this expansion, John Ford became interested in joining forces with the Navy. The Hollywood director, who had made *The Informer* and *The Grapes of Wrath*, was also a commander in the Naval Reserve. He met with little enthusiasm among the administrators of the Navy's film program, who felt that Hollywood was running the Army's motion picture production; they didn't want to follow suit. Ford then went to Colonel William Donovan, head of the Office of Strategic Services, and found that the budget there could accommodate him and a number of other Hollywood people, including cameraman Gregg Toland.

They set to work first on a historical treatment of Pearl Harbor Day, but one day while Ford was out from Honolulu on a cruiser with a friend, the cruiser ran into the battle of Midway. He took what pictures he could with his 16mm camera, most of them on the island itself afterward and brought them back for editing and later release through the OWI.[29] This seems to have been his major personal contribution to the recording of the war in the Pacific.

The OSS continued to produce films, however, in cooperation with the combat cameramen of the Navy, Marine Corps and Coast Guard. *With the Marines at Tarawa* and *The Battle for the Marianas* were produced by

27 Interview, Thomas Orchard, October 10, 1950.
28 Orville Goldner, "The Story of Navy Training Films," in *Business Screen*, Issue 5, Volume 8, June 1945. Lt. Comdr. Goldner was at that time head of the Branch. He reported that there were then 700 titles in various stages of production.
29 The battle of Midway took place in June, 1942; the film was released in September. See also Chapter 6.

the Marine Corps, but *Brought to Action* was based on photography by men in all three branches of the forces afloat, plus some footage from the Signal Corps and the Army Air Force. This OSS film was full of action sequences showing the Seventh Fleet scouring the seas to protect Mac-Arthur's landings on Leyte in the Philippines. It made some attempt to describe strategic concepts but also showed a partial change of plan in the middle of battle to meet reports of Japanese ships unexpectedly at hand— an element of suspense which served to make up in realism for the rather complacent opening scenes.

Fury in the Pacific was the first film produced jointly by the American Army, Navy and Marine Corps for public showings.[30] Nine photographers were wounded and one killed in the crew of 39 which took the footage for this story of the landings on Pelelieu and Anguar in the Palaus. *To the Shores of Iwo Jima* was the first American military picture made according to a carefully worked out battle-plan script. "This spectacularly beautiful and terrible film, by far the best and fullest record of a combined operation," [31] was the work of 106 Navy, Marine Corps and Coast Guard cameramen. *The Fleet That Came to Stay* told the story of Kamikaze attacks during the invasion of Okinawa and the role of the fleet in that invasion.[32]

During this later phase of combat reporting, Commander Edward Steichen, the widely known still photographer, had an important role, as did Captain Gene Markey, director of the Division of Photographic Services in the Office of the Secretary of the Navy, and Lieutenant Commander Fanning Hearon, who was in charge of a special Photographic Services Unit in Hollywood.

One of the important by-products of all this activity was the Twentieth Century-Fox feature picture, *Fighting Lady*. Louis de Rochemont looked on the combat footage as a good deal more than "a little film for Navy relief" (as it was once described to him), and built up the Navy's record of life on a carrier into one of the outstanding war documentaries to come out of Hollywood.[33]

Thus both the Air Force and the Navy chose to go beyond the primary, practical need of technical training. Both sought, with the help of Hollywood personnel, to make films of emotional quality for purposes of history and public relations.

[30] The commentary was written by Captain Charles Grayson of the Army; Warner Brothers distributed it for the OWI in March, 1945.

[31] *The Documentary Film, 1922–1945*, program for Museum of Modern Art Film Showing, January–June 1946. Lt. Comdr. John McLain was in charge of the photographic mission with Lt. (JG) Lothar Wolff of the Coast Guard assisting; Capt. Milton Sperling edited the film at Warner Brothers and it was released by United Artists for OWI.

[32] Lt. Collier Young wrote the commentary, and the film was released by Paramount in late July.

[33] Interview, Louis de Rochemont, November, 1950.

The Culmination of Army Documentary

Signal Corps cameramen were also writing history as well as informing the troops. *The Liberation of Rome* was as much for posterity as for the encouragement of the common soldier or the information of the American public.

Of the 200,000 feet of film which came into New York each week from overseas crews, not very much went into Information-Education films. More, for instance, went into weekly issues of *Combat Bulletins*, which were less confidential versions of the *Staff Film Reports*. The practical value to the Army—as well as the other services—in having film records of military operations to study filled an important function in officer training. This short-term historical value was no less important than the long-term value of history as a means of instilling pride.[34]

But somewhere in the middle distance, between these two values of immediate training and historical record, was the value of public information. Some of the most memorable motion pictures of the Army were made with public relations firmly in mind.

The first big undertaking of this kind was in November and December of 1942, when Darryl Zanuck, on leave as head of production at Twentieth Century-Fox, and 65 other Army and Navy cameramen took pictures at Algiers, Oran, Casablanca and in Tunisia. The immediate outcome was a production called *At the Front in North Africa*, toward which there were mixed critical reactions.[35] This pioneering effort was nevertheless a first evidence of what might be done in the way of reports from battlefields, and was an important response to the early leadership of the British in this respect.

The star of this later phase of military documentary turned out to be John Huston, the Hollywood screenwriter who had just begun to direct. In *Report from the Aleutians*, he brought back too much material and used too much, but the incidental observations were the best of it. There was

---

[34] *The Fighting First* (1946) is a good example of a "pride of outfit" film, tracing as it does a history going back to the Revolution, but spending most of its time on World War II, from Oran through Omaha Beach and Aachen to Czechoslovakia.

[35] *Life* called it "100% honest," and congratulated him for the "courage and foresight to shoot it entirely in color." The *New Republic*, disapproving the blurred effect of the colors, referred to Mr. Zanuck as an amateur photographer and said he didn't "get inside of the facts" because he was not used to filming actuality. Zanuck himself, in a book which he wrote about his exploits (*Tunis Expedition*, N.Y., Random House, 1943), remarked: "I don't suppose our war scenes will look as savage or realistic as those we usually make on the back lot, but you can't have everything."

Frame enlargement from *The Battle of San Pietro* (Dir. John Huston) for U.S. Army in World War II, 1945

a full-bodied record of an army mail-call, for example, and pictures of planes landing on a runway in half-a-foot of water. There were remarks about that runway: all one-and-a-half million square feet of it were put down—"by the infantry, of course"—in 36 hours. Such remarks foreshadowed Huston's uncompromising treatment of battle scenes in his next film, but there were softer highlights, too, as when he played his camera on the faces of individuals in the bomber crews and had the narrator speak against the roar of the motors: "The ride *back* from Kiska is the most beautiful ride in the world."

The Battle of San Pietro was a grim and grinding statement of how war looked to the infantryman in Italy. It was intended first as a message to the public explaining the slow progress of the war in Italy; later it was expected to be a training experience for green recruits. Officials at the War Department, however, found it rather more chilling than had been expected. They reduced it from 50 minutes to 30 and tacked on a solemn introduction by General Mark Clark, contradicting the over-all impact of the film with the statement that the "losses were not excessive." [36]

[36] Paul Rotha and Richard Griffith, *The Film Till Now*, pp. 463, 501. Griffith

There is not much excitement in *The Battle of San Pietro*. It does not stir hatred for the enemy nor a desire to fight. There is acid comment on a bombed church: "Note interesting treatment of chancel." There is dreary despair: "Each river seemed like five, each peak a little higher than the last." Rain falls at H-Hour. The enemy observation is excellent. Somewhere among the faceless hills a battalion keeps sending out patrols, and "not a single member of any of these patrols ever came back. . . . Many companies lost all their officers, and enlisted men came forward as inspirational leaders." *San Pietro* is a peculiarly inconclusive story, despite the introduction of liberated Italians at the end. It is as close to the real feeling of daily battle on the ground as any film since *All Quiet on the Western Front*.

Huston's third contribution to an understanding of war was never made available to the public. *Let There Be Light* revealed the treatment of psychiatric cases in a veteran's hospital. It is one of the most deeply moving of all documentary films. That it was not shown widely at a time when many young men were returning from experiences of terror is a thing to be regretted, for its spirit of compassion is such as to leave almost any audience chastened and changed. Regardless of the specific healing methods shown, and their effectiveness—and it apparently is true that the comebacks shown in the films were not all permanent ones—there is gained through watching these tortured men, with their torn memories and their longing for safety, a new awareness of the damages of war and the strange paths some men must walk when they return to peace.[37]

Probably the most important sequences from a documentary point of view (or from the point of view of psychology) are the group therapy sessions which the concealed camera caught with such steady honesty. The things these men share with each other about their early lives reveal the frankness and understanding the psychiatrists have achieved in working with them. It becomes very clear that not only the war, and not only themselves, but also the people who have lived near them, are responsible in part for their sicknesses.

In the final scene, the boy who has been freed from paralysis by the removal of a mental block and the boy who has surmounted incoherent speech by surmounting his terrified memories of German 88's are both

called it "an outright attack on all wars." Huston insists his attitude was one of "profound admiration for the courage of the men." (Robert Hughes, ed., *Film: Book 2—Films of Peace and War* [1962], p. 29.) A later version for the Defense Department's TV show, "The Big Picture," lost the characteristic scenes of death and burial, and with them the primary thrust of the film. This version should be avoided by film teachers. It has a shrugging introduction by Huston himself (in place of Clark) which seems to wink at the emasculation of his work.

[37] A transcript of *Let There Be Light* can be found on pp. 205-233 of Hughes, *Film: Book 2*.

playing ball in the hospital yard. The paralyzed boy is running the bases; the stutterer is umpire.

The largest achievement of wartime documentary was the presentation on film of the campaign of western Europe. It is difficult to assign credits for this achievement, since its British-American director-editors were Carol Reed and Garson Kanin, its scenario was constructed by five people in and out of the forces,[38] and it was produced by the Office of War Information and the British Ministry of Information. But the greatness of this film lies primarily in the pictures, which were taken by 1,400 Allied cameramen on the western front, of whom 101 were wounded and 32 killed. This extraordinary testimonial to the bravery and toil of the men who fought in France and Belgium and Holland and Luxembourg and Germany was based on 6,500,000 feet of film. It is a worthy testimonial to the men who took the pictures that the editing was done with skill and the narrative written with originality and warmth.

Of the technique of this narrative, Iris Barry wrote:

> The vernacular of a polygot Allied Army forms an integral part of *The True Glory*, a rough and rich cross-section of recent European and human history. The natural speech of the men, typifying those who wrote that history, enhances the message of the hundreds of battle pictures which compose the substance of the film. Blank verse, less effective but helpful as punctuation to mark the successive stages of the story, chimes in and, on yet a third level, the voice of General Eisenhower lends authority or adds elucidation to the saga. The whole is a broad, eloquent canvas compressing and suggesting much more than the visible facts, and doing it in a manner possible only to the motion picture: nothing else has so fully sustained or recorded the heroic story from D day to VE day.[39]

Certainly one of the enduring values of this powerful film is its reflection of the way Anglo-Americans thought and acted in this war of the 1940's.

> "We didn't think we'd spend fifteen days in the same field outside of Caen . . . each side mortaring each other all the time. . . . You get tired of being mortared . . . you think every one's coming straight for you."

> "We thought: God, are we going to have to go right across the world doing this to beat 'em? . . . Then we heard that the Third Army was taking off. . . . They'd pulled a rabbit out of a hat—and what a rabbit! A rabbit with pearl-handled revolvers."

> "Mortain . . . was where I got hit. . . . I get a belt in the face, left side, and I keel."

[38] Maj. Eric Maschwitz, Arthur MacRae, Flt/o Jenny Nicholson, Gerald Kerah, Sgt. Guy Trosper. (See Appendix, Rotha and Griffith, p. 686.) Capt. Peter Cusick was in charge of research.

[39] *The Documentary Film, 1922–1945.*

Frame enlargement from *The True Glory* (Dirs. Carol Reed & Garson Kanin) for British Ministry of Information and U.S. Office of War Information by 1400 cameramen in the Allied Armed Forces on the Western front, 1945

"I just kept 'em covered. . . . It wasn't my job to figure 'em. out. . . . But brother, I never gave 'em more than the Geneva convention, and that was all."

There were many examples of dangerous photography in this motion picture; one of the most intense is the matter-of-fact recording of that long moment when the side of the LCI goes down and the men start clambering out onto the Normandy beach. You have seen their faces before, but now you see only their backs and you strain your eyes ahead, as they do, to see what is beyond. In that moment, an infinitesimal trace of the fear and darkness of war is shared. To have shared even so much with a wondering and uncomprehending public, was the achievement of those brave men who happened to carry cameras.

The True Glory is 8o minutes of priceless film. Along with its final message addressed directly to the public—"It is not the beginning but the continuing of the same, till it be thoroughly finished, which yieldeth the true glory"—this motion picture stands as one of the enduring artistic monuments to men at war.

8

Film and Foreign Policy:
The USIA, 1962-1967

THE FOCUS of diplomacy, which used to be concentrated on diplomats and kings, has broadened in the last 50 years to include a wide variety of targets. An ambassador is increasingly concerned with public opinion. Foreign policy responds, as it always has, to basic economic needs and the dignities of national traditions. But its application is now irrevocably tied to the rattle of teletypes and the drama of "peoples speaking to peoples."

The changing nature of world interactions at the unofficial level has its personal symbol in the rise of the American public affairs officer. In small diplomatic posts he may work virtually alone. At critical centers, he is surrounded by a corps of specialists—poll-takers, news reporters, speechmakers, speech writers, librarians, photographers, educational advisers. He may have it in his power to bring prominent Americans to visit, tour and teach. He can often give favored local "specialists" free trips to America. But he is primarily in charge of the ambassador's relationships with press, radio, television and film.

The U.S. film officer in any major capital is primarily a distribution man. He tries to get informational movies shown in theaters, schools, clubs, churches and union halls. He takes 16mm shows on the road. Sometimes he is also responsible for special film production, tailored to the needs of the country or area to which he is assigned. In certain key places he may put out a periodic newsreel. Always it is his duty to fulfill over-all "directives," worked out by his own public affairs officer or in Washington.

Such semi-military coordination no doubt stems partly from the fact that information activities got their major growth during World War II.

The whole notion of 16mm screenings in villages was a wartime development. Adjustments to "area needs" around the world was also a wartime
public relations policy. The content and style of these policy guidelines,
however—and in fact the whole surviving apparatus of angling for approval
among the populace of foreign countries—is in large part a result of the
ritual of cold war competition.

Budgets for films, for the Voice of America, and for other expensive
representations of the U.S. image would never have been granted in such
large amounts by the U.S. Congress without the overshadowing threat of
Soviet infiltration, Soviet influence and huge Soviet outlays for overseas
information. Down through the years, the hearings before appropriations
committees have echoed this theme. The postwar information activities of
the State Department (August 31, 1945) were built on the precedent of
the Office of War Information. Later they were split off again as a separate
organization, the United States Information Agency (August 31, 1953).
In every case, the Russian budget for propaganda was part of the plea for
the American budget.

Documentary film production in the U.S. Government had a new
renaissance of activity and quality in the USIA during the five-year period,
1962–67. The pictures could not be seen in this country during that time
because the Senate and House appropriations committees, wary of domestic propaganda and jealous of the executive branch, refused to permit such
showings.[1] Meanwhile, the art of the film was notably, if somewhat secretly,
enriched.

Who should be credited for this burst of creative work? George
Stevens, Jr., to be sure, and Edward R. Murrow, who hired him as director
of the Motion Picture Service. But if Woodrow Wilson was responsible
in an earlier day for encouraging the open diplomacy that led to the new
publicity functions of foreign policy, Stalin and Khruschchev deserve some
credit for directly encouraging the U.S. Congress to support the documentary motion picture program of the USIA.

Postwar Programs

The transition from the flooding urgency of wartime to the shoals of
peacetime foreign policy almost swamped the idea of film as an ambassador.

[1] In 1972, just as the National Archives had completed plans for releasing to educators USIA films old enough to carry no taint of propaganda, Senator William Fulbright of Arkansas protested and the films were once more impounded.

World War II had shown conclusively the value of new documentary production on specific subjects to counteract Hollywood fictions and dramatize daily life in America. But as soon as the war was over, the Office of War Information was abolished outright. The film program might well have gone with it. The only reason for continuing film activities at all, in the minds of many Congressmen, was the fact that the costly prints still existed and might be used a few times more. Unlike the vanished words of the Voice of America or the news releases of bygone events, a movie was an artifact with a long-range usefulness. Some, of course, had to be put on the shelf; others took on historic values. A few were still relevant enough to be put to work in the regular channels of international information as a part of American diplomacy. Therefore, along with Voice of America transmitters, overseas libraries and other OWI investments, film distribution to foreign countries was swept into a corner of the State Department.

The whole notion of an information function serving world public opinion was being accepted with extreme gradualism and great reluctance by the diplomatic establishment. Under Edward Stettinius (first as Undersecretary and later as Secretary) an Office of Public Information had been established in 1944.[2] Soon afterward the information process was further dignified by the assignment of a full-time Assistant Secretary—Archibald MacLeish, who had been head of the Office of Facts and Figures before it was merged into the OWI. He created a new Division of International Information, which became the logical receivership for the OWI and the Office of Inter-American Affairs when both were transferred into the department on August 31, 1945.

President Truman's statement accompanying Executive Order 9608 set the tone for foreign information work for the coming years, especially in his phrase, "a full and fair picture of American life":

> The nature of present-day foreign relations makes it essential for the United States to maintain informational activities abroad as an integral part of the conduct of our foreign affairs. . . . The government's international information program . . . will be designed to assist American private enterprises engaged in the dissemination of information abroad, and to supplement them in those specialized informational activities in which commercial or other limitations make it difficult for private concerns to carry on all necessary information work. . . . This government will not attempt to outstrip the extensive and growing information programs of other nations. Rather, it will endeavor to see to it that other peoples receive a full and fair picture of American life and of the aims and policies of the United States government.

[2] Herbert Edwards recalls that in 1942, in the State Department's Cultural Affairs Branch, he was allowed $500 for motion pictures. He spent it on postage, borrowing and looking at free films sponsored by industry, finding a few that might be useful.

Nevertheless, this was the time of trial for the information process, as it was for the National Film Board in Canada. Assistant Secretary William Benton, planning for 1946–47, "cut to the bone and into the bone," leaving a proposed staff of 1,276 from the 10,000 in the OWI, offering a budget of $19,284,778 compared to the OWI 1945 request of about $59-million.[3] The appropriations committee of the House of Representatives was unimpressed. Suspicious of propaganda, as always, the House cut back the budget almost by half, to $10-million. Benton took his case to the Senate, where the cut was restored, the conference committee later confirming the $19-million for the first year of the new Office of International Information and Cultural Affairs.[4]

The best way to get Congressional support in the years following was to chart the propaganda activities of other nations (despite President Truman's disclaimer on this score). The United States was far behind in the race for attention. As Secretary James F. Byrnes noted in his letter to Truman, this was "a new departure for the United States, the last of the great nations of the earth to engage in informing other peoples about its policies and institutions." [5]

Not until a group of Senators and Congressmen visited Europe, however, was there a chance to observe firsthand the effects of Soviet propaganda. The direct result was the passage of Public Law 402 (80th Congress, 2d Session), the U.S. Information and Educational Exchange Act, signed by Truman on January 27, 1948. After that the appropriations for the information service began to go up, year by year: $24-million for 1948; $33-million for 1949; $47-million for 1950. Following the outbreak of the Korean war in 1950, the budget reached a peak of $120-million.

The new postwar period brought the usual reaction against information programs. Four investigations were underway after the Eisenhower inauguration in 1952, including the free-swinging inquiry of Senator Joseph McCarthy, who seemed especially sure that there were Communists in the Department of State. The upshot of various recommendations (a committee on foreign information under William H. Jackson; a committee on the executive branch under Nelson Rockefeller) was separation from

[3] Hearings before Subcommittee of Committee on Appropriations, House of Representatives: Department of State Appropriation Bill for 1947 (79th Congress, 2d Session).

[4] Report to Accompany H.R. 6056, State, Justice, Commerce, and the Judiciary Appropriation Bill for Fiscal Year 1947. Appropriations Committee, House of Representatives, April 9, 1946. House Report #1890, 79th Congress, 2d Session. See also Congressional Record, 79th Congress, 2d Session, pp. 3518–41, 4441–57, 4525, 7417–33.

[5] Department of State Bulletin, January 10, 1946. Benton pointed out that there were 58 nations engaged in international shortwave broadcasting, that world shortwave output in April of 1946 was 3,229 hours per week, of which 50% originated in Europe and only 14% from North America. Per day, the Soviet Union was putting out 48 hours and 23 minutes in 23 languages. Hearings, Department of State Appropriation Bill for 1947, pp. 29, 100, 503.

the State Department. On August 31, 1953, under Reorganization Plan No. 8, the U.S. Information Agency came into existence. Its first director was Theodore Streibert, former board chairman of the Mutual Broadcasting System. His deputy, Abbott Washburn, had been drawn from the public relations department of General Mills to be executive secretary of the Jackson committee; he stayed on at USIA until the appointment of Edward R. Murrow as director in 1961.[6]

The International Motion Picture Service was headed by Herbert Edwards in the early State Department days. His chief claim to cinematic fame is a satisfactory sound version of Robert Flaherty's silent film, *Nanook of the North;* he was also active in Democratic politics, as was his wife, India Edwards, who later became national committeewoman. His policy was suitable for the times: whenever a government documentary film is proposed, "there must be an overwhelming need to produce such a film." He felt keenly the opposition of both Congress and Hollywood. His concept of the role of documentary was that it should "set the stage, the background, for the actions we take in world politics." When a picture was planned, it was usually given to one of the well-known eastern documentary people, such as Affiliated (Willard Van Dyke, Irving Jacoby, Henwar Rodakiewicz), International Film Foundation (Julien Bryan), or Louis de Rochemont Associates.[7]

Few documentaries were made—23 in five years, according to the U.S. Advisory Commission on Information.[8] Two films about the arts were offered to literate viewers in Europe. One was a record of the Berkshire Music Festival at Tanglewood; another was called *The Photographer: Edward Weston.* The former depended on the music to carry the sound track with almost no commentary; the latter was an experiment in biography partly dependent on carefully edited still photographs. Two others were successful for the same reason as the OWI's *Autobiography of a Jeep* —they showed technical skills in action. *Hurricane Circuit,* with the help of animation sequences, explained Caribbean storms and how international warning systems work. *International Ice Patrol* followed the crew of a Coast Guard vessel as they patrol the Grand Banks, send out information to all ships in the vicinity and go off at full speed to pursue a newly reported iceberg, keeping it under spotlights until it melts. This and *The*

[6] Robert E. Elder, *The Information Machine,* pp. 36–38. Published by Syracuse University Press in 1968, this book is a thorough account of many USIA procedures and problems since its establishment. The designation, "U.S. Information Service" was retained for posts overseas although the Washington headquarters was now called USIA.

[7] Interview, Herbert Edwards, December 16, 1949.

[8] The Advisory Commission was set up under authority of Public Law 402 in 1948. See Semiannual Report to the Congress, March 1949. A list issued in late 1950 showed 23 productions since the war, excluding news and magazine films, and the Advisory Commission indicated that there was a great need for more and better documentary films.

Photographer, both made by Affiliated Films, were outstanding documentaries.

Various other movies were made about farms and homes and dams and schools. The only one of these that got inside a social subject with much success was a film about the University of California at Los Angeles, made by the Apex Film Corporation (Jack Chertok), a small independent in Hollywood. Called simply *UCLA*, it traced the lives of four students, with emphasis on outside activities and employment, student government and personal relations, but with some information alongside about campus and courses. Overplotted and overdramatized, it nevertheless explained to literate foreign audiences the way many American college students live.

During the Eisenhower era, there was more production, but it was done on a "low bid" basis, and quality suffered drastically. Turner Shelton, head of IMS under Streibert, had come up through civil service channels and was more of a cost accountant than a motion picture man. He appointed Cecil B. DeMille as his chief Hollywood consultant. Not long before the end of his stewardship, he described in rather plain language but with considerable insight the value of motion pictures in the USIA program. In response to a Congressman's question, he said:

> Motion pictures . . . create an atmosphere of receptivity. They create an aura that makes people receptive to what we specifically have to say to them.
>
> For example, if you know me well and you know my background and someone says something bad about me, you will be able to discount it, that is, if you understand me thoroughly. I think motion pictures can make America understood.[9]

Yet a knowledgeable viewer of the films Shelton supervised finds little to praise and much to mourn. Major effort was expended on film recordings of Eisenhower speeches, together with newsreel reports on the visits of heads of state to Washington. *Robert Frost* was a good subject, but the execution was pedestrian and patronizing. *In Search of Lincoln* was outclassed by a little film made by the University of Southern California called *The Face of Lincoln*; Shelton wisely decided to buy prints of the USC film as well, and distribute them to posts abroad. *Symphony Across the Land, Museum of Art, American Illustrator* and *Printmakers*, were intended to showcase the arts. The most promising one of this group, *Charley Russell's Friends*, is hardly up to its subject. The famous painter of western scenes is revealed, as he should be, through his paintings, but the narration is uninformative, the music and sound effects crudely laid in, and the panning and editing on the paintings themselves seem to have been done by one of the cowboys.

[9] Hearings before the Subcommittee of the Committee on Appropriations of the House of Representatives: Departments of State, Justice, Etc. for 1962 (87th Congress, 1st Session)—USIA, p. 555.

Shelton's best achievement overseas was provided for him by Walt Disney, whose Circarama tour of the United States seemed to surround the viewer with beautiful scenery and well-scrubbed faces.[10] It was a hit in Casablanca, Moscow and Djakarta. His favorite film, however, the agency production he showed most proudly to visitors, could not have been made by a man who understood the USIA's audience. Someone suggested a picture about important shrines throughout the world; *Pilgrimage of Liberty* became instead a slickly photographed tour of American historic and patriotic places. Perhaps he thought such a theme would improve his uncomfortable relations with the House appropriations committee.

Fear or Friendship?

The Motion Picture Service was deeply involved in the ups and downs of appropriations and also in the swings of USIA policy. With the intensification of the cold war and the outbreak of hostilities in Korea, the whole agency stance moved from a background operation to open propaganda. After President Eisenhower's speech to the American Society of Newspaper Editors in April 1950, the line grew steadily tougher, on the assumption that "we are the ones who must make sure that the truth about Communism is known everywhere." [11]

A hard-hitting approach, however, fits uncomfortably with the motion picture audience. While the medium itself can accommodate slanted newsreels and such open propaganda appeals as the Frank Capra pictures during World War II, the "attack film" gets tiresome after a while, especially in a neutral country, busy with its own affairs. Shown on a theater screen, just ahead of a feature the public has paid to see, it risks indignation and even a reverse effect.

Film is at its best when it reaches deeper levels of thought and emotion. Wavering or questioning attitudes may well be influenced by works of art that convey the rich background and warmth of spirit characteristic of America. The persuasion is indirect. It balances the picture put out

10 See "Circarama—A Tour of America," leaflet published by U.S. Information Service, New Delhi, printed at USIS, Bombay.

11 See the *Christian Science Monitor*, April 20, 1950, for partial text of the Eisenhower speech. See also speech before Overseas Writers, August 29, 1950, by Edward W. Barrett, Assistant Secretary of State for Public Affairs. Interview, John Devine, IMS, State Department, confirmed this stronger line, emphasizing use of straight newsreel coverage of the Korean War (October 1950). A later argument for a strong line and a highly selective approach to the "truth" about the U.S., because that's what the Russians were doing, can be found in Arthur E. Mayerhoff, *The Strategy of Persuasion*; also review by James F. Fixx in *Saturday Review*, January 9, 1965, p. 74.

by news media and official speeches, which may stress only military strength or productive power. Furthermore, a good movie takes a long time to complete, and this delay in production makes it logically a longer-range instrument for foreign policy.

The dilemma can be expressed with stark simplicity: Does the nation wish to be feared or loved? Does the United States wish to be known as rich and proud and powerful, or as a nation like any other, with problems and poverty and weaknesses, with joys and sorrows, with moments of unity and of trial, having pride in the achievements of many individuals and humility about the vast resources which have been inherited and used? It is far easier, from a technical point of view, to present the mailed fist, to let it turn and glisten in the spotlight, than to seek out the commonplace human stories which connect man with man across the world.

Such humane, long-range objectives are just as difficult to sell in Congress as in Hollywood. It is not easy to meet the questions of hard-headed, accounting-minded Congressmen on the appropriations committee when large sums are to be spent for nice, entertaining, informative films without a definite message or target. Direct propaganda sounds good in a budget hearing. The art of indirection which may lead to better human relations in the long run—this sounds like some kind of "soft" philosophy of foreign relations.[12]

An experienced diplomat might be able to take a Congressman aside and reason with him thus, off the record: "Joe, when you go home to see your constituents, part of what you do is highly specific, like answering questions, or taking care of somebody's grievance. But the main reason you go back there is to visit around, to let them see you and get re-acquainted. Just spending time with your constituents is valuable. It helps get you re-elected and it helps the natural flow of the democratic process. Well, it's the same in international relations. An ambassador, at least in modern times, tries to be friendly, available and full of general information about his home country. A film can do more of this, sometimes do it better, and certainly do it in more places than he can. A film can be like an extended visit with American families, a fascinating contact with the American scene. It shouldn't be wasted on gaudy, mile-long parades, when the viewers would rather have an intimate, ten-minute visit."

Such advice is useful and practical for most peacetime purposes. The choice is clear to any overseas information expert who knows his audience. Still, there are always going to be films of force and pride to represent the firm attitudes of Congressmen who vote billions for defense every year. The mailed fist is often dominant, while the good neighbor policy waits.

12 "No one could prove last year's funds had been well spent by producing a cage filled with 7,000 Russians who had deserted Communism. The committee . . . could not see ten million Indians or Britons who had been made a little less suspicious of America than they were a year earlier." Edward W. Barrett, *Truth Is Our Weapon*, p. 90.

James Reston said of America's overseas information policy in the 1950's: "It is loud and obvious, preferring rape to seduction." [13]

The emphasis was changing back again by the end of the Eisenhower era. Theodore Streibert had told the Motion Picture Industry Council in Hollywood in 1954: "We are limiting film production to subjects which support our foreign policy and to those which refute Communist lies. With limited resources, we cannot afford to produce and distribute purely Americana films." [14]

At the 1960 hearings of the House Appropriations Committee, George V. Allen, about to conclude his second stint as USIA director, declared: "We cannot restrict ourselves solely to the exposition of the fallacy of Communism. Rather, we devote most of our energies to setting out what the United States is. I believe that this positive approach is more beneficial to the United States and more in accord with the basic mission of the Agency." [15]

In earlier postwar years there was one moment when the choices were simple and the role of film happily fulfilled. In Europe, just after the war, the Economic Cooperation Administration was a giver of American millions on a wide variety of fronts. The Marshall Plan legislation specified that these gifts should not go unnoticed. The ECA information program under Roscoe Drummond (on leave from the *Christian Science Monitor*) included an active film production program supervised by Lothar Wolff (on leave from Louis de Rochemont Associates). About 70 subjects were produced, some for use in only one country, but many of them intended to be shown in all the European countries receiving Marshall Plan funds. European film-makers were used—men like John Ferno, Victor Vicas, and Arthur Elton.

These documentaries were direct reflections of physical changes in the face of Europe, as postwar reconstruction restored the land, rebuilt the towns and gave immediate hope to millions of individual men and women. Here was a subject film could easily cope with. Outward change, physical development, mechanical processes—these are natural subjects for the motion picture. ECA film directors followed the traditional paths of problem-and-solution laid out in years past by such American documentaries as *Power and the Land* and *The City*.

In *Village Without Water*, men and women who had grown used to carrying their water got a new aqueduct from the ECA. *Adventure in Sardinia* showed the defeat of malaria by a team of health experts. *Fuel Lines to Italy* reported on new oil pipelines from the Middle East and the building of new refineries. *Project for Tomorrow* showed how a 4-H club

[13] New York *Times*, January 29, 1961, Sec. IV, p. 100.

[14] USIA press release, March 15, 1954, for release after Streibert's speech March 17, 1954, in Hollywood.

[15] Hearings before the Subcommittee of the Committee on Appropriations: Departments of State, Justice, Etc. (86th Congress, 2d Session)—USIA, p. 7.

could be organized in Austria along lines familiar in the farm country of the American midwest. *Rice and Bulls* told the story of a change of mind: a cattle raiser in Southern France is persuaded to diversify by growing rice. There were general survey films, too, and reports on such projects as the Rhine barge fleet, a cutlery industry, electric power plants and the Corinth canal.[16]

The Marshall Plan films were not about American life. They did reflect the American spirit of change and progress—the ingrained attitude that "there must be some better way." They accompanied a historic moment and a magnanimous concept of free giving in the wake of disaster. It was a time when hearts were full, actions were generous and gratitude was freely spoken. The documentary film did its part by multiplying, intensifying and recording for posterity one of the greatest achievements of American foreign policy.

A Young Man From Hollywood

Hollywood is a major factor in foreign information policy. Movies are ambassadors whether they mean to be or not—and few dramas fit diplomatic needs. In the long run, the kinds of films Hollywood makes for boxoffice purposes are the best reasons in the world for the kinds of counter-movies the government must make for public relations purposes.

Out of the endless argument, pro and con, about the impact of American films abroad, one thing is clear. Hollywood cannot in all logic say that movies "sell the American way of life," or promote the triumph of good over evil (at least till recently) and yet deny that films can ever sell violence, eroticism, brutality or decadence. Those who try to speak for a peaceable, home-loving America in American embassies abroad are well aware that they are whispering against a gale.

In an ill-starred speech in Hollywood (soon after he became director of the USIA) Edward R. Murrow tried to state the obvious, the facts everybody knew about responses to Hollywood films abroad.[17] His listeners

[16] Glen Burch, "The Film Forum: Marshall Plan at Work," *Saturday Review*, February 17, 1951, p. 42. Also Arthur Knight, "Documentary—Rallying Point for Europe," pp. 40–42. Letter to author by Margaret Jones, ECA New York, December 6, 1950. Index of ECA Documentary Films, October 1, 1950. Interview, Lothar Wolff, November, 1950.

[17] "Films provide a high level of audience enjoyment and at the same time convey an equally high level of negative impressions about the United States. Because audiences like the extremities of storytelling is no reason to feed them that to the exclusion of all else. Children like candy. They will eat it to excess if fed only that. But no man in his right mind would prescribe a diet of chocolate bars and ice cream. Self restraint and

were alarmed. They upbraided him for trying to censor the art of the film. Like Lowell Mellett, 20 years before, he was attacked as a government czar speaking out of turn, as a traitor to freedom of information. Yet all he had asked for was a new approach now and then—a real try at the job of telling some different truths about the common life in America.

As producer (with Fred W. Friendly) of *See It Now* and *CBS Reports*, Murrow fully understood the historic role of nonfiction films.[18] At the very time he was chiding the entertainment industry, he was searching for a man who could take up the real challenge against the Hollywood film— someone who could sling against Goliath once in a while the small, smooth stone of the documentary.

As in the days of World War II (when there were 200 old gangster films available for newly liberated France but not a single satisfactory picture about the TVA) the Kennedy administration accepted the necessity for affirmative and creative activity. No vested interest in a free enterprise society could really be expected to make the documentaries needed for foreign policy themes. The government had to make them.

In his search for a new chief for the motion picture service, Murrow was faced with problems of qualification, representation and personality. Documentary people from the east, especially from television, might have been his first choice; such men were well qualified to turn out quickly the plain film statements needed overseas. On the other hand, there were many advantages in having a representative Hollywood "name." Such a man would not only please the industry but would carry prestige at all those diplomatic receptions connected with film festivals and special film showings. Finally, he knew he needed someone who could bend smilingly before the gusts of Congressional committee hearings and yet be firm enough to lead a whole new program.

One of Murrow's special friends in Hollywood was Samuel Goldwyn. In fact, one of his own CBS documentaries had explored the career of America's most independent motion picture producer. Murrow and Goldwyn talked about the staffing problem. Among others, they talked about Goldwyn's son, who had done some work with documentaries when he was on Eisenhower's Paris staff after the war; but Sam Goldwyn Jr. was bent on doing some producing of his own in Hollywood.

Next on the list was the son of one of the most respected directors in

---

control make a healthy child. I suggest that the image conveyed abroad of our land is not always a healthy one, and self restraint may nowadays be a good prescription. . . . I would be bold enough to suggest that the history of this land, done as only your skills could do it, would reap great benefits abroad and solidify the purpose of our own people." Edward R. Murrow, Speech to Representatives of Film Industry in Hollywood, November 5, 1961.

[18] See, for example, William Bluem, *Documentary in American Television*. Also *See It Now*, transcripts of some of the half-hour CBS-TV programs, and Alexander Kendrick, *Prime Time*, a biography of Murrow.

America. George Stevens, Jr., was invited to see Murrow at Goldwyn's house. He was not interested at all (he said afterward) in a government job, but "most interested in meeting Ed Murrow and exchanging some ideas about motion pictures," including one he wanted to make for the USIA on an independent basis. They talked for two hours. Murrow then asked him if he would come to Washington.

It was a difficult decision, and he took two more months to "sort it out." He was deeply involved in associate producer duties for his father on *The Greatest Story Ever Told*. There was a script he wanted to film on his own. Yet the possibility of making a unique contribution to his country's history and to film history could not be lightly put aside.

The most important factor, perhaps, was a picture in his head, remembered from Theodore White's *The Making of a President, 1960*. "Here were all these young men," Stevens recalled, "who had given up jobs to get behind JFK. It was an exciting atmosphere of fresh thought and action, of energy, of youth. I was young, and I thought I could fit in with that atmosphere." [19]

Ed Murrow told him later he was more than a little apprehensive about his new employee's tender years. In February 1962, when Stevens came to work in Washington, he was 28.

The Contract Problem

On November 8, 1961, three days after his first talk with Murrow, Stevens wrote him a letter about a film the USIA ought to make. Together with Leslie Stevens, a young Hollywood producer, he proposed "special film coverage" of Jacqueline Kennedy's forthcoming visit to Pakistan. The purpose would be to "show to all of the nations of the world the seriousness with which our country takes the Indo-Asian peoples. By catching the moment-to-moment attitude of the First Lady as she encounters the peoples of Pakistan, we can demonstrate both the stature and dignity of America and, at the same time, provide eyewitness proof of our true democratic spirit. The key, as we see it, is that Mrs. Kennedy comes to *learn* from Pakistan: who its people are, what they hope for, their wants and needs, their culture and their accomplishments. By virtue of her warm personality and her intense curiosity, Mrs. Kennedy is ideal for such a film."

In Washington, as the new head of the motion picture service of the USIA, this was the first project Stevens tried to make come true. The

[19] Interview, George Stevens Jr., February 1965.

trip had been postponed, and it now included India. Perhaps he could not afford to hire Ted McCord, a leading Hollywood cinematographer, as he had urged in his letter, but he could try to get one of the leading documentary film-makers in the East—someone like Leo Seltzer.

Now he came up against his first governmental roadblock. Films, tradition said, are like desks or dams. Each purchase must be open to competitive bids. The lowest bidder gets the job. Imagination, effective scripting, personal suitability—to such matters a contract must be blind.

Stevens had run into this problem before. When he was a first lieutenant in the Air Force, from 1954 to 1956, with the 1365th Photographic Squadron at Orlando Field, Florida, he had observed the solemn bidding by competitive companies for the privilege of filming *Meat Cutting by the Rail Method* and *Walk-Around Inspection of the F86D*.

If he really wanted to catch "the moment-to-moment attitude" of Jacqueline Kennedy, however, there had to be some better way. The USIA film program had been hobbled for years by government accounting routines which assumed that art could be bought by the yard. He talked over the problem with Anthony Guarco, veteran deputy director of the motion picture service, who wanted as much as anybody to find a way around this unfeeling, unseeing obstacle to international communication. "Tony is a man who can facilitate anything," Stevens says. "He is thoughtful, progressive, enormously effective and helpful." They prepared their case and took it "upstairs":

> We had several meetings on this in Murrow's office, trying to figure out ways to attract better film-makers. We decided that we could successfully defend, at the General Accounting Office and before Congress, a procedure of assigning pictures to people because they were best qualified, and then keeping a budget control at the usual professional stop-points—research, script, production, completion.
>
> In the meantime, we had already put the Jackie Kennedy film out for bids. We were entitled to send bids to a selected list of people, and we included Leo Seltzer. His bid, of course, was quite high; Hearst and Fox Movietone, as usual, were low. I was pretty much in despair about the whole thing. I knew we couldn't get the picture we wanted if we were restricted to the mentality and methods of low-budget newsreel production.
>
> Well, what we finally did was to give the contract to Hearst and persuade them to hire Seltzer as director and his wife as writer. The budget had to be amended later on—it came to about the original high bid after all, because of our requirements. We also divided it into two separate films for overseas use.[20]

The result was very nearly what Stevens had hoped for—two fresh and friendly films that pleased theater audiences and 16mm viewers all

[20] Interview, February 1965.

over the world. He also got more than he bargained for: a groundswell of
pressure for release in this country. He willingly helped this movement
along by making the films available for private showings in Hollywood.
Eventually Congress voted, by joint resolution, that theatrical release
would be a good thing, and the India and Pakistan films, recombined,
were widely seen as a single short subject in American movie houses.

The contract problem remained. Guarco says it was worn down in
large part because of Stevens' adamant insistence on using outstanding
film-makers:

> He came in at just the right time. Herb Edwards had used the choice
> method, too, under Truman, and the climate of the Congress allowed
> it. Under Eisenhower, Turner Shelton was badgered unmercifully by
> the Democrats in the House and being a financial type himself he was
> not inclined to seek out any new procedures.

> Under Kennedy, the administration and Congress were both Demo-
> cratic again, and the committees were disposed to let us try a few
> things. We were, of course, completely justified in doing it this way
> because of the nature of film, and so long as we had successes, nobody
> quarreled with our way of working. I think now it has been pretty well
> established that the matching system can be kept financially under
> control.[21]

It is this latter concept, as much as anything, which may be remembered as Stevens' contribution to government film production precedents
—the matching of talented young documentary directors with specific
public relations themes.

Stevens studied hard the aspects of the American way of life the USIA
directives told him to emphasize—racial and ethnic progress, economic
strength, economic democracy, scientific and educational strength, and
cultural diversity. He kept in mind the agency's policy directives, too,—the
pursuit of peace, strength and reliability, free choice, the rule of law and
support of the United Nations. He kept them at hand to show his
prospective film-makers.

Then he started looking for individuals, not companies, who could
make films that would be notable for liveliness, warmth and originality—
films reflecting some knowledge of film's own expressive possibilities. He
laid this general proposition before the young directors he wanted to work
for him: "Here are the wide variety of subjects we need to have covered.
For example, we want to get across to people overseas the way government and business can successfully work together for social betterment.
Is there some case study in this area that would appeal to you?"

Not a critic or theorist of the art of the film, Stevens nevertheless was
keenly aware of the long-standing claim by film-makers in Hollywood that

[21] Interview, Anthony Guarco, February 1965.

the best results come from essential control by a single artist. He had been, for a short time, a TV film director, and his associations, through his father, were with members of the Screen Directors Guild. He tried, so far as possible, to give to each man freedom to choose a subject and, after that, freedom to make the film. Supervision was mainly to touch four points—the selection of the man in the first place (usually on the basis of someone's recommendation and the submission of an existing film), approval of preliminary treatment and of script, and approval of the final edited film.

This is not to say that he avoided the responsibility of the executive producer. Some would say that he was all too active in shaping each and every film, much in the manner of the youthful Irving Thalberg, whose meteoric career at MGM in the early 1930's is interpreted variously by those he curbed and those he left free. Stevens fancied the role of teacher-producer from the beginning. He gave projects to students in university film departments. He sought out others who had only one or two films to their credit. He worked closely with some of these and assigned others to "project supervisors." Always he was fascinated, like his father before him, by the possibilities for adjustment and change in the cutting room. A screening was only a chance to find out how it could be done better.

As director of the Motion Picture Service, Stevens in fact selected the subjects and controlled the development of all domestically produced USIA films. The important thing is that USIA control was relatively loose in the early stages of production. A man could develop a treatment and work out a rough script in his own way, as long as the budget and shooting schedule fitted in with governmental ideas of expense. Thus Stevens could get freshness and variety and still fulfill his basic function as a tax-paid communicator of American policy and the American way of life.

Documentaries for the World

During the five years he was director of the Motion Picture Service, Stevens kept a balance among newsreels, special projects supporting foreign policy, and the art of the documentary film. But it was clear from the first that his major effort would go into the kind of film-making which went beyond the crisis of the moment. The year before, at the time of his appointment, he had told the committee:

I was disappointed by the number of documentaries made. I recalled that my unit in the service, commanded by a major, produced between 40 and 60 documentary films each year solely for the consumption of the men of that service. Last year USIA produced in this country 13 documentaries for the consumption of the world.[22]

As he brought his own tastes and interests to bear on the quality of film production, Stevens found that he could not increase the quantity very much.[23] This was partly a matter of budget; it also reflected the difficulty of procuring talent which could supervise as well as create.

It took a year or more to begin to find directors.

Leo Seltzer, who had received an Academy Award and a silver medal from Venice for *First Steps*, continued to work for Stevens after *Invitation to India* and *Invitation to Pakistan*. In *Friendship and Independence*, *Poland Abroad* and *Saturn*, Seltzer showed his capacity to handle assigned projects of a topical nature and develop them with documentary depth.

In St. Louis Stevens found Charles Guggenheim. He owned his own production company for industrial and educational films and had stirred some interest with a study of integration and education called A *City Decides*. For the USIA, he made *United in Progress*, a survey of the moves toward a common market economy in Central America. *Nine From Little Rock* reported on the later lives of the first Negro children who stepped into that famous, beleaguered Arkansas high school. Their faces were full of courage, but the narration made clear the step upward they had achieved—most of them had moved away from Arkansas.

Later, Guggenheim was asked to produce one of the most propagandist of all USIA films, *Night of the Dragon*. Its all-out support of the American effort in Vietnam was to be expected; its chilling feeling of the danger of living through any night in Saigon was prophetic and paradoxical in its underlying feeling that the war was not being won.[24]

Among the many commercial producers of 16mm films in Los Angeles, Stevens found Bruce Herschensohn. He had already edited and scored a space flight film for the USIA, *Friendship Seven*. For Stevens, he

[22] Hearings, Subcommittee of the Committee on Appropriations, House of Representatives: Departments of State, Justice and Commerce, the Judiciary and Related Agencies Appropriations for 1963 (87th Congress, 2d Session)—USIA, p. 422.

[23] Each year, about 15 USIA documentaries were produced within the United States. These were basic films intended for most of the areas of the world, prepared in multiple-language versions. Some 200 or 300 more, of widely varying lengths, were made overseas, in single language versions, to meet needs for understanding within a special geographical area; they were usually assigned to local directors and crews in the countries where they were to be seen. Newsreels from various posts were released at the rate of about 300 a year. Not till Stevens' fourth year, when television and motion pictures were consolidated under his direction, did the quantity of domestic film-making increase.

[24] An Associated Press story of January 13, 1965, revealed what were described as "fake" scenes photographed in Vietnam by the director, Richard Heffron. Because of the uproar over this and over the use of American troops for close-ups and other connecting scenes so often necessary in any well-made film, Carl Rowan, USIA director at the time, ordered a stop to any "mock battles" (the United Press phrase) for *Night of the Dragon*.

made *Bridges of the Barrios,* in which the Ecuadorian army found peace-time pride in helping to build a better water system. Then, in *Five Cities of June,* produced by Hearst Metrotone News, he struck a vein of parallel reporting which seemed to please the USIA's far-flung audiences; it particularly impressed President Kennedy. The film (27 minutes in length) attempted to show scenes of world importance during June 1963, including the death of Pope John and the election of Pope Paul, the activities of a Soviet female cosmonaut, and the admission of two Negro students to the University of Alabama. More time and emphasis were devoted, how-ever, to foreign policy elements: the presence of John Kennedy in West Berlin and his fighting speech to a vast multitude there, and the menacing presence of Viet Cong infiltrators (soon defeated) in a hamlet in South Vietnam.

Herschensohn became the man to lean on for the more didactic essays on foreign policy. His ability to write, direct, edit and compose music brought an unusual degree of economy and directness to USIA film-making, and his skill in compilation was important when speed was neces-sary. After the assassination of President Kennedy, Stevens turned to him for a short film intended to reassure viewers abroad that the American constitutional system survives such shocks. *The President* was a simple, informative introduction of Lyndon Johnson to the world, produced in something like three days and nights for distribution to all diplomatic posts abroad.

Herschensohn, too, directed the feature-length film about the Ken-nedy years for which Stevens himself took producer credit. *John F. Kennedy: Years of Lightning, Day of Drums* was an attempt to connect the personality of the dead president with his own statements about foreign affairs, linked at intervals with shots of the funeral in Washington. Civil rights, the space program, the Alliance for Progress and the Peace Corps were major themes. There was impressive footage (borrowed from the earlier film, *Five Cities of June*) of Kennedy addressing the throngs in Berlin. A strong plea to remember Kennedy and his policies, the picture nevertheless could not easily carry its double burden of personal affection and public policy. It reached large audiences overseas, but when it was finally released for theaters in the U.S. in 1964 (by special joint resolution of Congress) it seemed anticlimactic to those who remembered the direct eye of television during three days of mourning.

The following year Herschensohn was working on still another compi-lation, this time comprising "20 stories without beginnings or ends," all taking place at the same moment in the "two-thirds of the world living in freedom." Entitled *Eulogy to 5:02,* it included a bazaar in Baluchistan, a wedding in the Himalayas, a village well in Africa, a library in Latin America, a fish-and-chips store in England, and a Los Angeles salesman driving home on the freeway. While the educational value of this kind

Still photograph from *The School at Rincon Santo* **(Dir. James Blue) for USIA, 1963**

of breathless simultaneity might have been questioned by those who wanted to get across deeper messages, the format offered a further expansion of detail through the use of multiple images, a process already experimented with in a brief sequence in the Kennedy film.

At the Cannes film festival, Stevens discovered James Blue. A young man from Oregon who had gone far afield for his film study, Blue was fortified with some camera and editing experience at the Institut des Hautes Etudes Cinématografiques in Paris. His feature film, *The Olive Trees of Justice*, impressed Cannes critics with its quiet documentary quality and its resolute attempt to get behind the scenes of one family's involvement in the Algerian war. Stevens decided to try him out in Latin America. U.S. aid through the Alliance for Progress was being poured into Colombia and President Kennedy was eager to see the story told on film. In the manner of the old Marshall Plan films, Blue was to find some village or event where the aid was visible and try to catch the new spirit of change with his camera.

He brought back a trilogy of ten-minute films, and one of them was a triumph. *Letter from Colombia* reported in a general way on the moves

Still photograph from _The March_ (Dir. James Blue) for USIA, 1964

toward land reform and agricultural training, with a false note in the middle which joked about the film's own message of progress. _Evil Wind Out_ told more plainly the story of the overcoming of superstitious fears and the acceptance of simple rules of diet and hygiene. _The School at Rincon Santo_, which received unanimous praise from posts overseas, was one of those rare achievements which make ten other false starts worth-while.

There had never before been a school in this little Colombian town. The Alliance for Progress was providing building materials, and the people were doing the labor. A familiar theme in the history of the documentary film, it is handled here with almost perfect simplicity. Blue did not arrive in time to catch the early stages of construction. With wise equanimity, he photographed in close-up the wall of bricks, telling us by narration how many people had worked on it. He showed children wandering at large in the fields—and the same children, later on, being brought to the first day of class. In this graceful and dramatic finale, each pupil is firmly seated in his proper place by the teacher, herself a bit tense with joy and appre-hension; the camera then turns to show the proud faces of parents peering through the window. The lesson begins: it is the Spanish alphabet. The

chanting aloud of the letters continues over an extreme long shot of the
school, seen below in the ancient valley, which will never be quite the
same again.

Another film by James Blue is probably the most memorable one of
the Stevens era at USIA. *The March* (1964) has something of the epic
quality of *The River*, and in the manner of that poetic government documentary, it reflects the sharp excitement of a great contemporary issue. The
civil rights march on Washington had to be reported. To have ignored it
would have been foolish, when newspapers had already brought daily
reports on it to readers all over the world. Then how should it be handled?
As a simple parade? As a kind of disaster? Stevens and Blue had no doubt
that the important thing was to keep the moral issue firmly in view in a
framework of free speech. After some lighthearted footage on the preparations—bus riders, sandwich packers, poster-carriers—and the mingling of
faces in the crowds, the strong climax of the half-hour film was the stirring
speech of Martin Luther King.

Southern repression in all its harshness, the Northern ghetto with its
cold segregation—these were not pictured in *The March*. Liberal critics
who later saw or heard about the film thought these elements should have
been shown, rather than implied. Conservative critics, on the other hand,
wondered why the story had to be told at all.[25] Responses from Africa and
Asia were answer enough: the United States was not afraid of a march, and
the United States government was not afraid to show it on film.

These, then, were the men the USIA depended on the most—Seltzer,
Herschensohn, Guggenheim, Blue.[26] From the beginning, however, Stevens
had wanted to use young film-makers on single projects. His first experiment in this direction was an invitation to young movie-makers to try to
communicate by means of film with other young people around the world.
He pulled apart a budget for a single $30,000 film and offered $5,000 apiece
to six University students. Selection proved to be a ticklish process and the
staff settled for recent graduates of university film departments, in order
to be assured of receiving completed films. Technical logistics were even
more difficult, and Richard Kahlenberg, a graduate of the Northwestern
and Boston University film programs, was asked to supervise the five
campus facilities being used. Stuart Hanisch, a graduate of the University
of Southern California department of cinema, then working in the film
unit at the University of Wisconsin, undertook to show how education

[25] See, for example, "Look Who's Selling Mob Action," editorial in Phoenix,
Arizona, *Gazette*, January 24, 1964. Secretary of State Dean Rusk was greatly disturbed.
He required all ambassadors to pass on the film; some refused to let it be shown. A
defensive statement by USIA Director Carl Rowan was filmed as a special introduction.

[26] Guggenheim eventually moved his company to Washington, as more national
contracts came his way. After a year on a Ford Foundation grant, Blue was called back
to help Stevens strengthen the monthly newsfilms beamed at Latin America. Herschensohn, after the creation of the American Film Institute in 1967, became Stevens' successor at USIA as Stevens moved on to be director of the AFI.

schools give actual classroom training in *Student Teacher.* Stuart Hagmann and Robert Ford, of Northwestern University, offered a study of the daily life of a *Student Engineer.* Alvin Fiering showed the life and work of a fellow student at Boston University in *The Sculptor.* Other contributions were *Patterns in Jazz,* by Dugald McArthur of Baylor University, and *I Hear the Carpenter Singing,* by Hart Sprager of the University of Southern California. Except for the jazz film, which was made at a school with no film resources or tradition, all of these pictures were fresh and appealing. Their youthful origins and technical limitations made them of special interest to their expected audiences abroad.[27]

Thereafter, Stevens developed a somewhat more cautious open-door policy, letting the major film schools know that he was receptive to applications, but handling everything on an individual basis. Inquiries (like his own inquiry to Murrow) came in from prospective young film-makers. He would suggest that they send him a film. If their work looked promising, he might invite them to Washington and offer them a project in the *Young America* series. If they were interested in joining the agency, they might become "interns" and help make pictures either in Washington or overseas. Two of the best-known west coast film graduates were directly invited to propose subjects. Terry Sanders (with his brother Denis) had made the Civil War story, *A Time Out of War,* at UCLA and had gone on to do minor feature directing in Hollywood. He was eventually assigned a lengthy report on the 1964 political conventions. Kent Mackenzie had made *Bunker Hill, 1956* at the University of Southern California and *The Exiles* afterward, a feature-length documentary about displaced American Indians in Los Angeles. He agreed to do a short documentary on the vocational training programs of the Department of Health, Education and Welfare.

A later discovery was Carroll Ballard, who had impressed his professors at UCLA with *Waiting for May,* a bittersweet impression of an old woman's memories. He delivered a remarkable study of an Oregon farm family, *Beyond This Winter's Wheat.* Thematically a testament to the goals of foreign aid and foreign trade, the film refers with pride to U.S. wheat shipments to the Soviet Union and India. The young narrator (who incidentally declares that his grandfather came from the Ukraine) is preparing to depart for a stint with the Peace Corps, sharing his inherited skills and scientific know-how with less fortunate lands. Meanwhile we

---

[27] See USIA press release, November 13, 1962, for announcement of grants. One of the planned projects, "a counselor in a California conservation camp," did not materialize. One report from USIS Fort-de-France in Martinique: "Though we frequently rent a local downtown theater in Fort-de-France for the showing of USIS films, we have rarely had as enthusiastic a response to our flms as that which greeted the first showing here of the *Young America* series. Quite characteristically—and without any USIS prompting—the audience broke into applause at the end of five of the six films, failing only to applaud the film on jazz, for reasons we have not determined."

see his close family ties and feel his closeness to the soil itself and to those great machines that drew the close-plowed furrows stretching to the horizon.

Documentaries about government agencies fitted well into USIA policies. They tended to modify the commonly held view of a harsh American capitalism by showing the many humane collective decisions Americans have made. *Joe*, a film by Robert K. Sharpe, attempted to convey the importance of social security benefits to an old man retiring from work in a machine shop. *Labor of Love* (written, produced and directed by John G. Fuller) showed the work of three public servants—a forest ranger, a social worker and a therapist. A plain film, it nevertheless managed to be informative and revealing about some ordinary people in the United States. More ambitious was Gary Goldsmith's *Born a Man*. The retraining of a blinded man (by a state agency with the help of federal funds) was shown to be complicated by the man's starchy personality. There are some brilliant moments in this rather theatrical film, and the idea in one narrative line is thought-provoking: "No man truly sees with his eyes. He sees with his mind. But he must truly believe what he can do." At the end, we watch the blind man take up once more his trade as an electrician —his senses of touch and hearing expanded and confident, his ability to get around with a cane finally accepted.

Kent Mackenzie's approach to a similar theme placed more emphasis on the documentary detail of a man's life. *A Skill for Molina* is not only about the classroom work and examinations Molina must go through to improve his wage rate. It also mirrors a particular Mexican family in all its quarrels, fears and solidarity. We learn from a series of still photographs the story of Molina's early struggles for jobs and education. In other sequences, Mackenzie's unobtrusive camera captures moments of family tension and relaxation with natural grace.

The sense of multiplicity in the melting pot was attempted more indirectly in an editing exercise directed by William Hale and photographed by Haskell Wexler called *Grand Central Market*. It showed, without comment, the mingling of races in a downtown market in Los Angeles amid the sounds of paper sacks snapping and cash registers ringing. This pattern of purely visual exploration of America was continued in a special semi-experimental series. *Faces of America*, by Ed Emshwiller (known as the most technically accomplished of the so-called underground film-makers) led the viewer across the country for shots of men and boys on motorcycles and bicycles, girls dancing and women reading, people working in factories, on farms, moving earth, sawing lumber—a kaleidoscope that might fascinate and also confuse an outsider. *Architecture USA*, directed by Tibor Hirsch, an American from Hungary, photographed briskly the latest buildings shining in the sun—morning, noon and night—but made no attempt to contrast older styles of architecture which might have interested many foreign viewers.

Whatever one might say about individual films, the essential thing was that an atmosphere of experimentation was maintained in the very midst of a mundane propagandist mission. In the tradition of John Grierson, Stevens managed to draw into a program of national publicity a variety of individualists. The U.S. Information Agency became the only place in the United States where young film-makers might advance from college projects or first efforts for industrial sponsors to a filmic statement on a broader theme.

Certain programs had to be covered and foreign policy points made. *President Tito in the U.S.A.* and a dozen other colorful pictures about heads of state were produced and sent to the countries concerned. Newsreel footage was unspooled in quantity in accordance with regional requests, USIA "country plans," and subject priorities. But when it came to documentaries about America, there was always the chance for insight and for art. In *A Bridge to Tomorrow*, Nicholas Webster could put some of the excitement of modern trends in scientific education at Massachusetts Institute of Technology, including the new emphasis on the humanities. In *My Friend the Enemy*, something of the real impact of invention and automation on the lives of union members could be dramatized, and the slow acceptance of solutions through retraining and retirement. Even the theme of national strength could be somewhat infused with human values as William Jersey showed the practical problems met by idea men and craftsmen working in the background *Behind the Spaceman*. And occasionally there was the opportunity for Ed Emshwiller to zoom into a survey like *Art Scene USA*, or young film-makers like Mike Ahneman and Gary Schlosser to examine the relaxed home life of a third-generation *Cowboy*.

Arthur Schlesinger, Jr., who was a film critic for *Show* magazine at the same time he was an adviser to President Kennedy, had this to say about the USIA film program: "There have not been so many striking films stimulated in Washington since the days of Pare Lorentz and the Department of Agriculture film program a generation ago." The best ones —*A Skill for Molina, Born a Man, Beyond This Winter's Wheat*, and especially *Invitation to India, The School at Rincon Santo* and *The March* —are in the great tradition of government documentaries in England and Canada as well.[28]

---

[28] An Academy Award went to *Nine From Little Rock* in 1964 and a nomination to *Five Cities of June* (1963) and *Cowboy* (1966), and *Harvest*, the Carroll Ballard film (1967), for best documentary. *The March* won first prize at the Bilbao documentary festival (1964) and the Cannes Youth Festival (1966). At Venice, *The School at Rincon Santo* won a first prize for human relations and *Letter from Colombia* won a Lion of St. Mark for documentary (1963). See also Hollis Alpert, "Movies That Carry the Freight," *Saturday Review*, December 12, 1964.

The Burdens of Public Communication

It is not the primary purpose of film-makers, or any artist for that matter, to create an image of their country; it is their job to express their perceptions to the best of their ability.

If Stevens could have operated on this basis alone, his troubles would have been chiefly artistic ones. He could have subsidized promising young directors to express themselves and waited for critics to judge the results. But as he further pointed out to the Los Angeles Rotary Club in June, 1964:

It is the responsibility of USIA to seek to have us better understood and to make known our aims and ideals, so that all in the world who seek a better life in peace may feel that the United States stands with them.

The patriotic demand on the artist is only one aspect of this basic dilemma in linking film and foreign policy. The artist has agreed to become more or less willingly a propagandist. The matching game, which offers him a choice of several subjects, makes him, for a while, an advocate of some part of his country's way of life. But he also needs to be aware of a more professional matter—his intended audience, and the intended effect on that audience. He should be able to justify his efforts—before, during and after production—in terms of attitudes to be reached, touched and changed. This is a wearisome, nettling and sometimes destructive burden for creative film-makers. Many of the young artists Stevens hired were unable to talk very knowledgeably about audience effect and in fact were reluctant to be concerned about it at all.

Stevens and his production staff members usually undertook to mediate between the writer-director and his worldwide audience. This meant that Stevens also had to be the buffer between the artist and his sponsor— the USIA itself—a task involving continuous, elaborate and hazardous intra-agency diplomacy. Not only did he have to justify each film to a battery of assistant directors at the top of the agency. The logic of USIA organization also calls for divisions representing major regions, as it does in the State Department. The head of each division—Latin America, Far East, Middle East, Africa, Europe—must see and judge every proposal, every script, every finished film. However beautiful and cinematic the completed project might turn out to be, if these division chiefs decided it wasn't useful in their areas, then money would not be forthcoming for translated versions, and the motion picture division would be left with an expensive production available only to Great Britain and its English-speaking dependencies, dominions and former possessions, most of which were friendly enough already.

Division chiefs are usually people who have had years on the firing line in various consular and diplomatic posts. Trained in journalism or academic work, inured to the necessities of formal speechmaking by ambassadors and others, they are happy with hard-sell techniques and straight news, impatient with the indirect and subliminal effects that films can best accomplish. It is fairly easy for such men to respond to the simple emotional impact of an extraordinarily likeable film once it is made. They will be able to guess that its effect may be similar in many places overseas. It is harder for them to assess the long range approval that may come from mildly *avant-garde* films like *Art Scene USA* because intellectual groups abroad are pleased to see it.

Stevens did not try to experiment too much. If division heads and assistant directors tended to be dubious, the appropriations committees were likely to be totally unsympathetic. He defended the impressionistic films on an economic basis: they needed no narration or dialogue in multiple languages. Beyond that, he simply tried to have a balanced program, serving many subjects and interests.

There had to be audience studies, of course. A special staff kept track of showings, number of viewers and the presumed effects on attitudes. Sometimes the audience surveys consisted merely of quotations from friendly newspapers or theater owners. But one impressive report by a professional polling organization gave strong support to the persuasiveness of a particular documentary film. *The School at Rincon Santo* was shown to 500 Latin Americans. They were asked questions afterward about U.S. aid given through the Alliance for Progress. Of this test group, 72 per cent approved of the Alliance. A control group, selected in the same way from similar backgrounds, did not see the film. Of these, only 54 per cent expressed approval. Here was evidence that those faces on the screen carried conviction far beyond the general knowledge gained already through other media. Yet the response to this film could not have been predicted or planned in advance of production.[29]

Film is a medium directed at large audiences. Pinpointing its effects is as hard as limiting its purposes. *The School at Rincon Santo* was effective precisely because it was not a hard-sell, calculated message fitted like a glove to some pre-selected purpose. It was an unexpected work of art, and it accomplished far more than its budget or its intended objectives foretold.

[29] The report on the survey by "a professional polling organization" of the response to *The School at Rincon Santo* appeared in various speeches of the period, including Stevens' talk to the American Film Festival luncheon in New York, April 22, 1965.

This is the paradox, the challenge and the mystery of film-making. The challenge does not change merely because the artist is put to work within a set structure of policy objectives. The policy planner in a government film agency should be content with very little planning, if he wants more than mediocre results. He may well be grateful for whatever "policy points" remain in the final version. What he really needs most of all are those rare and shining communicative achievements which emerge sooner or later from any representative group of artists who are hardworking, skilled and free.

Stevens knew this instinctively. When he had to defend a new project, he leaned not only on his professional background but on the perpetual hope of unpredictable bonanzas. He educated his advisers about film, even as they were educating him about regions. He dazzled them with talk of interlock sessions and *cinéma vérité*; he invited them to Hollywood premieres at the Motion Picture Association headquarters in Washington. Most of all, he worked—day and night—to bring each film up to the best possible standard in every technical and creative aspect. In 1965, he expressed it this way:

> We have tried to set a certain standard of style. We try never to have a voice-of-doom narrator, for example. Sometimes it is the man himself, the man whose story we are telling, or an actor who sounds like him. Again, we don't want to depend too heavily on narration. We certainly can't go to dialogue, ordinarily, or even synchronized sound (except for Presidential speeches, when we override with translation). Narration is the essential technique for our program of translation into many languages. But we like to leave room for pause, for thought, and often that means letting the pictures carry most of the meaning. We have also tried to avoid depending on garish musical scores to bolster ineffectual scenes.
>
> We have to keep asking for quality, that's all—quality in the best documentary tradition, without losing the simple educational effect we need. After all, in those first months I was here, Ed Murrow saw most of our films in the rough cut stage. We couldn't show anything corny to him! [30]

If Stevens was determined to avoid corn, he had no desire to avoid emotion. From his Hollywood background, he brought a strong conviction

[30] Interview, February 1965, is basis for this and the following quotation. For a critical statement about USIA motion picture policies, see especially "Use and Abuse of Stock Footage," in *Film Comment*, Fall-Winter 1967. Gordon Hitchens made a film called *Crossroaders in Africa* for the USIA. Some of the footage about this privately sponsored group was admittedly misused to represent Peace Corps work in the Kennedy film, *Years of Lightning, Day of Drums*. For transcript of sound track of the latter flm and other background, see *Film Comment*, same issue. See also USIA-related articles in *Film Comment* No. 3, 1962; Vol. 3, No. 2, Spring 1965; Vol. 3, No. 3, Summer 1965, and "Films in Vietnam," Vol. 5, No. 2, Spring 1969, with follow-up letter from William Bayer in Vol. 6, No. 2, Summer 1970.

of the role emotion plays in the lives of the world audience. In speeches he was fond of quoting Carl Sandburg: "Anything that brings us to tears by way of drama does something to the deepest roots of our personality."

Stevens may have overemphasized this interpretation of his job. The Hollywood tradition often showed through—especially in the longer films —to :he detriment of the straightforward informational stance that has traditionally won respect for government films abroad. Yet when the emotion perfectly fitted the frame, as in *The March*—an emotion that was drawn honestly and directly from the material itself—all the risks became justified. His reply to such criticism is persuasive, and suggests the particular role he envisioned for the film medium in the no-man's-land of propagandist public communication:

> Do we think propaganda is going to change peoples' minds in some direct, conscious way? No, I think we have a much more subtle responsibility to try to open people's minds, get them in the frame of mind that is willing to evaluate events in somewhat different terms. If we can get people moved to tears about Kennedy, for example, they will be more likely to hear the things we say at other levels. If we can stir them in their hearts, their ideas are moved as well. Maybe their ideas come down scrambled a little bit—that's when education begins.
>
> On the racial question, there is very little use in making up lists of logical arguments to defend our record. If we involve people in the emotional aspects of the problem, they will see what we are up against and sympathize with the depth and difficulty of it.

At the other end of the scale, Stevens was sure he could not afford to appeal—in the Hollywood tradition—to the lowest common denominator of audience reaction. Talking down is as ineffectual as talking on too high a level. A single film should contain a wide enough range of appeals to hold the attention of a varied audience. It does not have to offend the educated man, but at the same time it can be suitable for nearly everybody else. "Why should a bright Latin-American student," he asked, "come downtown to the USIA to see a dull film? Why should anybody?"

In a speech at the American Film Festival in April 1965, Stevens told the 16mm producers of the nation a few of his feelings about "advertising America":

> Selling is too simple a word for our needs. The circumstances and complexities of the civil rights movement in the United States are not going to be sold to the people of Africa. Perhaps our adversaries have *sold* the simple concept that America is a land of bigotry. This, reinforced by front-page photographs from Selma, cannot be outdone by selling of any kind. What is required is understanding. The oversimplifications of what has been "sold" must be rounded out by a vigor-

ous and unending communication with curious people of other lands. For this task the motion picture is eminently qualified.[31]

[31] Under the Nixon administration, there was new controversy over the short-term propaganda role of USIA films. *The Silent Majority* offered some logical support for the traditional refusal of Congress to permit USIA films to be seen in this country. Made in two weeks on a "crash" basis, according to a *Chicago Daily News* story November 23, 1969, this 15-minute film "minimizes the mass antiwar demonstrations and suggests that most Americans back President Nixon's Vietnam policies." Rep. John E. Moss (Democrat, Calif.) chairman of the House Government Operations Sub-committee on Foreign Operations and Government Information, protested: "I think it most appropriate to show demonstrations for or against [U.S. Vietnam policy] or both." A partisan defense of a particular policy would naturally call into question the capacity of the USIA to represent what President Truman, in his original charge to the Foreign Information Service of the State Department, called "a full and fair picture" of American life. At the same time, it may be recalled that USIA support for President Kennedy's less controversial policies in Berlin and Latin America was enthusiastic and steady.

9

Television for
President and Congress

DOCUMENTARY FILMS made by government have only rarely grappled with the decision-making process in government itself. Films about problems are far more common than films about processes of reaching solutions—that is, politics and administration.

The Plow That Broke the Plains and *The River*, radical and thought-provoking as they were, did not undertake this task. The problems were there, in all their visual glory, with poetic descriptions to match, and at the end of *The River*, the TVA dams offered emphatic physical solutions. But the politics had to be inferred by the contemporary audience, and the administrative agencies were barely referred to. Even in *Power and the Land*, which took the trouble to act out a solemn scene of farmers talking together, the results of their cooperation with the REA seemed more magical than practical, as electric appliances suddenly turned up on the farm in abundance and life was transformed.

One film of the immediate postwar period made a halting attempt to show working relationships between government and people. In *Bob Marshall Comes Home*, a young veteran applies to the Rural Electrification Administration to extend electric service to his farm. The board of the local REA cooperative has judged his farm to be too far away from the main road to justify the expense of a line. Bob asks for reconsideration. He can't forget the vast technical miracles of World War II and he feels certain this small step of progress is owing to him. Someone on the board speaks up in his support. "Look at us!" he says. "Not one of us looked like good investments" to the old utility companies in the 1930's. He points to

President John F. Kennedy press conference on Viet Nam using visual materials

a board member now taking a conservative position: "You were one of the people who lived 'too far out.' "

Bob wins, of course, because the film is intended to persuade local cooperatives to keep extending electric service to farmers less able to pay. But this dramatization of a grass-roots decision was more than propaganda. Crudely conceived and performed, it nevertheless made an effort to show the inside of a political and administrative process. It even revealed a citizen talking back to a government agency—in this case to his friends and neighbors.

Neither the OWI nor the State Department tried to cope with the realities of American politics in their films for foreign viewers. The Motion Picture Service of the USIA did make a film about political conventions, and other documentaries revealed the impact of employment services and social security on individual lives. A dramatization of the Gideon case, in which the Supreme Court required that lawyers be provided for accused persons, was filmed by the USIA Television Service.

But of course no executive department—least of all the USIA—is specifically charged with educating the American people about the operations of government. This kind of education, insofar as it is undertaken within government at all, is essentially the task of political leadership.

The President as Educator

At the Presidential level, there have been three important innovations in political communication since 1933, innovations which have used the mass media as instruments of public education about government.

Franklin D. Roosevelt introduced the "fireside chat." He talked to the nation from the White House—rarely, not regularly—on the radio. He spoke in a relaxed, informal style, directly to his listeners as individuals, and the fireside chat seemed a simple extension of the President's personality. It also accomplished a difficult substantive task. The way he spoke conveyed to the citizens of the United States a feeling of the step-by-step thinking that went into the policies he was proposing. It made them feel close to the basic processes of government.

The televised Presidential press conference is another matter entirely. It is useful, of course, but it does not go deeply into the substance of decisions or of issues. It reveals something of the personality of the President and is an ideal framework for conveying the President's personal grasp of issues—the wide range of problems he has to cope with. But a press conference is McLuhanism *à la carte*. It inevitably comprises a grab bag of unrelated items, a rambling tour of the peaks of public policy to satisfy knowledgeable newsmen in search of headlines. The John F. Kennedy conferences tended to be brilliant but not really educational.

Campaign debates on television carry greater handicaps. The format, adapted from the TV program "Meet the Press," tends to reflect the conflicting news-entertainment paradox of contemporary journalism. The Kennedy-Nixon debates were historic and informative. Their chief contribution to the campaign was to exhibit the extensive knowledge, calm style and brisk humor that made Kennedy a winner. In this respect, television probably swung the election of 1960.[1] It gave the voters the new information they needed. But the peculiar nature of a question-answer format limits the teaching function of such a program. The search for

[1] See Sidney Kraus, *The Great Debates*; Bernard Rubin, *Political Television*; Gene Wyckoff, *The Image Candidates*.

quick answers, however honestly and seriously conducted, is often closer to the suspense and shock of entertainment than it is to the slow logic of exposition, the exploration of *pro* and *con*, which can build an educational experience.

Neither the TV press conference nor the TV campaign debate have accomplished the same kind of closeness to the processes of government achieved by the fireside chat. Because they bring in a conflict between questioner and answerer, they seem more objective, less spoon-fed than the Roosevelt approach. Yet they allow little time for depth, little opportunity to become acquainted with the substance of contemporary issues. They inform us more about personalities than about problems.

The last television appearance of Robert Kennedy, his so-called debate with Eugene McCarthy before the 1968 California primary, was less rigid in format (and might well have been followed four years later by George McGovern and Hubert Humphrey). The two Senators sat around a coffee table with three network correspondents, a whole hour ahead of them. There was much less of a feeling of confrontation with the press. Because they knew each other well, the two protagonists even insisted on talking to each other from time to time. This drifted at one point into a notable revelation. McCarthy wanted black families to move to the suburbs near existing factories which might provide them with jobs; Kennedy was more cautious, willing to wait for another educated generation, proposing that some new industry be moved into the ghettos; McCarthy was surprised to learn that this was Kennedy's position. The topic then shifted, but for one moment we had the exhilarating experience of watching two first-rate men begin to hammer out a difference between them, as they might in the cloakroom of the Senate, or at a committee meeting.

It requires only a small effort of imagination to picture an expanded setting for discussion of public issues on TV. Out of the limbo of the sound stage would appear two research assistants with position papers, charts, projectors. When the speakers mention the budget, it appears on the screen. If supporting testimony is needed, a face is called up from the file and the voice speaks. As they talk about the ghetto, the ghetto confirms its presence in motion picture form. The purpose of such visuals is to humanize the issues—to show what is so often forgotten because it is so hard to describe: the basis in actual experience for what seems to be an abstract governmental decision.[2]

Soon, of course, this format will become as routinized—and as suspect —as the old-fashioned stump speech. Pictures used as illustrations for an argument will inevitably become disembodied emotional gestures. The face from the ranks of the unemployed will become a crude exploitation of an

[2] This is in fact not unlike the format developed by "The Advocates," a program on stations of the Public Broadcasting System covering contemporary controversial issues.

economic issue. The woman with her supermarket basket will become a visual cliché in the battle of inflation.

This transitional phase of public communication is already upon us. President Nixon's use of photographs in his televised report on weapons captured during the Cambodian invasion may be the first such instance in Presidential speechmaking. It was long overdue. Lawrence O'Brien took the technique one step further by his attack on the Nixon policies using pictorial quotations from Presidential speeches.[3]

The incorporation of visual passages in political dialogue is the modern successor to the fireside chat. The next step is the conscious artistic development of public information by means of the documentary film. The introduction and commentary might be by the President himself or by members of his administration. The natural distribution for such messages in the 1970's is television.

There should be more than rudimentary TV facilities in the White House—and more than the occasional hospitality of private networks— if the President's messages are to reach the public as often as the public needs them.

It was only a short time ago that President Lyndon Johnson had to jump into a car and roar downtown, with sirens wailing, in order to get on the evening newscast with the story of the end of a strike.[4] He did it because he knew he would have a big audience. His political and publicity motives were obvious, and we may expect that the indignity of such a spectacle will not be repeated. The basic fact, nevertheless, is that only by the claim of some crisis or some "major statement" can the President get on the private airwaves today. For lesser officials there is essentially no access at all.

If the President wants to sit down in his office and have a talk with the American people, showing them a documentary film of a long-range problem they should be thinking about, his staff has to negotiate with the heads of three networks. They willingly accede to his request—the first time. Later on, there are doubts, especially if it is necessary to give equal time to the opposition party after the President's first broadcast. In the end, the networks complain more and more, as the dollars for sponsored entertainment go down the drain while the President speaks. If he asks for additional time for someone in his official family to present in depth a governmental problem, he will simply find the whole thing recorded and put off till 11:00 p.m. in the manner of the Eisenhower press conferences.

[3] Nixon's report to the nation on TV was June 3, 1970. O'Brien's speech was on July 7 and opened with a segment from the President's inaugural address; his 25-minute broadcast on prime time was on CBS and was transmitted without charge. See *Facts on File*, Vol. 30, Nos. 1545 (June 4–10, pp. 393G2) and 1549 (July 2–8, p. 486B1) 1970.

[4] The end of a railway strike was thus announced on WTOP, Washington, at 6:55 p.m. April 22, 1964. Later announcements of this sort came from a "theater" in the White House. See *Published Papers of the Presidents of the United States:*

President Nixon's televised "conversation" with network newsmen. From left, Howard K. Smith, ABC, Eric Sevareid, CBS, John Chancellor, NBC

From 1969–1972, Richard Nixon repeatedly preempted time on all three networks for statements on the Vietnam war and other policy decisions he thought important. These were interspersed with special favors like the invitations for special White House "conversations" with TV newsmen. In the background, however, were Vice President Spiro Agnew's intermittent attacks on network handling of news.[5]

This stick-and-carrot system of media relations may have advantages in a primitive communicative situation. It is not good enough for an era in which television is a necessary instrument of democratic life.

The President and his staff have no suitable way of coming before the American people directly and frequently in the television age. Press releases and speeches can be timed to fit newspaper and broadcast deadlines, but this is essentially a technique of the past. Television is potentially a town meeting technique. To begin to use it as an educational and political instrument is the obligation and the natural function of a modern President. That his political proposals should be answered by the opposition party is equally natural, and in fact is required by law.

There are at least four ways for the government to get access to prime television time on any regular basis: (1) the purchase with tax money of

Lyndon B. Johnson, 1963–64, Book I, Item No. 284, pp. 517–519. Also introduced and speaking were Roy E. Davidson, Chief of the Brotherhood of Locomotive Engineers and J. E. Wolfe, Chairman of the National Railway Conference.

[5] See *Broadcasting* Magazine, January 11, pp. 46–47 and January 18, p. 52, 1971.

enormously expensive evening hours from the networks; (2) a law directly
regulating the networks which would require them to deliver free time
for political and governmental purposes; (3) a contract with the growing
community antenna television systems to use one channel on certain
nights; (4) a Federal network which would accommodate both political
and governmental programming.

Most taxpayer-viewers would consider the first course of action a
criminal misuse of money. The second alternative may eventually come
to pass, but it will require a long legislative battle, with little chance that
anything more than political campaigns will be covered. Transmission by
CATV implies mailing videotapes to a thousand local stations—hardly a
form of fast, simultaneous communication. But wherever CATV now
extends the reach of educational television, it could also extend a Federal
network.

The last alternative is probably the most feasible, both financially and
politically, and satisfactory for everything except the most critical public
reports (which would be taken by all networks as before). The Corporation for Public Broadcasting is already helping to pay for educational TV
programs. ETV stations may never reach the entire country, but network-
linking among them is now commonplace. During certain hours of the
week, National Educational Television could become a Federal network.
Such preemption of educational time would hardly raise such an outcry
as preemption of popular shows in commercial TV.

It should be one of the essential and regular aspects of public broadcasting that government officials (the President, the Secretary of Transportation, the chairman of the Senate Foreign Relations Committee, the
minority leader of the House) can turn to it at any time to reach the citizens of the republic. It should not be true that a major public figure has
no place to go on television except the conflict-centered interview panels,
the headline-focused news, or the night and morning "talk" shows.

If it is true that the government should not withhold news, it is also
true that the communications media should not be left with a monopoly
of the machinery of broadcasting. Just as speeches should be freely available
to reporters, so should the techniques of speaking to the people—books,
magazines, platforms, film production, TV stations—be accessible to those
in government who have legitimate information to offer.

Format is important. It should be possible once in a while for a government or party official to speak to citizens in his own style—however
boring that is, or however much he chooses to conceal it with audio-visual
techniques. He should not be forever compelled to sit in some kind of cage
and toss back time-bombs to a panel of newsmen, in "Meet-the-Press"
fashion. He should not be forced, in order to get time on the tube, to rub
shoulders with practiced pitchmen, schooled to interrupt him at the first
sign of seriousness. It is fine if the mayor of New York is adept at trading
barbs with the master of ceremonies on the "Tonight" show. But what

happens if this is the only extensive TV exposure available to him? The public begins to think he is not serious about anything.

Melvin Laird, Secretary of Defense, turned down an invitation in 1971 to be part of a documentary about prisoners of war, unless CBS would put him on the air "live," that is, unedited. The CBS News bureau manager in Washington refused, suggesting that documentaries must be on film or tape because TV always has to edit—and that "newspapers and magazines" would never give him "a certain number of column inches to fill as he sees fit." The fact is that if the Secretary of Defense did prepare an article for a magazine, he would probably not be edited. The issue here is not freedom of the press but commercial television's inevitable nervous fear of losing the audience. On TV news, the speaker gets summed up in a one-sentence extract. Ninety per cent of the time, this is an act of violence (like so much else on TV). There appears to be no place in our most powerful and popular national communications medium for the "full text" of anything—not even for the speaker's own chosen extract or summary.[6]

It is no wonder, surely, that a defensive and private person like Richard Nixon would discover his own alternatives in dealing with commercial television: (1) very few open press conferences; (2) handy tricks for changing the subject when unacceptable questions are asked; (3) totally managed sessions ("spontaneous" or otherwise) for paid political programs. Such withdrawal is not healthy for public communication. What is needed is some form of alternative transmission system, more hospitable toward the substance of public affairs.

The President should not have to beg time from the public broadcasting system any more than from the other networks. He should have his own TV station, with origination facilities in or near the White House. "Studio facilities" are not enough; he should have broadcast capability and a spot on the spectrum. Federal programmers should be able to go on the air directly and not merely pass out to stations packages of tapes—costly equivalents of press releases. The Federal network would then be expected to pick up programs as they are broadcast in Washington. Delayed broadcasts might well occur, and some stations might refuse them altogether. But most programs would reach the country because anything actually broadcast in Washington is news.

There is no direct precedent for an open line from President to people. The fireside chats occurred only occasionally and only by courtesy of the radio networks. The Government Printing Office is a close comparison, but its massive output is for the most part so specialized as to be nonpolitical, while its coverage of Congress and the committees is strictly in the form of transcripts, without editorial selectivity. The notion that a President might have his own newspaper while in office has never been

[6] See Sedulus, "Melvin Laird and CBS," New Republic, July 10, 1971, a good statement on the peculiar problems of excerpting news on TV.

seriously put forth. Thomas Jefferson felt driven to it while he was Secretary of State. In his day there were plenty of newspapers, each offering distinct and heated political views. A group of friends published his paper, in competition with Hamilton's, then Secretary of the Treasury. Such an idea might have been attractive to Franklin Roosevelt—who was steadily opposed by a vast majority of newspaper publishers—but the nearest he came to it was the publication of his papers and addresses in books.

Will the Corporation for Public Broadcasting become the captive of the party in power? The heavy hand of Charles de Gaulle on the centralized television system of France is still fresh in our memories. The total control of all media in China and Russia, the manipulation of minds by print, radio and film in Nazi Germany—these are grim precedents that offer little encouragement. The CPB is intended to be something quite different—more like the BBC in England, which has long prized its independent status. For a while in the late 1960's the British Broadcasting Corporation even carried on an open feud with Prime Minister Harold Wilson.

It is certainly true that either Congress or the President can try to dominate public television, in spite of its carefully planned independent structure and multiple financing. Its dependence on the federal budget is heavy, and this insecure income should be replaced by an automatic tax on all TV sets, as in England. Otherwise its vulnerability is clearly illustrated by Nixon's veto of the CPB budget in 1972. That veto, proposing a familiar Republican policy of "decentralization," was essentially an attack on the independent programming and the conflicts of opinion characteristic of NET. Decentralizing by turning program control back to the stations is like turning social legislation or civil rights back to the states. It would devitalize and destroy the strong alternative TV system the CPB was intended to be.

Much of this hostility and tension between President and CPB might never have developed if broadcasting time and facilities had been freely and habitually available to the President and his staff for policy presentations and conversations with the people. Perhaps such proposals have at some time been made, from one side or the other. It seems more likely that there was an ideological preference for the traditional journalistic mode of skeptical opposition to the government. No one thought of the CPB as providing a new channel of contact between government and people.

The President of the United States is the nation's leading educator. If he fails to undertake this task, his other functions will suffer and his authority as leader of the people, the party and the executive branch will slowly wither away. In modern terms, this means he may occasionally have to be master of ceremonies of his own educational television show. After that, it is the function of the opposition party, especially in the Congress, to propose and explore contradictory themes, further enriching the public's acquaintance with its problems.

The very necessity of creating lucid informational programs can help to clarify public policy, not only for the public but for President and Congress. Documentaries made in the heat of controversy will not only reflect the battle but help to shape the attitudes of those who produce them. Communication is often a fruitful discipline.

Congress Makes a Film

On Thursday, Friday and Saturday, May 12–14, 1960, the Committee on Un-American Activities of the U.S. House of Representatives held a subcommittee hearing in the city hall at San Francisco. There were ten "friendly" witnesses and 36 who were uncooperative, including a group of men and women described by the committee as longstanding Communist Party agitators on the west coast. A crowd of people milled around in the corridors and outside, many of them young college students from the Bay area. Some carried placards calling for the abolition of the committee. There was a lot of booing, chanting and singing.

Sometime during the course of Friday's festivities, city authorities were asked to clear the halls. Fire hoses were not enough. The police had to shove and carry demonstrators down the city hall's massive stairway, slippery with cascading water. For their resistance, 68 people were arrested. All but one were let off by a municipal judge.

Cameras had been grinding busily throughout the proceedings, and some of the footage had been seen on San Francisco TV stations. The committee told KRON-TV and KPIX-TV they wanted to "take a look at it," and subpoenaed the total footage. No payment was given or asked. Before the reels of film were sent back, however, duplicate negative was made of much of it and turned over to a company called Washington Video Productions to construct a new film. Presumably the committee participated fully in editing the picture material and writing the commentary. Three of the members made brief speeches which were filmed and cut in with the news footage. The narrator was Fulton Lewis III, a committee staff member.[7]

Operation Abolition was issued as an official document of the House of Representatives, a 45-minute film report "attached" to the committee

[7] See *Time*, March 17, 1961, p. 17; Paul Jacobs, "A Movie With a Message," *Reporter*, November 24, 1960. A *Washington Post* editorial on November 26 called it "Forgery by Film."

report issued by the Government Printing Office. It was an answer to the committee's foes, in and out of Congress, who were trying to abolish the committee or at least cut down its appropriation. The film unquestionably played a major role in winning a lopsided 412-6 vote in the House for continuing the appropriation another year.

But this film was not just an internal matter. *The Plow That Broke the Plains* had begun as a proposed training film for agency employees, but its inherent purpose, like most documentary films, was to reach people and change their minds. In the same way, *Operation Abolition* eventually reached a mass audience. Prints were offered for sale at the modest price of $100 apiece, and by June the little company in Washington was close to a $100,000 gross.

The film was circulated widely and was sometimes bought sight unseen by ideology-conscious businessmen, especially by building and loan companies. They then offered it, usually free of charge, to thousands of private groups across the country. On the one hand, middle-class parents were shocked into a new wave of fear about the resurgence of communism. On the other hand, the film was shown to overflow crowds on many college campuses, accompanied by outbursts ranging from tense debate to fisticuffs.[8] The whole episode was like a small preview of the marching youth, the police action and the television coverage in Chicago at the time of the 1968 Democratic National Convention.

Certain key events were a matter of dispute between the film-makers and the students. According to the tense, present-tense commentary of the film, by Friday noon "the hallways are in complete chaos" and "officials are unable to maintain order." Judges in other courtrooms in the city hall order the police to remove all demonstrators, and "the mob surges forward to storm the doors." According to the students, there were no such threatening moves; the hoses, they said, were turned on by the city police without warning and without immediate provocation.[9]

Robert Meisenbach, the one student held for trial, was accused of hitting a policeman with his own billy club and thereby starting the riot. A jury acquitted him on May 2, 1961. There were some documented reports of police brutality, but the committee's film showed none of this; it may have been recorded in the television out-takes that were not used. Instead the film-makers emphasized an elderly policeman who was overcome by the excitement and was supposed to have had a heart attack. The editor lingers long on shots of his stretcher and his face.

[8] See, for example, editorial in *Yale Daily News*, February 17, 1961, and news reports in University of Southern California *Daily Trojan*, March 9, 10, 1961.

[9] See a series of articles by Wes Willoughby and Hadley Roff in *San Francisco News-Call Bulletin*, January 23–31, 1961. See also pamphlet by Northern California chapter of Americans for Democratic Action, "San Francisco and the Un-American Activities Committee." Extensive material may be found in Albert T. Anderson and Bernice P. Biggs, *A Focus on Rebellion* (1962), taken from news accounts.

There are other, more subtle shadings of bias in the film, including repeated rearrangement of the order of events and significant psychological emphasis in camera viewpoints. But *Operation Abolition* is not so much a trick film as it is a one-sided film. It is a throw-back to the old days of personal political journalism, a stump speech for a special point of view, a propaganda film. Its opponents could hardly have been surprised that the film failed to give them equal time.

The Committee on Un-American Activities clearly made an ethical and probably a constitutional mistake when it subpoenaed footage from private TV stations without payment and then allowed another private company to profit from making a film. In this way, the committee alone had the power to state its case. (The San Francisco stations impounded the unused footage.) Not until some months later was there an "answer" on film: the American Civil Liberties Union of Northern California prepared a rewritten sound track to be used with the same footage, calling it *Operation Correction*. Meanwhile the National Council of Churches asked that the original film not be shown without providing at the same time some corrective material—clippings of editorials, an informed speaker, or some other source of balanced skepticism.[10]

Operation Abolition deserves harsh criticism. Yet can we say that the Congress, which every day publishes a mountain of reports on its committee hearings, has no right to make such a report to the people on film? Further, is such a report not entitled to have a point of view? How does a film differ from a TV interview, a committee report or a transcript of hearings? Any of these may be politically biased. A hearing may be surprisingly dramatic. And when a committee has been subjected to a chanting crowd of students and others, is it not entitled to make a more effective report than can be conveyed in that mild parenthesis in transcribed hearings: "(Disturbance)"?

If Congress is to make films, for itself or for the public, its obvious responsibility is to hire writers, directors and editors trained in the skills of film-making and alert to the hazards of bias and partisanship. Their obvious challenge is to tell the truth. But like the expanding corps of lawyers and investigators and assistants hired by Congressional committees in recent years, these communications experts will be only as objective as the committee requires. Some of the films may be sharply partisan, calling forth a minority report. Others may be statesmanlike contributions to nonpartisan debate.

Ever since television has been a familiar part of the American scene, Senators and Congressmen have been making film clips of themselves and

---

[10] Letter to author by Harold See, general manager, KRON-TV, April 3, 1961. The original footage was "available to anyone presenting us with a bona fide subpoena; which method was employed by the committee." Associated Press article printed December 6, 1961, in the *Christian Science Monitor* gave some details of the reversed narration for *Operation Correction*. Superimposed subtitles also indicated actual days when pictured events occurred.

sending these back to TV stations in their states and districts. This activity is not going to decline. The televised hearings of the confrontation between the Army and Senator Joseph McCarthy settled once and for all the importance of first-hand visual communication in helping the American people to make up their minds. Is the Senate hereafter going to leave to private researchers like Emile de Antonio (who produced *Point of Order*), the summary version of such hearings? Or is the Congress of the United States also capable of setting up a rational system for sharing with the people the glamor and grind of the legislative process? If so, then we may eventually salute the House Un-American Activities Committee for inflicting on us, as a precedent, its attachment to House Report 2228, 86th Congress, 2d Session—which can well be called Public Film No. 1 of the U.S. House of Representatives.

The members of Congress are very much aware of the advantage the President holds in the new communications environment. Television can focus far more successfully on one man and his proposals than on a variety of conflicting viewpoints in a legislative situation. Yet even if the drama of this conflict could be orchestrated, the forum for response is essentially lacking. The Senate and House as institutions are cut off from the television audience.

The press conferences of Harry Truman and John F. Kennedy were often followed by the "Ev and Charlie" show. Senator Everett Dirksen and Representative Charles Halleck were Republicans. But there was something beyond this struggling to be born. The Congress was claiming the right to be seen and heard on its own terms—seeking some new invention which would bring to public communication a counterpart of the American system of checks and balances.

The Congressional feeling of isolation has become more acute in recent years. After a series of appearances by President Nixon on prime TV time—and after a group of Senators were refused and then reluctantly granted some network time to oppose the President's Cambodian adventure—some of the members of the legislative branch began to think in terms of an institutional right to be heard.

Senator William Fulbright introduced a resolution amending the 1934 Communications Act to require TV stations to "provide a reasonable amount of public service time" to members of the House and Senate to talk about "issues of public importance" at least four times a year. Dean Burch, chairman of the Federal Communications Commission, objected. In testimony (August 6, 1970) before Senator John O. Pastore's communications subcommittee of the committee on commerce, he declared that any such notion of a "right of access" to private broadcast media would represent a "sharp departure from the basic scheme of broadcasting in this country." [11]

[11] Hearings, Communications Subcommittee, Committee on Commerce, U.S. Senate, 91st Congress, 2d Session, S.J.Res. 209, p. 142.

Senator Edmund S. Muskie, also appearing before the committee, doubted that a particular scheme should be forced on the networks, but supported "wholeheartedly" the idea behind the resolution. His statement provides a valuable perspective on the relationship of television to government today:

> Television has changed totally the whole system of checks and balances. It has changed the nature of the political process, making the value judgment of the people on specific issues far more significant than ever before in history.
>
> Heretofore, the entire governmental process has been largely indirect. This, of course, is the nature of a republican form of government. Its control over the purse strings kept Congress at least in a competitive position in relation to the executive. Both branches enjoyed the detachment granted by a benign electorate. Television has changed all that. . . .
>
> The televised veto of the HEW appropriations bill in January [1970] of this year provides a splendid example. The entire viewing audience of one of television's most popular programs—the "Laugh-In" show— sat captured while the President spoke. . . .
>
> The position the President advocated was contested by overwhelming majorities in Congress with equal access to information. That congressional position was never heard or seen by those Americans. If the President happens to be wrong, there is little that can be done to make that known to the people.
>
> At an evening press conference on January 30, 1970, the President stated that the antiballistic missile system against China is now "virtually infallible." As a result, that statement was imbedded in the minds of millions although there is unanimity among scientists and admissions by the administration subsequently that the statement was dead wrong. The awesome potential of this use of television could be brought home by other less striking examples. . . .
>
> The tax relief and tax reform measure developed last year by Congress would be a recent example. What Congress conceived and achieved single-handedly with that issue was of such importance to the American people that a national airing of its many facets on television would have been highly justified. . . .
>
> The allocation of television time to Congress should be afforded as the need is justified. The issue will establish that need and when it does, then Congress must have the ability to determine its own format and its own participants. It is the only way. . . .[12]

[12] Hearings, pp. 40–43. Julian Goodman, president of the National Broadcasting Company, reported that on NBC's "Today" show "45 pro-administration federal officials and 35 opposition spokesmen appeared between January 1970, and mid-June." (The list appears on pp. 77–78.) A good many cabinet members, Senators, and Representatives were included. He did not say how many minutes they were allowed.

A Few Practical Predictions

Joint production of films or TV programs by President and Congress is not to be expected. The familiar chasm of the separation of powers lies in wait to swallow up any such hopeful attempts at cooperation in the field of publicity.

A strange and wonderful attempt at a joint film project was reported by United Press International on October 15, 1965. It bore all the earmarks of an attempted diplomatic coup—a bow and a flourish on the part of the executive branch toward the Congress of the United States. Like some other proposals by the Johnson administration, however, this one apparently was preceded by insufficient consultation.

A Hollywood-style movie spectacular on the 89th Congress flopped before it was finished, the White House reported today.

Joseph Laitin, assistant White House press secretary, said the film had been designed to show what the first session of the 89th had accomplished.

Gregory Peck, the actor, narrated a script by Bernard Asbell, the writer.

The film was apparently to have been shown for the first time on Oct. 7 at a salute to Congress held in the State Department Auditorium. However, when a preview was held on the still incomplete film, it was decided to shelve it.

Mr. Laitin said he did not know who had paid for it.

According to Mr. Laitin, the Department of Health, Education and Welfare "came up with some unique ideas" for the Congressional salute and was asked to assemble more material from other Government sources.

The *Washington Post* said today that one proposed title for the film was "the fighting 89th—the Congress that wouldn't quit."

John Naisbitt, an aide to Health Secretary John W. Gardner, was the producer. A producer for the American Broadcasting Company, John Lynch, was called in as the top creative consultant, the newspaper said.

Also it was reported that different Federal agencies had contributed movie clips to illustrate problems solved by the 89th Congress.[13]

[13] The *New York Times* headline on this story was: "White House Nixes Flix of 89th Sesh; Pic Rates Floperoo."

There may be moments when a President and a majority in Congress are in tune, harmony prevails, and a film can be proposed by all concerned. Such moments seldom last long enough for a film to be conceived, produced and released. Of course administrative agencies will often find it reasonable or politic to include Congressional personalities in program-oriented films, but they are well advised to leave to Congress the pleasure of telling its own story.

The House and Senate can also be expected to find their own forms of self-expression. For a time, Congressional formats may be clogged with "talking faces." Even reports to local constituents, however, will eventually get away from that. Viewers will demand more imaginative and visual presentations. For similar reasons, it would seem advisable not to undertake vast surveys of the year's work. Somehow 535 faces would have to be—or want to be—included. The total effect would be tiresome in the extreme.

The story of a single Congressional decision—an appropriation, perhaps, or a new kind of statute, or even the party process of organization to do business—offers a more manageable number of participants. As Senator Fulbright said when the commerce committee was considering his resolution on equal time for the Congress, it should not be so hard to pick the television performers for a report on a particular bill: certain men and women are naturally identified with the debate, for and against, in the committee and on the floor. Eventually it might even be possible to select two or three popular "masters of ceremonies" and hire a director of programming.

Some of the basic input for decision making, too, can be on tape or film. The members of Congress have just as much right to modern methods of informational presentation as do the Joint Chiefs of Staff, who have spent millions of dollars over the years on filmed reports (some of them about secret weapons, shown only to them and shown only once). Major committee witnesses will still come in person. But a good deal of the testimony from faraway places and from people who need not take a trip to Washington can be recorded on film. Added to their speaking likeness would be the visual record of conditions the committee is investigating. Committee counsel and other assistants can ask questions in the field, with cameramen present; editors in Washington can sort out the most significant material for the eyes of the committee. Members who are absent during the film showing can see it later in the projection room or on their office TV set, with every gesture and intonation exactly as the other members saw them.

As the drama of committee decisions begins to be seen as the most fascinating and at the same time the most significant visual material for Congressional reports to the people, the leading committees will eventually schedule their sessions to fit the availability of the six or eight camera crews hired to cover public hearings. The party caucuses will take up the question of the communicative calendar along with the regular one.

The old taboos against television inside the House and Senate chambers will yield before long to the convenience of automatic cameras, installed to focus on a few podiums convenient for all members to approach when speaking. Film editors will be hard at work around the clock, like the editors of the *Congressional Record*. They won't print it all (as the *Record* must), but the best "takes" will be made available for use by individual Congressmen, by the mass media (public and private), and by editors of the valuable topical compilations in preparation during and after the session.

Historians and political scientists—already beginning to be aware of the values of film in research and teaching—will no longer have to depend upon the two-minute takes of nightly TV news programs for visual records of the work of our nation's lawmakers.

Will there be retakes and flattering close-ups added in the studio at the end of the day? Of course: just as speeches are rewritten for the *Record*. Will there be more haranguing and "playing to the gallery" by long-winded speakers as a result of the everpresent TV eye? Probably not. The new medium imposes brevity and succinctness, as Hubert Humphrey found out in the 1968 campaign, and the chances are that the end result will actually be a somewhat slimmer *Congressional Record*.

The best of the summaries and some of the daily "rushes" will no doubt be made available to the executive branch. The President's advisers will sort out the ones he "must see," and he will be under the necessity, perhaps, of commenting on the style as well as the substance of such performances at the next White House breakfast for Congressional guests. At the same time, administrative agencies will provide their own documentaries for viewing at convenient times by members of key committees or by the whole membership of House or Senate. The most important ones may become Presidential messages. The agencies will remember that their job is not to be dramatically overwhelming, but to use their production funds with simple effectiveness. In fact, agencies will vie with one another to make the most informative in-depth reports at the lowest cost and with the least apparent use of technique.

All of this material will be available to news writers and program producers. Networks and stations all over the world should be able to plug in by satellite and pick it up live, tape it for later use, or get completed prints of films from press representatives at the White House or Capitol. Any special program or portion of it would be available to public and private users in later years from the National Archives.

The President's own films will reflect, of course, the special style of the master of ceremonies himself, and the documentaries he asks for will relate intimately to the subjects he is currently pursuing. This does not demand a large permanent staff. He needs a conceptual group—a film writer who can work with his speech writer, a producer who will keep in close touch with his television adviser, and a film editor who is alert to the President's tempo and style. After that, the projects may best be carried out by independent contracting companies or with *ad hoc* crews under freelance directors. Existing facilities in Washington or agency regional offices can often be used, especially for camera, graphics, studio and laboratory work. A good deal of illustrative stock footage may be needed for speech inserts. But the temptation to build up a large permanent unit of production people would be self-defeating.

Up-to-date public communication does not call for some sort of vast central film production center. This is proposed from time to time. Sometimes it is an accounting-minded Congressman who assumes that large sums could be saved by centralizing studio space in Washington and letting all work orders go through the same bottleneck. Sometimes it is a hungry Hollywood producer who deplores the failure of the U.S. government to use all the studios and artistic talent in Southern California. But the actual needs of government publicity would not be served by consolidation: each agency has its own clientele, approach and priorities.[14] And film itself in recent years has moved away from the studios and the old "production values" of Hollywood. The government film-maker, like any other, nowadays is out in the open air, catching things as they happen. His *cinéma vérité* has a very special significance in the service of government.

It is doubtful, in any case, that the overnight development of a domestic U.S. film center with in-house production by a big Civil Service staff would be anything like the National Film Board of Canada. Within five years it would be just as cautious, conservative and crotchety as the Congressional committees appropriating its funds. Motion picture people should be assigned to the specialized departments that need their services; this has been the tradition in Washington and it would be foolish to change it. A central agency would have no constituency to attach itself to. Like the U.S. Film Service of 1940 it would probably not last long.

None of the above speculation about the future should be viewed as a plea for some unique role for film, unattached to the realities of daily needs. Many of these developments do seem likely if film is to be used to serve the public interest. But the moving image has no more magic in it than any other form of communication. Men and women, not machines, are the originators of messages. If their motives are sincere—if they persist in seeking just solutions for public problems—then communication has a

---

[14] See Zecharaiah Chafee, *Government and Mass Communications*, Vol. II, pp. 780–781: "An over-all information service lacks expertness in any one field, and yet this is indispensable if the law and the practical situation are to be satisfactorily explained. . . . Moreover, even if Congress should unexpectedly consent to a centralized information service, there would still have to be separate publicity groups in many federal agencies. . . . It is inconceivable that the establishment of a centralized service in peace would enable the Department of Agriculture to stop distributing bulletins to farmers. . . ." See also Chafee, p. 754, for a suggestion that the Congress "institute an information service of its own."

chance to be successful and may even be mercifully brief. Film can facilitate understanding, but only if understanding is truly desired.

A motion picture can be used for vicious subjects and for insignificant ones. It can be as dull or as agonizing as a bad speech. Senators and Congressmen are not going to be herded into dark rooms to peer at a lengthy Presidential report consisting of a talking face when they can get the information quicker from an Associated Press printout.[15] Nobody in Washington, D.C., on the other hand, is likely to win votes by producing a daytime TV show about the love life of a Senator's overworked secretary. Nor are laws about to be written in some form of audio-visual scroll, intercut with dancing girls for easier public reading.[16]

Film, videotape and live TV should be reserved for the things they can do well. They can transmit quickly and at long distance the tone and emphasis of an expert witness. They can probe the human complexities of the regulatory process. They can bring together far-flung activities of Congress and of government agencies and show how these relate to the general welfare. And it may be that they can provide a new form of feedback mechanism within the democratic process—the people themselves talking back to their government, conveying the intensity of feeling and the actual economic background of a single constituent, a protesting group or a whole town.

[15] It might also be observed that the Congress is not easily overwhelmed by dramatized symbolic events. The reporters on PBS' "Washington Week" wondered at the time why two-thirds of the House and Senate were missing when Nixon came to the Capitol by helicopter just after his arrival from Moscow. They may have resented the contrivance, but they could also much more conveniently watch the speech at home on TV.

[16] Herbert Mitgang, in his novel *Get These Men Out of the Hot Sun*, has predicted a horror story for 1976, when Acting President Agnew provides a nightly "Good News Hour" about the happy side of America as seen from the White House, with five sponsors, including a headache formula and Dr. Pepper.

IO

The Documentary
Dialogue

The paradox of the film in public information is that the peculiar powers of the medium are not engaged except there is warmth of seeing.

—John Grierson [1]

G OVERNMENT PUBLICITY and government film-making have come a long
way from 1908 and those first surreptitious flickers in the Department of Agriculture. Today the National Aeronautics and Space Administration makes impressive color films about moon landings, and the Department of Defense turns out thousands of films a year.[2]

There have been three wars and five Presidents since a young film critic and firebrand of the New Deal took the dry words of a government report and turned them into a documentary film poem called *The River*. Pare Lorentz dramatized unforgettably the great conservation problems of the 1930's. Drama was the danger Congress feared most. Senator Robert Taft sounded the skeptical warning that still applies: "A U.S. documentary film is a U.S. propaganda film."

Today the atmosphere is different. Motion pictures and multi-media are as familiar at nominating conventions and during Presidential cam-

[1] From his preface to Paul Rotha, Documentary Film (p. 19, 1963 ed.).
[2] A report by James Gibson for the National Archives found that there were at least 7,500 motion pictures made by or for the U.S. Government in 1967. Of these, the following were the major sponsors: Defense Department, 6,640 films; USIA, 300; NASA, 180; Health, Education, Welfare, 179; Agriculture, 90; Transportation, 21; Atomic Energy, 20; Interior, 18; Office of Economic Opportunity, 17; Post Office, 10; Labor, 9; Veterans Administration, 8; State Department, 6; Small Business Administration, 6; Commerce, 6; Treasury, 4.

paigns as they are at world fairs. The arts are officially in the ascendant. Government grants are being made—not merely to keep artists employed, as in the days of the WPA, but as a matter of pride in the republic, an investment in the future. The American Film Institute became part of this new scene in 1967, with the Motion Picture Association as a founding partner, plus the National Endowment for the Arts and the Ford Foundation. A Corporation for Public Broadcasting was authorized in 1969 to add public to private money in support of programs on educational TV channels.

Yet those who propose to speak to the people in the 1970's find it harder than ever. The 1960's had a destructive impact on the credibility of governmental spokesmen and on the faith of young people in the responsiveness of the democratic process. On one hand, there was a retreat into privacy, either naive or cynical, doubting all cooperation as futile "compromise," rejecting all messages as mere TV commercials. On the other hand, among college students there was much romantic talk of revolution—the same yearning for simple action and fast results which characterized the bourgeois Babbitts of business who were their fathers.

To bridge these gaps would require a rediscovery of essential values and their application to present discontents, with the support of effectively focused public attention. In the long run, there might come to be a redefinition of politics not as a game to be won but as a life of endless persuasion. In the short run, new inventions in communication seemed urgently needed.

A flood of bland information, on paper or on film, could hardly help. But documentary, at its best, might provide some true and healing confrontation.

When the Gap Becomes Incredible

As the Johnson administration gave way, more or less imperceptibly, to the Nixon regime, the prevailing public mood was restless and pessimistic. The assassinations of Martin Luther King and Robert Kennedy, together with the interminable tragedy of the Vietnam War, filled many Americans with feelings of despair and impotence. Deeds seemed so much more powerful than words, and the traditional Jeffersonian faith in the basic values of education and information seemed to be shaken. The desperate desire of many young people to mass their bodies outside the Chicago Democratic convention was only a symptom of this national *malaise* that insisted: "What good does it do to talk?"

Lyndon Johnson's approach to government public relations had been proprietary and high-handed. His early press conferences were often unannounced. His relationship with individual correspondents was marked by erratic favoritism and an intense desire for praise. He installed three TV sets in his White House office, watching all major channels for the handling of the news he provided. If the name of a proposed appointee somehow "leaked" to the press, he took peculiar pleasure in switching the appointment to someone else. If bad news was coming up, he often tried to smother it by making headlines with some other exciting announcement on the same day.

The war brought with it unimagined contradictions in public information. Based as it was on a questionable prophetic vision (the domino theory of Southeast Asian politics) and a whole series of missteps, misinformation and lies, the war became a tragedy both for American self-respect and for hundreds of thousands of American families. A ritual of retarded communication began when Johnson denied each "escalation" of troops just before the troop movements took place. The Tonkin Gulf resolution was extracted from Congress in a great hurry on the basis of information later proved by Congressional study to be false. After that came the bombings of Hanoi and the manipulation of the bombing as a stake in the poker game, followed by peace negotiations which were wrongly assumed (like the war itself) to follow the pattern of Korea. The rhetoric of optimism became hollow, and reports from the battlefields began to sound like sales talks. "Body counts" and other statistics made headlines that seemed like victories, as enclaves of security for the South Vietnamese grew smaller. The Viet Cong suddenly struck hard at Saigon itself at the very time our hopes were high.

An effort was made to look on the bright side—rebuilt villages, orphans' homes, business-as-usual in Saigon in the daytime. The Defense Department set up special teams of cameramen to accentuate the positive. But the war went on, lacking only an act of courage to cut it off, airlift 5,000 vulnerable Vietnamese bureaucrats to Australia or the U.S., and turn over the country to its people, admitting finally that another Yugoslavia in Southeast Asia would not degrade American foreign policy.

Film in the service of national self-delusion: such could be the subtitle of a study of documentary in Vietnam. It would tell of an indigestible stew of production by Army, Navy, Air Force and Defense Department— by television, independent companies, and cynical or dedicated individuals. The story of government information and government films in Vietnam will not be attempted here. There is too much of it, and it is too intricate, distorted and shameful; the possibility of a full and fair history lies too far in the future. Yet it cannot be ignored, because it gave rise to that condition in Washington and in Saigon so politely labeled the "credibility gap." It was a time of manipulation of the media against the grain—that is, not only by providing publicity but by suppression, contradiction, "leakage" and denial. Of course it was actually, if not officially, a war—and all's fair in war, as the CIA and the James Bond films affirmed. But it had not been that way in World War II, and an honest publicity man sometimes wondered whether it was worthwhile to stay in government. It was a time that warned us all against putting too much trust in government as a source of information.

Then, with the Nixon administration, nothing was essentially changed, and the country gradually went into shock. There was talk, to be sure, of "de-escalation." But this could no more be confirmed, timed or measured than escalation had been. In fact, there was an uneasy feeling that dramatic troop withdrawals were accompanied by build-ups of special strike forces and air squadrons. The truth continued to disappear behind Pentagon releases. Denials of military actions in Laos were found to be untrue. Denials that Americans were killing prisoners were found to be untrue. Were civilians being slaughtered wholesale by the infantry as well as by air force bombings? That, too, was vehemently denied and in the face of the denials came the revelation of the multiple murders at My Lai.

What could blot out that grisly announcement? Only an ultimate fantasy of still more sacrifice. Nixon, who had earnestly pledged that "Vietnamization" of the war would soon lead to withdrawal by American troops, suddenly accepted the view of Pentagon strategists that a strike against Cambodia would scare Hanoi, collect some armaments and influence peacemaking. He sent American soldiers across the border and told the American people that this invasion was "not an invasion." He reaped the greatest spontaneous national outcry ever unleashed against a President of the United States.

For the second time in a year, every anti-war college student who could afford it converged on Washington in protest. Even though they remembered the last time, they still came, hoping that something would get through to the people, even to the President, perhaps by means of television. TV had brought the war home, every night, to the American people. Could it be made to speak against the war? A national network cannot take a political position as a newspaper publisher can—just the news, and a tough documentary now and then, offering the public the kind of information that can help it decide. Could the people themselves create a series of events that would make TV into a two-way channel?

How naive that question was—and how strangely hopeful! The drama of war on television countered by the drama of the streets: as the Paris mobs raised pitchforks in 1789 against the parading of wealth by the governing classes, so the youth of 1969 would have their say by putting their bodies on the line against the cruel spectacle of the Vietnam War. It was peaceful protest, clearly in the tradition of the First Amendment. Instead of a futile "letter to the editor," it was the talk-back of the times. It had misfired horribly at the Chicago convention. It had produced no effect in October. It had accomplished little in 1967. Yet they tried again.

This time there was more TV coverage, and this time Nixon evidently watched. He even went out to converse at 2 a.m. with a random group at the Lincoln Memorial, trying to add his own closet drama to the major scenes. But it was impossible for young people to forget his first intransigent response, eight months before. Ringed by a battery of buses hastily drawn up around the White House, he had watched a TV football game instead. This galling image of a President refusing to listen would stay with them to their graves.

Across the credibility gap and across the everpresent gap of knowledge that lies between a government and its people, a large and thoughtful segment of the American public was trying to find a way to reach the hearts of the nation's leaders. It was live documentary—incoherent, inadequate as a source for public policy—but a signal that something was wrong with the communicative media of the age. Youth, faced with the unyielding constitutional barrier of the Presidential four-year term, wanted to know if the forces of business-as-usual would always be tuned to another channel. Nixon appointed a commission, headed by a former Pennsylvania governor, William Scranton, to listen for him. National Educational Television put the hearings on the air. The verbal communication multiplied once more. But the war went on.

The need for a two-way channel was the issue. In an era of such rich communicative variety, surely there must be some better way, some new invention in communication. Traditional feedback might be by speeches or by polls. The documentary way would be to reveal the experience behind the speech, the intensity behind the answer to the poll.

Community Action Films

Two notable contributions to political communication came out of the last activist gasp of the Johnson administration—the Office of Economic Opportunity. In films about VISTA volunteers, poor people were encouraged to take part in political decision-making.[3] And in the OEO's

---

[3] VISTA (Volunteers in Service to America), sometimes known as the domestic Peace Corps, drew much of its inspiration from that continuing experiment in international relations. The Peace Corps had its own group of film-makers for a while, some of whom had moved over from the USIA. Early VISTA training films sought to caution overeager young people against expecting to accomplish much very soon—in Navajo country or in the ghetto (A Year Toward Tomorrow). Such training films served also to report on VISTA activities to interested taxpayers.

community action films (following a Canadian model) the people were asked, by talking to the camera, to talk back to their government.

Before the Mountain Was Moved is a re-enacted documentary about a group of home owners in West Virginia with a visible and shocking grievance. Strip miners take the top off the hills and go away. Later, the rains come. Mud roars down on unprotected houses and farms below. And "nobody can do anything about it." Laws about such things? Maybe, but "how's a poor man going to get the law to work?"

Harder to move than the mountains are the ingrained doubts and the hopelessness of the poor people in the valleys. Into such a situation come two young people, plugging at the idea that political action can work. The older men and women, some on social security, say they can't afford a lawyer and the legislators won't listen anyway—"our representative is a strip miner himself." And the big insurance companies just call it "an act of God."

Finally they persuade a group to go to the capital and get one old man to speak for them. "I've been had by the strippers," he tells the lawmakers grimly, his fear overcome by his outrage and despair. "I've had to sell my cattle at a loss—an awful loss—there's no place for them to drink, the creek beds are all filled up. And it's impossible to go fishing. You just can't enjoy life any more. I love that flag, but I believe the flag is for living, not just dying. And a mountain coming down on your house *is not living.*"

We do not see the deliberations of the state senate, but we hear on the radio, as the people of the valleys did, that the new law has been agreed to without a dissenting voice. During the debate in the lower house, "the people are trapped in their homes by rains," but an attempt to soften the new requirements on strip mining is defeated 98-1. The voice of the people has been heeded.

Before the Mountain Was Moved has some moments of lingering exaggeration, as when the little delegation of protestants looks up in awe at the capitol dome from the steps outside. But the feeling of working steadily through a problem in human relations is well maintained, and the occasional injection of *cinéma vérité* technique adds bite to the proceedings. As a study of the roots of the political process, this film by Robert K. Sharpe is a landmark among government productions.

The OEO experienced a distinct cooling in the ardor for community action under the Nixon administration. The film program, too, was reduced and then abolished in little more than a year.[4] Under President

---

[4] The OEO was active on many film fronts under the leadership of Anne Michaels, who set up the audio-visual department in 1965, and Ronald Capalaces, who moved over from the USIA Television Service and eventually took charge of film production. Leading documentary film-makers—William Jersey, Herb Danska, Robert Drew, Francis Ford Coppola, Charles Guggenheim, and John Sutherland—were brought in to do films on contract. An OEO documentary was nominated for an Academy Award each year for the five years the film unit existed. (Interviews, Washington, D.C., March 20, 1970.)

Johnson and Sargent Shriver, however, another extraordinary experiment had been tried, inspired by the work of the Canadian National Film Board on Fogo Island in Newfoundland. Film crews were sent to a Mexican-American town, Farmersville, California (and later, briefly, to Hartford, Connecticut) to study and reflect on community life.

Here the traditional pattern of film-making was reversed: documentary was no longer an art form handed down from on high. Documentary film has served, from time to time, as a description of community experience—a description or enactment which can be passed on to other communities as example and inspiration. A film would be made, for instance, about the building of a bridge or a school, and the film then becomes a pattern of suggestions for other towns that may need to develop cooperative action to build bridges or schools.

The community action film is something else. It sets up a new cross-current of communication by asking the people themselves to speak. In the NFB and OEO programs, film had a totally new role. It became a tool of direct dialogue among groups within the community, a substitute for the tension of physical confrontation. It forecast the possibility that communication, like government, can be of the people and by the people, as well as for the people.

The technique is simple—so simple it requires a new kind of self-effacement for camera operators, editors and directors. Men and women representing various points of view are photographed as they express their opinions and feelings about current problems in the town and about their own life and work. Each one is entitled to see the film and make changes before it is shown to anyone else. Then the film interaction begins: the worker sees the film of the mayor, the mayor sees the film of the worker. On Fogo Island, merchants, teachers, fishermen and cabinet ministers were interviewed singly and in groups. The outcome of the whole effort was that the dying island community was encouraged to survive.

Julian Biggs, NFB production director who supervised the project, reveals the heart of the process:

> Now if you take fishermen to the Cabinet, they won't talk about the problems of their lives the way they will among other fishermen. But if you let the government people look at films of the fisherman talking together, the message comes across.

> And if you in turn let the fishermen see films of the government people discussing the same problems, you have established a new communication with each group remaining in its own context.[5]

[5] Michael Kernan, "A Way of Social Change Through Film," *Washington Post*, March 2, 1969. See also William Selover, "Blacks and whites get together via film-exchange technique," *Christian Science Monitor*, December 4, 1968. A private enterprise application of community action film techniques has been worked out in some places in the U.S. through community antenna television. George Stoney, the American

When this new communication happens, it is profoundly different from merely seeing a problem and then its solution. What is going on is actual participation, and after that, a ripening acquaintanceship with "the other side"—or some other side—of the social and political framework. As long as it is truthful and imperfect and deeply felt, it can provide a cushion of understanding against violence and distrust. Of course it takes time, as any process of persuasion, of social amelioration, takes time. But it may forestall the dangers of a physical encounter. And it is far more effective than the embarrassment of such an encounter, because the interviewer and the film, as agents of the participants, have stepped between them to encourage personal expression without interruption.

Of course movies in community action can only be one step in the democratic process—and that process can only be as good as the people who take part in it. Some talkers will always be slicker—and therefore more self-defeating—than others. Excess of communication, too, may be self-defeating: too much talk can lead to strife, and it is possible to know one's opponents too well. The effectiveness of any direct dialogue depends on a combination of honesty and diplomacy—a readiness to speak freely and a willingness to stop at the right time.

Then there is the question of the film-making process. The art of directing a community action film is not just the art of recording something on film. It is not random or blankly "objective" but based on a knowledge of human nature and society. The director must know how to select representative people. He must be deeply involved and aware of the meaning and value of every gesture and word, and he must be alert to the meaning of certain kinds of backgrounds. Such cameraman-directors are hard to find.

Still, the community action film offers special promise as a healing experience in an alienated time, an instrument of change that carries with it some of the built-in patience of the town meeting. Such films need not be expensive. The emergence of new reusable videotape techniques, as well as super-8-mm film (with sound) make the cost of materials reasonable. Local camera operators and editors can be trained on a budget any community can afford.

Can this sort of thing be done at the national level? In this day of highpowered public relations and political image-making on television, can a dialogue be achieved simply by offering it, by bringing the people to the camera and microphone? Will the President take the time to listen to this new kind of letter, with its underlining of emotional expression?

What we are really asking is whether democracy can manage to regain

documentary director who was for two years head of the Challenge for Change program in Canada, returned to take a position with New York University and to prepare, on a foundation grant, program ideas for CATV. "Public access" channels may come to mean the voices of the people—fascinating and unpredictable public affairs programming. The only problem is to get the right people to watch.

any of its directness, its feeling of face-to-face honesty, in an increasingly technological age. The answer, of course, cannot depend on technology, but on the motives and the persistent effort of those who care about the democratic process.

The only way democracy has ever worked is by enlisting mutual interest in the happiness of others—by what William Hazlitt once called "the power of sympathetic identification." [6] Without that, no man or woman can presume to guide the affairs of others. Without that, no park can be planned, no school built, no regulation of injustice, greed and crime maintained.

It is an inventive and creative process, this renewing of the sense of sympathy for others, and it puts a heavy burden on the artists and reporters of this busy age. But the documentary film can do that kind of work, and it therefore has a natural place at the heart of the process of public communication.

[6] See W. P. Albrecht, *Hazlitt and the Creative Imagination*, pp. 57–59.

INDEX